"I Thank the Lord I Am Not a Yankee"

ALSO BY STEPHEN DAVIS

Atlanta Will Fall: Sherman, Joe Johnston and the Yankee Heavy Battalions

What the Yankees Did to Us: Sherman's Bombardment and Wrecking of Atlanta (Mercer)

A Long and Bloody Task: The Atlanta Campaign from Dalton through Kennesaw Mountain to the Chattahoochee River, May 5–July 18, 1864

All the Fighting They Want: The Atlanta Campaign from Peachtree Creek to the City's Surrender, July 18-September 2, 1864

100 Significant Civil War Photographs: Atlanta Campaign

100 Significant Civil War Photographs: Charleston in the War (with Jack W. Melton, Jr.)

Texas Brigadier to the Fall of Atlanta: John Bell Hood (Mercer)

Into Tennessee and Failure: John Bell Hood (Mercer)

The Atlanta Daily Intelligencer Covers the Civil War (with Bill Hendrick)

"I Thank the Lord I Am Not a Yankee"

Selections from Fanny Andrews's
Wartime and Postwar Journals

Edited with Commentary by

STEPHEN DAVIS

MERCER UNIVERSITY PRESS
Macon, Georgia

MUP/ H1036

© 2023 by Mercer University Press
Published by Mercer University Press
1501 Mercer University Drive
Macon, Georgia 31207
All rights reserved

27 26 25 24 23   5 4 3 2 1

Books published by Mercer University Press are printed on acid-free paper that
meets the requirements of the American National Standard for Information
Sciences—Permanence of Paper for Printed Library Materials.

Printed and bound in the United States.

This book is set in Adobe Garamond.

Cover/jacket design by Burt&Burt.

ISBN   978-0-88146-889-2
Cataloging-in-Publication Data is available from the Library of Congress

MERCER UNIVERSITY PRESS

Endowed by

TOM WATSON BROWN
and
THE WATSON-BROWN FOUNDATION, INC.

Contents

Prelude

Editor's Introduction

A week before Christmas 1864, twenty-four-year-old Eliza Frances ("Fanny") Andrews set out with her younger sister, Metta ("Mett"), to travel from the family home near Washington, in northeast Georgia, to their sister's home in the opposite corner of the state. Sherman had already marched to the sea, and the Confederacy was collapsing. Fanny expected to see a lot, so she started a diary that spanned eight months, through August 1865. The latter half was written after Fanny and Mett had returned to Washington in the final days of the war.

Late in life she edited her journal for publication. She deleted remarks of an insignificant or personal nature, "whole paragraphs and even pages." But the bedrock remained, published by D. Appleton of New York in 1908, offering such intelligent observations about the last days of the Old South that it has been termed by Richard Barksdale Harwell, the Confederate bibliographer, as equal to Mary Boykin Chesnut's famed *Diary from Dixie*.[1] Indeed, Spencer B. King Jr., who prepared an introduction for a reissue of Andrews's journal in 1960, calls it "more meaningful and even better written" than Mrs. Chesnut's well-known work.[2]

Miss Andrews's writings are also more vindictive toward the Yankees. "I can't believe that when Christ said 'love your enemies' he meant Yankees," she wrote at one point in her journal.[3] Indeed, as the chronicle of a fierce Rebel, *The War-Time Journal of a Georgia Girl* has

---

[1] Richard Barksdale Harwell, *In Tall Cotton: The 200 Most Important Confederate Books for the Reader, Researcher and Collector* (Austin: Jenkins Book Publishing Company, 1978), 1.

[2] Spencer Bidwell King, Jr., "Introduction" in Eliza Frances Andrews, *The War-time Journal of a Georgia Girl 1864–1865* (Macon: Ardivan Press, 1960), vii. Future references to Andrews's *War-Time Journal* will be to the Ardivan edition of 1960.

[3] King, "Introduction," xviii.

few equals. More important for the historian, the titles of its seven chapters suggest the journal's value as a personal record of both the last four months of the war and the start of Reconstruction:

I. Across Sherman's Track
II. Plantation Life
III. A Race with the Enemy
IV The Passing of the Confederacy
V. In the Dust and Ashes of Defeat
VI. Foreshadowings of the Race Problem
VII. The Prologue to Reconstruction

Eliza was the daughter of Garnett and Annulet Andrews. Her father was a prominent attorney and superior court judge living in Washington, a good-sized town in northeast Georgia. He was prosperous, too, as shown by his spacious estate, "Haywood"—Dr. Gilbert Hay had built his mansion in 1791. "The big house" was surrounded by a dozen outbuildings. The judge owned more than a hundred slaves, in addition to plantation lands elsewhere in Georgia and the Yazoo delta of Mississippi.

Born August 10, 1840, at Washington, Fanny received an excellent education. The Andrews family prized learning; a big library filled a room at Haywood, and newspapers and magazines sparked conversations about current events. Her two older brothers embarked on professional careers: Henry as physician, Garnett as attorney. After attending the Washington Female Academy, Fanny graduated from LaGrange Female College in 1857. She liked literature and languages, conversed in French (having learned it "from an amiable old French master" who taught at a boarding school in Washington) and was not averse to sprinkling Latin in her writing. She was also a strong-willed individual. When, in February 1865, she wrote at the age of twenty-four, "I am never going to marry anybody. Marriage is incompatible with the career I have marked out for myself," she was probably thinking about teaching—one of the few vocational tracks open to women in nineteenth-century America.[4] She was also thinking about writing—another career possibility for educated women. A few months after the war, Capt. Paul Semmes, son of the famed Confederate admiral, asked Fanny for her photograph, "and I told him he should have it when I get to be a 'celebrated female.'"

It is at this point in her life that we turn to Andrews's *War-Time Journal.* She wrote a prologue for it, in which she terms the diary "an informal contemporaneous record," but one that possesses "unpremeditated realism, which is more valuable as a picture of life than detailed statistics of battles and sieges." She declares that she originally composed it not for publication, "with absolutely no thought of ever meeting other eyes than those of the author."

The diarist was a stern critic of her work. Fanny tells us that she maintained her diary "with more or less regularity" for a period of up to ten years, but that at various times, reading her entries, she experienced "fits of disgust" and destroyed large sections. Only the intervention of a relative, she explains, saved her *War-Time Journal* from a similar fate.

As best as we can discern, Miss Andrews edited her wartime diary in the early 1900s. For instance, she adds a footnote to her journal entry of August 25, 1865, in which she writes, "at present (1907)." She speaks of her feelings "forty years ago," and writes that the "pale, home-made ink" on the pages of the "old day-book" she used for her diary had faded "after nearly fifty years." At that time, by her own admission, Fanny was a "gray-haired editor"; she would have been in her early 60s. We may also infer that she spent considerable time in preparing her journal for publication, as she admits candidly that she "may be pardoned a natural averseness to the publication of anything that would too emphatically 'write me down an ass.'"

---

[4] Anne Firor Scott, *The Southern Lady: From Pedestal to Politics 1830–1930* (Chicago: University of Chicago Press, 1970), 118. Fanny's remark about the "amiable old French master" in Washington is in her article "The Art of Lying," *Scott's Monthly Magazine* 7/4 (April 1869): 268. The essay was published under her postwar pen name, "Elzey Hay"—about which more, anon.

In her editing, though, she was restrained, choosing not to correct rather harmless grammatical lapses, or even to undo erroneous statements of fact. For instance, at one point she states that Ben Butler was, like Sherman, a West Pointer. About this she admits that she probably knew better at the time (April 23, 1865), "but my excited brain was so occupied at the moment with thoughts of the general depravity of those dreadful Yankees, that there was not room for another idea in it."

She also deleted "thoughtless criticisms and other expressions that might wound the feelings of persons now living." As example, she changed the name of a gentleman to "Gen. Graves" (the only instance in which she did so) because of his evidently well-known "bibulous propensities."[5]

One measure of a book's distinction is the extent to which its text has been quoted by other writers. Francis Butler Simkins and James Welch Patton repeatedly quote Miss Andrews's journal in *The Women of the Confederacy* (1936), paying particular attention to her observations in summer 1865 as she became aware of the consequences of Confederate defeat and the onset of Reconstruction. They term this part of her diary "perhaps the fullest available account of Southern feminine thoughts immediately after the war." The two historians take note of Frances crossing the street to avoid encountering Federal soldiers in occupied Washington; of her wanting "to run a knitting needle" into a Yankee insolently taking a meal at her aunt's house; and of her terming the newly afloat Stars and Stripes "a hateful old striped rag."[6]

In 1955 Katherine M. Jones' *Heroines of Dixie* appeared, including excerpts from Andrews's journal entries from April 25 to May 4, 1865. "This I suppose, is the end of the Confederacy," the twenty-four-year-old diarist lamented. In a later work, *When Sherman Came* (1964), Jones reprinted a five-page section of the *War-Time Journal* in which

---

[5] *War-Time Journal*, 4–8, 105.

[6] Francis Butler Simkins and James Welch Patton, *The Women of the Confederacy* (Richmond: Garrett and Massie, 1936), 55, 249–50.

Andrews describes her and Metta's travels from Washington to Macon, December 19-24.[7]

Mary Elizabeth Massey is another historian to repeatedly cite Andrews's journal in *Bonnet Brigades* (1966), on topics from Andersonville to the flight of Confederate leaders through Washington. As to be expected, Burke Davis quotes Miss Andrews's description of the "Burnt Country" in his *Sherman's March* (1980). Anne Sarah Rubin has done the same in her study of Sherman's march and American memory (2014). George C. Rable makes extensive use of *The War-Time Journal* in his study of Confederate women, quoting it on everything from the luxury of linen nightgowns to class distinctions ("nothing is more contemptible than broken-down gentility trying to ape rich vulgarity"). Moreover, it is not just as a wartime journal that historians cite Miss Andrews; in their book on the opening year of Reconstruction, Thomas and Debra Goodrich quote Frances's diary entries of April–July 1865 two dozen times.[8]

Another measure of popularity is frequency of reprint. After publication in 1908, Miss Andrews's journal was notably republished in 1960, with introduction by Spencer Bidwell King Jr., and in 1997, with introduction by Jean V. Berlin.[9] After that, a casual search suggests several more reprints in recent years.

Even today, *The War-Time Journal of a Georgia Girl* reads like a travel through time, honestly reflecting wartime passions; the author's

---

[7] Katherine M. Jones, ed., *Heroines of Dixie: Winter of Desperation* (New York: Ballantine Books, 1975 [1955]), 234; Katherine M. Jones, *When Sherman Came: Southern Women and the "Great March"* (Indianapolis: Bobbs-Merrill, 1964), 76–81.

[8] Mary Elizabeth Massey, *Women in the Civil War* (Lincoln: University of Nebraska Press, 1994 [1966]), 232, 307–308; Burke Davis, *Sherman's March* (New York: Random House, 1980), 79–80; Anne Sarah Rubin, *Through the Heart of Dixie: Sherman's March and American Memory* (Chapel Hill: University of North Carolina Press, 2014), 18–19; George C. Rable, *Civil Wars: Women and the Crisis of Southern Nationalism* (Urbana: University of Illinois Press, 1989), 93, 270; Thomas and Debra Goodrich, *The Day Dixie Died: Southern Occupation 1865–1866* (Mechanicsburg, PA: Stackpole Books, 2001), *passim*.

[9] *The War-Time Journal of a Georgia Girl* (Lincoln: University of Nebraska Press, 1997).

prologue makes clear that this is a journal of a reconstructed but unregenerate Rebel. "I have never been able to bring myself to repent of having sided with my own people," she admits; "the word 'rebel,' now so bitterly resented as casting a stigma on the Southern cause, is used throughout the diary as a term of pride and affectionate endearment." This simple but revealing statement goes far to define the heart of her book. She adds,

> In the desire to avoid as far as possible any unnecessary tampering with the original manuscript, passages expressive of the animosities of the time, which the author would be glad to blot out forever, have been allowed to stand unaltered—not as representing the present feeling of the writer or her people, but because they do represent our feelings forty years ago, and to suppress them entirely, would be to falsify the record.

As an unregenerate Rebel, Miss Andrews wrote excoriatingly of Yankees as well rhapsodically on the nature of antebellum Southern society:

> It was a medieval civilization, out of accord with the modern tenor of our time, and it had to go; but if it stood for some outworn customs that should rightly be sent to the dust heap, it stood for some things, also, that the world can ill afford to lose. It stood for gentle courtesy, for knightly honor, for generous hospitality; it stood for fair and honest dealing of man with man in the common business of life, for lofty scorn of cunning greed and ill-gotten gain through fraud and deception of our fellowmen— lessons which the founders of our New South would do well to lay to heart.... The Old South, with its stately feudal regime, was not the monstrosity that some would have us believe, but merely a case of belated survival, like those giant sequoias of the Pacific slope that have lingered on from age to age, and are now left standing alone in a changed world.

At one point, she frankly laments, "It is a pity that this glorious old plantation life should ever have come to an end."

She also fashioned an explanation of how the war between the South and North had erupted as result of "economic determinism," the conflict between a system of agricultural "chattel slavery" versus one of industrial "wage slavery...a question of dollars and cents." Indeed, she reflects that "the influence of this factor is generally so subtle and indirect that we are totally unconscious of it." As a result, "we of the South honestly believe to this day that we were fighting for State Rights, while the North is equally honest in the conviction that it was engaged in a magnanimous struggle to free the slave."

Fanny could not refrain from sympathizing with the Lost Cause and the Confederate soldier who fought for it:

> He fought a losing battle, but he fought it honestly and bravely, in the open—not by secret fraud and cunning. His cause was doomed from the first by a law as inexorable as the one pronounced by the fates against Troy, but he fought with a valor and heroism that have made a lost cause forever glorious. He saw the civil fabric his fathers had reared go down in a mighty cataclysm of blood and fire, a tragedy for all the ages—but better so than to have perished by slow decay through ages of sloth and rottenness, as so many other great civilizations of history have done, leaving only a debased and degenerate race behind them.

In other words, it was better to have fought and lost than never to have fought at all.

Such are some of the ideas and sentiments one sees in *The War-Time Journal*, as it retains, after all these years, the author's wartime emotionalism.

> The diary was written in a time of storm and tempest, of bitter hatreds and fierce animosities, and its pages are so saturated with the spirit of the time, that to attempt to banish it would be like giving the play of Hamlet without the title-role. It does not pretend to give the calm reflections of a philosopher looking back

dispassionately upon the storms of his youth, but the passionate utterances of the stormy youth itself. It is in no sense a history, but a mere series of crude pen-sketches, faulty, inaccurate, and out of perspective, it may be, but still a true picture of things as the writer saw them. It makes no claim to impartiality; on the contrary, the author frankly admits that it is violently and often absurdly partisan—and it could not well have been otherwise under the circumstances. Coming from a heart ablaze with the passionate resentment of a people smarting under the humiliation of defeat, it was inevitable that along with the just indignation at wrongs which ought never to have been committed, there should have crept in many intemperate and indiscriminate denunciations of acts which the writer did not understand, to say nothing of sophomorical vaporings calculated now to excite a smile. Such expressions, however, are not to be taken seriously at the present day, but are rather to be regarded as a sort of fossil curiosities that have the same value in throwing light on the psychology of the period to which they belong as the relics preserved in our geological museums have in illustrating the physical life of the past.

"Youth is impulsive, and prone to run with the crowd," she explains.

We caught the infection of the war spirit in the air and never stopped to reason or to think. And then, there were our soldier boys. With my three brothers in the army, and that glorious record of Lee and his men in Virginia, how was it possible not to throw oneself heart and soul into the cause for which they were fighting so gallantly? And when the bitter end came, it is not to be wondered at if our resentment against those who had brought all these humiliations and disasters upon us should flame up fiercer than ever.

It is in the pages ahead.

Part 1

Selections from
The War-Time Journal of a Georgia Girl
(1908)

December 19–24, 1864

Under this date Miss Andrews wrote a preamble to her war journal, explaining why she and her younger sister, Metta, had set out across Georgia. Fanny's eldest sister, Cora, lived at Pine Bluff, a plantation between Albany and Thomasville in southwest Georgia. Her husband, Brother Troup (as he is called throughout the journal), was in the army, and Cora had no "male protector," save the servants in the house. So Fanny and Mett set out to provide some company for their sister. They were in the habit of traveling there in wintertime anyway; in return, Cora came to Haywood, Judge Andrews's estate at Washington, during the summers.

There was another element, one of timing. Sherman's army of 60,000 Federals had marched out of Atlanta on November 16, 1864, and by Christmas had taken the city of Savannah. Thus in their trek across the state there was no threat of the young ladies encountering the dreaded Yankees. But they had left their tracks. Fanny explains the destruction the Federals had wreaked on the several railroads running across the state, damage that complicated and prolonged the sisters' journey, but did not halt it. The young journalist does not routinely offer specifics on how the two pilgrims conveyed themselves on trains and wagons. A map prepared for the 1960 edition of *The War-Time Journal*, showing a continuous rail line from Washington to Albany, is clearly incorrect.

On Monday, December 19, Fanny, Mett, and a Black "reliable man" (whom she does not name) set out from Washington for Camak, twenty miles south, a station on the railroad connecting Atlanta eastward to Augusta. On a short spur line from Camak, the trio traveled to Mayfield, a dozen or so miles to the southwest. Then came a wagon ride to Gordon, fifty miles by direct line, but for the weary travelers, "65 miles of bad roads and worse conveyances, through a country devastated by the most cruel and wicked invasion of modern times," as Frances characterizes Sherman's "march to the sea."

Miss Andrews does not note the mileposts in this trek from Mayfield through Sparta and Milledgeville to Gordon, a town maybe twenty miles east of Macon. We merely know that by December 24, a Saturday, she and Metta had reached Macon. For part of their trek, Fanny and Mett were accompanied by their older brother, Fred, a Confederate second lieutenant in the artillery. Shortly after the group left Mayfield, Fred departed, heading back to his post at Augusta. "I felt rather desolate after his departure," the diarist admits. But in their carriage, she and Metta also enjoyed the company of a Confederate colonel and his pretty young bride, plus several men who followed the tram on foot. "We sang rebel songs and became very sociable together," she notes. One may guess what "rebel songs" they sang (one was "The Confederate Toast," which Fanny mentions later). More important, though, and easy to overlook, was that, here, in December 1864, with perhaps a quarter of the Confederacy overrun or occupied by the enemy, Lee's army starving in the Petersburg trenches, and Hood's army shattered at Nashville, this convivial coterie not only joined merrily in song, but defiantly chose "rebel" ones at that.

Here we begin to offer excerpts and comment on *The War-Time Journal of a Georgia Girl*.

December 24, 1864

We had a royal breakfast, and while we were eating it, Mr. Belisle, who had spent the night at the hotel, drove up with a four-mule wagon, in which he had engaged places for us and our trunks to Milledgeville, at seventy-five dollars apiece. It was a common plantation wagon, without cover or springs, and I saw Mr. Simpson shake his head ominously as we jingled off to take up more passengers at his hotel. There were several other conveyances of the same sort, already overloaded, waiting in front of the door, and a number of travelers standing on the sidewalk rushed forward to secure place in ours as soon as we halted. The first to climb in was a poor sick soldier, of whom no pay was demanded. Next came a captain of Texas Rangers, then a young lieutenant in a shabby uniform that had evidently seen very hard service, and after him our handsome young captain of the night before. He grumbled a little at the looks of the conveyance, but on finding we were going to ride in it, dashed off to secure a seat for himself. While we sat waiting there, I overheard a conversation between a countryman and a nervous traveler that was not calculated to relieve my mind.[1] In answer to some inquiry about the chances for hiring a conveyance to Milledgeville, I heard the countryman say:

"Milledgeville's like hell; you kin get thar easy enough, but gittin' out again would beat the Devil himself."

I didn't hear the traveler's next remark, but it must have been something about Metta and me, for I heard the countryman answer:

"Ef them ladies ever gits to Gordon, they'll be good walkers. Sherman's done licked that country clean; d—n me ef you kin hire so much as a nigger an' a wheelbarrer."

---

[1] "Countryman" was the Southern term of the time for rural folk.

At Sparta, where they had spent the night, Fanny and Mett heard this conversation. The Yankees had not marched through Sparta, but they had most definitely reached Milledgeville. The then-state capital lay twenty southwesterly miles ahead, and the young travelers were already hearing tales of Sherman's devastation. No wonder Fanny recorded this as a conversation "not calculated to relieve my mind."

As Mrs. Chesnut did in her diary, Miss Andrews clustered days upon days of events—indeed, most of her first chapter—under "December 24." It is under this date that she describes how the two sisters passed through the "Burnt Country"—the area of central Georgia through which Sherman's soldiers had marched the previous month. (Mrs. Elzey, the perfume-profferer mentioned below, was Ellen [Irwin] Elzey, wife of the Confederate brigadier and a good friend of the Andrews family.)

About three miles from Sparta we struck the "Burnt Country," as it is well named by the natives, and then I could better understand the wrath and desperation of these poor people. I almost felt as if I should like to hang a Yankee myself. There was hardly a fence left standing all the way from Sparta to Gordon. The fields were tramped down and the road was lined with carcasses of horses, hogs, and cattle that the invaders, unable either to consume or to carry away with them, had wantonly shot down to starve out the people or prevent them from making their crops. The stench in some places was unbearable; every few hundred yards we had to hold our noses or stop them with the cologne Mrs. Elzey had given us, and it proved a great boon. The dwellings that were standing all showed signs of pillage, and on every plantation we saw the charred remains of the gin-house and packing-screw, while here and there, lone chimney-stacks, "Sherman's Sentinels," told of homes laid in ashes. The infamous wretches! I couldn't wonder now that these poor people should want to put a rope round the neck of every red-handed "devil of them" they could lay their hands on. Hay ricks and fodder stacks were demolished, corn cribs were empty, and every bale of cotton that could be found was burnt by the savages. I saw no grain of any sort, except little patches they had spilled when feeding their horses and which there was not even a chicken left in the country to eat. A bag of oats might have lain anywhere along the road without danger from the beasts of the field, though I cannot say it would have been safe from the assaults of hungry man. Crowds of soldiers were tramping over the road in both directions; it was like traveling through the streets of a populous town all day. They were mostly on foot, and I saw numbers seated on the roadside greedily eating raw turnips, meat skins, parched corn—anything they could find, even picking up the loose grains that Sherman's horses had left. I felt tempted to stop and empty the contents of our provision baskets into their laps, but the dreadful accounts that were given of the state of the country before us, made prudence get the better of our generosity.

The roads themselves were in a better condition than might have been expected, and we traveled at a pretty fair rate, our four mules being strong and in good working order. When we had made about half the distance to Milledgeville it began to rain, so the gentlemen cut down saplings which they fitted in the form of bows across the body of the wagon, and stretching the lieutenant's army blanket over it, made a very effectual shelter. Our next halt was near a dilapidated old house where there was a fine well of water. The Yankees had left it, I suppose, because they couldn't carry it away. Here we came up with a wagon on which were mounted some of the people we had seen on the cars the day before. They stopped to exchange experiences, offered us a toddy, and brought us water in a beautiful calabash gourd with a handle three feet long. We admired it so much that one of them laughingly proposed to "capture" it for us, but we told them we didn't care to imitate Sherman's manners.

Eliza Frances Andrews here proves herself one of the bitterest chroniclers of the devastation observable in the wake of the Federals' march through Georgia.[2]

In planning his next campaign after the capture of Atlanta—leading 60,000 veteran troops through Rebel territory undefended save by a few thousand scattered Confederate cavalry and local militia—General Sherman envisioned a "sweep" across Georgia, "breaking roads and doing irreparable damage" to "cripple their military resources." Lest he be mistaken, he promised General Grant on October 9, "I can make the march, and make Georgia howl."[3]

Against the backdrop of this vengeful boasting, however, Sherman's orders to his troops before they set out actually appear rather restrained. In Special Field Orders No. 120, issued November 9 (a week before the army headed out from Atlanta), the commanding general directed that "the army will forage liberally on the country during the march," but the gathering of meat, vegetables, cornmeal, *et al.* was to be done by designated forage parties "under the command of one or more discreet officers." At the same time, when the march columns were at halt or in camp, soldiers were allowed within short distances "to gather turnips, potatoes, and other vegetables, and to drive in stock in sight of the camp." Moreover, the cavalry and artillery were authorized to "appropriate freely and without limit" horses and mules, especially from rich landowners, "who are usually hostile."

Sherman's forces comprised four infantry corps, organized as right and left wings (also designated as the Army of the Tennessee and the

---

[2] Miss Andrews's observations on the animal carcasses strewing the roads are quoted in John B. Walter, *Merchant of Terror: General Sherman and Total War* (Indianapolis: Bobbs-Merrill Company, 1973), 177.

[3] Stephen Davis, *What the Yankees Did to Us: Sherman's Bombardment and Wrecking of Atlanta* (Macon: Mercer University Press, 2012), 360; Sherman to Grant, September 20, 1864, U.S. War Department, *The War of the Rebellion: Official Records of the Union and Confederate Armies* (cited hereafter as *OR*), 128 vols. (Washington: U.S. Government Printing Office, 1880–1901), vol. 39, pt. 2, 412 ("60,000 men"); to Grant, October 9, vol. 39, pt. 3, 162 ("cripple their resources"; "make Georgia howl").

Army of Georgia). Corps commanders were authorized to order the destruction of civilians' property, such as "mills, houses, cotton-gins, &c." Yet there was an important caveat: "in districts and neighborhoods where the army is unmolested no destruction of such property should be permitted." If, on the other hand, guerrillas or bushwhackers fired on his troops, Sherman directed army commanders to "order and enforce a devastation more or less relentless according to the measure of each hostility." Then, for the record, he issued the order that "soldiers must not enter the dwellings of the inhabitants, or commit any trespass.[4]

To judge from *The War-Time Journal,* though—and substantiated by the standard histories of the "march to the sea"—Sherman's men deviated from these instructions. In the preceding passage alone, Miss Andrews catalogs six different forms of Federal vandalism:

a) destruction of fencing;
b) slaughter of livestock and expropriation of grain, chickens, etc. for the apparent purpose of denying the people such food;
c) looting and pillaging of private residences;
d) burning of cotton mill equipment and of the cotton itself;
e) torching of civilian homes (note reference to "Sherman's Sentinels"); and
f) destruction of farm outbuildings.

For years afterward, such destruction as witnessed by Fanny Andrews was considered to have been so demoralizing to Southern civilians that it weakened their war-will and hastened the collapse of the Confederacy. General Sherman himself believed this, as when he wrote, "thousands who had been deceived by their lying papers into the belief that we were being whipped all the time, realized the truth." Confederate president Jefferson Davis acknowledged this as well:

---

[4] Noah Andre Trudeau, *Southern Storm: Sherman's March to the Sea* (New York: Harper, 2008), 52–53.

"Sherman's campaign has produced [a] bad effect on our people. Success against his future operations is needed to reanimate public confidence." Historians' acceptance of the psychological impact of Sherman's march was drily summarized by James G. Randall in 1937: "That it did in fact contribute materially toward ending the war is the general opinion of authorities."[5]

More recent scholarship has yielded a different view. Since the home fronts "visited" by Sherman's soldiers were predominantly overseen by women, female historians have taken a close look at what ladies like Fanny Andrews wrote. Prof. Jacqueline Glass Campbell acknowledges that, to be sure, Southerners were stunned and shocked by the Yankees' excesses, but that gradually such initial impulses morphed into more virulent hatred of the enemy and more deeply rooted Confederate patriotism. (Fanny would have strongly agreed.) Campbell explains that encountering Federal soldiers turned Southern women into something like soldiers as well: "confronting the enemy face-to-face allowed these women to share in a sense of responsibility for actually defending the Confederacy, with a consequent upsurge in patriotism." Prof. Anne Sarah Rubin sees a similar transformation, from "helpless victims" to "brave resisters."[6]

Our journalist resumes.

> Before crossing the Oconee at Milledgeville we ascended an immense hill, from which there was a fine view of the town, with Gov. Brown's fortifications in the foreground and the river rolling at our feet. The Yankees had burnt the bridge, so we had to cross on a ferry. There was a long train of vehicles ahead of us, and it was nearly an hour before our turn came, so we had ample time

---

[5] Herman Hattaway and Archer Jones, *How the North Won: A Military History of the Civil War* (Urbana: University of Illinois Press, 1983), 655; J. G. Randall, *The Civil War and Reconstruction* (Boston: D. C. Heath and Company, 1937), 561.

[6] Jacqueline Glass Campbell, *When Sherman Marched North from the Sea: Resistance on the Confederate Home Front* (Chapel Hill: University of North Carolina Press, 2003), 6, 59, 69, 74; Rubin, *Through the Heart of Dixie*, 2.

to look about us. On our left was a field where 30,000 Yankees had camped hardly three weeks before. It was strewn with the *debris* they had left behind, and the poor people of the neighborhood were wandering over it, seeking for anything they could find to eat, even picking up grains of corn that were scattered around where the Yankees had fed their horses. We were told that a great many valuables were found there at first,—plunder that the invaders had left behind, but the place had been picked over so often by this time that little now remained except tufts of loose cotton, piles of half-rotted grain, and the carcasses of slaughtered animals, which raised a horrible stench. Some men were plowing in one part of the field, making ready for next year's crops.

On November 22, troops of the Union XX Corps had marched into Milledgeville. Gov. Joseph E. Brown and members of the legislature had fled, taking whatever they could after sending important papers into southwest Georgia—the very "Land of Goshen" to which the Andrews sisters were heading. In addition to blowing up an arsenal, burning the train depot and various buildings, the Federals burned the Oconee River bridge—Miss Andrews is correct on this point though she overestimates the number of blue-clad occupiers (which was closer to fourteen thousand). Sherman's troops marched out of Milledgeville on November 24, leaving behind the usual debris cast off by thousands of marching men, as Fanny observed, but also a statehouse that had been thoroughly vandalized, which she did not remark upon.[7]

Fanny Andrews saw more traces of the Yankees' destruction the farther she went. At Scottsboro, a village four miles south of Milledgeville, she observed (concerning the old women there) that "Sherman's army marched through and gave them such a shaking up that it will give them something to talk about the rest of their days." Taking

---

[7] William R. Scaife, *The March to the Sea* (Saline, MI: McNaughton & Gunn, 1993), 50f. (map); Rubin, *Through the Heart of Dixie*, 17–18; Trudeau, *Southern Storm*, 75; James C. Bonner, *Milledgeville: Georgia's Antebellum Capital* (Macon: Mercer University Press, 1985), 187–88.

lodging in a Scottsboro inn at the end of the day—again, we don't know which day in December—Fanny was told by Mrs. Palmer, the landlady, that she had no supper to serve "because the Yankees had taken all her provisions." After she pulled from the chimney a hidden jar of pickles, Mrs. Palmer disclosed that the Yankees had left her but few plates on which to serve them. One of the sisters' traveling companions brought forth some coffee, which was served, but the landlady had been left with only one spoon to stir all the cups. Afterward the group amused itself with more singing of "The Confederate Toast." The charm of the ditty provided for the vocalists to make up their own couplets. "This started up a rivalry in verse-making, each one trying to outdo the other in the absurdity of their composition, and some of them were very funny." One of Fanny's compositions ran like this:

> Here's to the Southern rebel, drink it down;
> Here's to the Southern rebel, drink it down;
> Here's to the Southern rebel,
> May his enemies go to the—[8]

After the songfest, Fanny continued to feel the Yankees' presence in Scottsboro: "The weather had begun to turn very cold, and the scanty supply of bed-clothes the Yankees had left Mrs. Palmer was not enough to keep me warm."

The travails of the travelers are on full display in the following passage, still under the date of December 24:

> About noon we struck the Milledgeville & Gordon R.R., near a station which the Yankees had burnt, and a mill near by they had destroyed also, out of pure malice, to keep the poor people of the country from getting their corn ground. There were several crossroads at the burnt mill and we took the wrong one, and got

---

[8] "Rebel Toasts: Or Drink It Down," which begins with "O, here's to South Carolina! drink it down," is published in *Allan's Lone Star Ballads* (Esther Parker Ellinger, *The Southern War Poetry of the Civil War* [New York: Burt Franklin, 1970 (1918)], 56, 143).

into somebody's cornfield, where we found a little crib whose remoteness seemed to have protected it from the greed of the invaders. We were about to "press" a few ears for our hungry mules, when we spied the owner coming across the fields and waited for him. The captain asked if he would sell us a little provender for our mules, but he gave such a pitiful account of the plight in which Sherman had left him that we felt as mean as a lot of thieving Yankees ourselves, for having thought of disturbing his property. He was very polite, and walked nearly a mile in the biting wind to put us back in the right road. Three miles from Gordon we came to Commissioners' Creek, of which we had heard awful accounts all along the road. It was particularly bad just at this time on account of the heavy rain, and had overflowed the swamp for nearly two miles. Porters with heavy packs on their backs were wading through the sloughs, and soldiers were paddling along with their legs bare and their breeches tied up in a bundle on their shoulders. They were literal *sans culottes.* Some one who had just come from the other side advised us to unload the wagon and make two trips of it, as it was doubtful whether the mules could pull through with such a heavy load. The Yankees had thrown dead cattle in the ford, so that we had to drive about at random in the mud and water, to avoid these uncanny obstructions. Our gentlemen, however, concluded that we had not time to make two trips, so they all piled into the wagon at once and trusted to Providence for the result. We came near upsetting twice, and the water was so deep in places that we had to stand on top of the trunks to keep our feet dry.

Safely over the swamp, we dined on the scraps left in our baskets, which afforded but a scanty meal. The cold and wind had increased so that we could hardly keep our seats, but the roads improved somewhat as we advanced, and the aspect of the country was beautiful in spite of all that the vandalism of war had done to disfigure its fair face. Every few hundred yards we crossed beautiful, clear streams with luxuriant swamps along their borders, gay with shining evergreens and bright winter berries. But when we struck the Central R.R. at Gordon, the desolation was more complete than anything we had yet seen. There was nothing left of the poor little village but ruins, charred and black as Yankee hearts. The pretty little depot presented only a shapeless pile of bricks capped by a crumpled mass of tin that had once covered the roof. The R.R. track was torn up and the iron twisted into every conceivable shape. Some of it was wrapped round the trunks of trees, as if the cruel invaders, not satisfied with doing all the injury they could to their fellowmen, must spend their malice on the innocent trees of the forest, whose only fault was that they grew on Southern soil. Many fine young saplings were killed in this way, but the quickest and most effective method of destruction was to lay the iron across piles of burning cross-ties, and while heated in the flames it was bent and warped so as to be entirely spoiled. A large force is now at work repairing the road; as the repairs advance a little every day, the place for meeting the train is constantly changing and not always easy to find.

Miss Andrews was an alert chronicler. "The Milledgeville & Gordon R.R." was a branch of the Central of Georgia line that connected Gordon with the state capital and on to Eatonton. More than likely, the burned rail station she mentions had been destroyed by Union brigadier general Judson Kilpatrick's cavalry, which rode from Gordon to Milledgeville before heading east on November 25.[9]

Yankees throwing dead animals in wells is an oft-repeated Southern legend about Sherman's march, but Frances's observation of carcasses in Commissioners' Creek seems substantive. As for Gordon, her remark, "there was nothing left of the poor little village" seems to contravene General Sherman's strictures against burning towns. Miss Andrews had seen Gordon in earlier travels to visit her sister in southwest Georgia, so she was able to recall "the pretty little depot." But Gordon was, in the words of historian Noah Andre Trudeau, merely "a whistle-stop town, just in the middle of nowhere." If indeed most, if not all, of the structures in Gordon were railroad-related (depot, woodsheds, water tanks, even a wayside tavern), according to Sherman's Special

---

[9] Scaife, *March to the Sea*, 50f. (map).

Orders No. 120, soldiers of the XVII Corps who entered Gordon on November 22 would have been authorized to burn them. In the hands of the Federals, Trudeau writes, "the structures in the town linked to the railroads didn't last long."[10]

Fanny has mentioned "Sherman's sentinels"—the isolated chimneys standing amid the ruins of burned houses. She has not referred to "Sherman's neckties," but she describes them well. William Tecumseh Sherman never tired of lecturing his officers on how he wanted his soldiers to wreck Rebel track. Typical was this:

> My own experience demonstrates the proper method to be: To march a regiment to the road, stack arms, loosen two rails opposite the right and two opposite the left of the regiment, then to heave the whole track, rails and ties, over, breaking it all to pieces, then pile the ties in the nature of crib work and lay the rails over them, then by means of fence rails make a bonfire, and when the rails are red-hot in the middle let men give the rail a twist, which cannot be straightened out without machinery.[11]

Moreover, Miss Andrews observed that after Sherman had marched, even before the war had ended, Southern railroad officials were overseeing the repair of track that had been wrecked by Union troops. By January 1865, for instance, the Central Railroad from Macon to Gordon had been rebuilt—the very work she was witnessing the month before.[12]

At one point Frances heard how some captured Yankees were being handled by their captors. In the vicinity of Sparta, she encountered a local resident, Sam Weller, and recounted her conversation with him. The exchange allowed her to distinguish between two sorts of Sherman's soldiers.

---

[10] Trudeau, *Southern Storm*, 190–91.

[11] Davis, *What the Yankees Did to Us*, 357.

[12] T. Conn Bryan, *Confederate Georgia* (Athens: University of Georgia Press, 1953), 117.

He told awful tales about the things Sherman's robbers had done; it made my blood boil to hear them, and when the captain asked him if some of the rascals didn't get caught sometimes— stragglers and the like—he answered with a wink that said more than words:

"Yes; our folks took lots of prisoners; more'n'll ever be heard of agin."

"What became of them?" asked the lieutenant.

"Sent 'em to Macon, double quick," was the laconic reply. "Got 'em thar in less'n half an hour."

"How did they manage it?" continued the lieutenant, in a tone that showed he understood Sam's metaphor.

"Just took 'em out in the woods and lost 'em," he replied, in his jerky, laconic way. "Ever heerd o' losin' men, lady?" he added, turning to me, with an air of grim waggery that made my flesh creep—for after all, even Yankees are human beings, though they don't always behave like it.

"Yes," I said, "I had heard of it, but thought it a horrible thing."

"I don't b'lieve in losin' 'em, neither, as a gener'l thing," he went on. "I don't think it's right principul, and I wouldn't lose one myself, but when I see what they have done to these people round here, I can't blame 'em for losin' every devil of 'em they kin git their hands on."

"What was the process of losing?" asked the captain. "Did they manage the business with firearms?"

"Sometimes, when they was in a hurry," Mr. Weller explained, with that horrible, grim irony of his, "the guns would go off an' shoot 'em, in spite of all that our folks could do. But most giner'ly they took the grapevine road in the fust patch of woods they come to, an' soon as ever they got sight of a tree with a grape vine on it, it's cur'ous how skeered their hosses would git. You couldn't keep 'em from runnin' away, no matter what you done, an' they never run fur before their heads was caught in a grape vine and they would stand thar, dancin' on nothin' till they died. Did you ever her of anybody dancin' on nothin' before, lady?"—turning to me.

16

I said he ought to be ashamed to tell it; even a Yankee was
entitled to protection when a prisoner of war.

"But these fellows wasn't regular prisoners of war, lady,"
said the sick soldier; "they were thieves and houseburners,"—
and I couldn't but feel there was something in that view of it.

The sick soldier was distinguishing between foragers—troops authorized to scavenge the countryside in search of food, forage and livestock (as designated in Special Orders 120) and "bummers," undisci-
plined soldiers who entered homes (against Sherman's orders), looted
freely, and sometimes burned them. Burke Davis, another historian of
Sherman's march, reasons that *bummer* came from the German word
bummler, idler or wastrel, and notes that a decade before the war
"'bummer' had come to mean tramp." Nor was the execution of
Northern soldiers caught looting or burning a rare instance. Davis tells
of one such that occurred in the same area of middle Georgia through
which the Andrews sisters were traveling: how the Kentucky cavalrymen of Maj. J. P. Austin came upon a group of foragers who were
looting a plantation. After rounding them up, the Confederates shot
every one.[13]

This passage further leads Miss Andrews to add a footnote, which
is also telling:

In justice to both sides, it must be understood that the class of
prisoners here referred to were stragglers and freebooters who
had wandered off in search of plunder, and probably got no
worse than they deserved when they fell into hands of the enraged country people, who were naturally not inclined to regard
the expropriation of their family plate and household goods and
the burning of homes as a part of legitimate warfare. There were
doubtless many brave and honorable men in Sherman's army
who would not stoop to plunder, and who did the best they could
to keep from making war the "hell" their leader defined it to be,
but these were not the kind who would be likely to get "lost."

---

[13] Davis, *Sherman's March*, 40–41, 72.

Those readers who care to inform themselves fully on the subject, are referred to the official correspondence between General
Sherman and Gen. Wade Hampton in regard to the treatment of
"foragers."

Here again Eliza Frances Andrews proves herself to be a good historian. In August 1880, to a group of Union veterans assembled in
Columbus, Ohio, General Sherman declared, "There is many a boy
here today who looks on war as all glory, but, boys, it is all hell." The
speech was published in the *Ohio State Journal* on August 12, 1880,
and from there the phrase worked its way into the literature—such that
Miss Andrews could refer to it with familiarity.[14]

She was also aware of an incident that occurred in the closing
months of the war.

In February 1865 Sherman's army, having spent a month at Savannah, started marching into South Carolina. Even more than in
Georgia, bummers wreaked harsh vengeance on the state, which had
initiated secession and arguably started the war. Southerners struck
back. Sherman learned that some of his troops had been found dead,
with signs on their bodies reading "death to foragers." On February
24, he addressed a letter of protest to Lt. Gen. Wade Hampton, in
command of Southern cavalry in the Carolinas. Sherman asserted that
foraging was a long-accepted war practice and that soldiers captured
when so engaged should not be murdered. He threatened to retaliate
for his men's deaths. Hampton countered, writing that Sherman's "foragers' were actually house-burners, and that he had ordered his troops
to shoot on sight any arsonist. He further threatened to execute two
Union prisoners for every Confederate's death that Sherman ordered.[15]
(Nothing happened further from this incident.)

---

[14] Lloyd Lewis, *Sherman Fighting Prophet* (New York: Harcourt, Brace &
World, 1958 [1932]), 635–36.

[15] Manly Wade Wellman, *Giant in Gray: A Biography of Wade Hampton of
South Carolina* (New York: Charles Scribner's Sons, 1949), 169–70; Edward G.
Longacre, *Gentleman and Soldier: A Biography of Wade Hampton III* (Nashville:
Rutledge Hill Press, 2003), 230.

The lively Sherman-Hampton correspondence made its way into Southern newspapers, which would have been how Miss Andrews learned of it. In the end, recognizing Northern soldiers as "thieves and houseburners" did much to fuel Fanny's longstanding animosity toward Yankees.

January 1865

When Fanny Andrews begins the second chapter of her *War-Time Journal*, it is under date of January 1, 1865; she was writing from the Butlers' plantation, Pine Bluff, a few miles southeast of Albany, Georgia. The trip from Washington had taken perhaps ten days; we only know that by January 1, 1865, Fanny and Mett were at their sister's plantation.

Along the way the two sisters had experienced much. Making their way toward Macon, Fanny states that a mile and a half east of there a creek bridge "had been damaged by Stoneman's raiders last summer" and was recently so weakened by a storm that the engineer stopped his train, refusing to cross. Someone sent for cars from Macon and a few hours later the two pilgrims were trudging across the trestle on foot to board the train that would carry them into the central Georgia city.

Miss Andrews proved to be an able historian. In late July 1864, Maj. Gen. George Stoneman had led a mounted column from Sherman's army near Atlanta, riding south toward Macon. There Stoneman hoped to free the several thousand Federal officers confined at Camp Oglethorpe. He failed in that effort, but on July 30 his men burned the bridge across Walnut Creek.[1] The storm-weakened trestle that had halted the sisters' trek had soon been rebuilt by Confederates.

The Southwestern Railroad from Macon to Albany, ninety miles by direct line, had not been touched by enemy raiders, so Fanny's journal entries about that part of her trek would likely have been much less dramatic than her observations on "the Burnt Country." The journalist closes her first chapter by noting "several pages are torn from the manuscript here." Frances Andrews made her way from Macon to Albany without further comment.

---

[1] David Evans, *Sherman's Horsemen: Union Cavalry Operations in the Atlanta Campaign* (Bloomington: Indiana University Press, 1996), 309.

General Stoneman ended up at Camp Oglethorpe, but not as liberator. Concluding that an attack on Macon's defenders (several thousand, with artillery) was unfeasible, he led his column in retreat back toward Sherman's army. About twenty miles north of Macon, however, Stoneman's force was so strongly assailed by pursuing Southern horsemen that the general and half his men surrendered on July 31; he sent the rest off to make their escape as best they could.

If Stoneman had been successful in liberating Camp Oglethorpe's inmates, he envisioned riding fifty miles farther south in an attempt to free the thirty thousand Union soldiers imprisoned at Andersonville. Stoneman obviously did not get that far. After the fall of Atlanta on September 2, with Sherman's army ensconced there, the Confederate War Department telegraphed Brig. Gen. John H. Winder to begin sending Andersonville inmates to other POW camps elsewhere in Georgia and South Carolina. By mid-November, about the time Sherman started marching for the sea, only fifteen hundred Federal prisoners remained at Andersonville.[2]

This did not keep Miss Andrews from focusing on Andersonville. As she was editing her journal thirty years after the war, Fanny addressed the question of whether Confederate authorities such as Capt. Henry Wirz, commandant at Andersonville, should have been charged with deliberate cruelty to prisoners, as was being propagated in the North during postwar decades. (Wirz had been hanged in November 1865 after trial by a Federal military court.) Fanny's consideration of the matter demonstrates that she was, in the words of the Andersonville historian Ovid L. Futch (who quotes her), "an ardent rebel and a cultured Southern belle."[3]

---

[2] Stephen Davis, *All the Fighting They Want: The Atlanta Campaign from Peachtree Creek to the City's Surrender, July 18–September 2, 1864* (El Dorado Hills, CA: Savas Beatie, 2017), 69; Stephen Davis, *Into Tennessee and Failure: John Bell Hood* (Macon: Mercer University Press, 2020), 24; John K. Derden, *The World's Largest Prison: The Story of Camp Lawton* (Macon: Mercer University Press, 2012), 71.

[3] Robert Scott Davis Jr., "Andersonville Prison" in John C. Inscoe, ed., *The Civil War in Georgia* (Athens: University of Georgia Press, 2011), 145–46; Ovid

It is not my purpose to dwell upon public events in these pages, nor to revive the dark memories of Andersonville, but a few words concerning it are necessary to a clear understanding of the allusions made to it in this part of the record, and to a just appreciation of the position of the Southern people in regard to that deplorable episode of the war. Owing to the policy of the Federal Government in refusing to exchange prisoners, and to the ruin and devastation of war, which made it impossible for the Confederate government to provide adequately for its own soldiers, even with the patriotic aid of our women, the condition of our prisons was anything but satisfactory, both from lack of supplies and from the unavoidable over-crowding caused by the failure of all efforts to effect an exchange. Mr. Tanner, ex-Commander of the G. A. R., who is the last person in the world whom one would think of citing as a witness for the South, bears this unconscious testimony to the force of circumstances that made it impossible for our government to remedy that unhappy situation:

"It is true that more prisoners died in Northern prisons than Union prisoners died in Southern prisons. The explanation of this is extremely simple. The Southern prisoners came North worn and emaciated—half starved. *They had reached this condition because of their scant rations.* They came from a mild climate to a rigorous Northern climate, and, although we gave them shelter and plenty to eat, they could not stand the change."

This argument, intended as a defense of the North, is a boomerang whose force as a weapon for the other side it is unnecessary to point out. Whether the conditions at Andersonville might have been ameliorated by the personal efforts of those in charge, I do not know. I never met Capt. Wirz, but I do know that had he been an angel from heaven, he could not have changed the pitiful tale of suffering from privation and hunger unless he had possessed the power to repeat the miracle of the loaves and fishes. I do know, too, that the sufferings of the prisoners were viewed with the deepest compassion by the people in the

L. Futch, *A History of Andersonville Prison* (Gainesville: University of Florida Press, 1968), 138–39.

neighborhood, as the diary will show, and they would gladly have relieved them if they had been able. In the fall of 1864, when it was feared that Sherman would send a raid to free the prisoners and turn them loose upon the defenseless country, a band of several thousand were shipped round by rail to Camp Lawton, near Millen, to get them out of his way. Later, when he passed on, after destroying the railroads, these men were marched back overland to Andersonville, and the planters who lived along the road had hampers filled with such provisions as could be hastily gotten together and placed before them. Among those who did this were my sister, Mrs. Troup Butler, and her neighbors, the Bacons, so frequently mentioned in this part of the diary. My sister says that she had every drop of milk and clabber in her dairy brought out and given to the poor fellows, and she begged the officer to let them wait till she could have what food she could spare cooked for them. This, however, being impossible, she had potatoes and turnips and whatever else could be eaten raw, hastily collected by the servants and strewn in the road before them. I have before me, as I write, a very kind letter from an old Union soldier, in which he says that he was one of the men fed on this occasion, and he adds: "I still feel thankful for the help we got that day." He gives his name as S. S. Andrews, Co. K, 64th Ohio Vols., and his present address as Tularosa, Mexico.

But it is hardly to be expected that men half-crazed by suffering and for the most part ignorant of their own government's responsibility in the matter, should discriminate very closely in apportioning the blame for their terrible condition. Accustomed to the bountiful provision made for its soldiers by the richest nation in the world, they naturally enough could not see the tragic humor of their belief, when suddenly reduced to Confederate army rations, that they were the victims of a deliberate plot to starve them to death!

Another difficulty with which the officers in charge of the stockade had to contend was the lack of a sufficient force to guard so large a body of prisoners. At one time there were over 35,000 of them at Andersonville alone—a number exceeding Lee's entire force at the close of the siege of Petersburg. The men actually available for guarding this great army, were never more than 1,200 or 1,500, and these were drawn from the State Reserves, consisting of boys under eighteen and invalided or superannuated men unfit for active service. At almost any time during the year 1864–1865, if the prisoners had realized the weakness of their guard, they could, by a concerted assault, have overpowered them. At the time of Kilpatrick's projected raid, their numbers had been reduced to about 7,500, by distributing the excess to other points and by the humane action of the Confederate authorities in releasing, without equivalent, 15,000 sick and wounded, and actually forcing them, as a free gift, upon the unwilling hospitality of their own government.

But even allowing for this diminution, the consequences of turning so large a body of men, naturally incensed and made desperate by suffering, to incite the negroes and ravage the country, while there were only women and children and old men left on the plantations to meet their fury, can hardly be imagined, even by those who have seen the invasion of an organized army The consternation of my father, when he found that he had sent us into the jaws of this danger instead of the security and rest he had counted on, cannot be described. Happily, the danger was over before he knew of its existence, but communication was so slow and uncertain in those days that a long correspondence at cross purposes ensued before his mind was set at rest.

Several points are apparent in Miss Andrews's disquisition.

1. The Federal government bore some major degree of culpability for the suffering among Andersonville inmates by ending POW exchanges. In July 1862, the two governments had arranged a cartel for the exchange of prisoners of all ranks (e.g., sixty privates equaled one general). On April 17, 1864, however, the recently promoted Union general-in-chief Ulysses S. Grant ordered the exchanges to cease,

believing that they aided the South more than the North, with its larger manpower resources.[4]

2. That Northern prisoners suffered and died at Andersonville was not in dispute, Miss Andrews concedes, but the Confederate government was not to be blamed for their malnutrition and starvation. By February 1864, when Camp Sumter (as it was officially called) began receiving inmates, much food-providing territory in the South lay under enemy occupation. Moreover, the Confederate railroad "system" was in widespread disrepair and strained by overuse. Nevertheless, in early May a Southern officer reported that prisoners' rations were "the same as those issued to Confederate soldiers in the field." When General Winder asked that ten days' rations be kept on hand at the prison camp, the Confederate commissary general in Richmond exploded, replying Confederate soldiers were given only one day's ration, and that Federal prisoners should not get anything more. In October 1865, when he heard that Captain Wirz was in prison, the chief commissary officer in Georgia wrote him that "the Andersonville prisoners were supplied from this post with precisely the same rations as our army in the field."[5]

3. Fanny made certain to mention the good-heartedness of Southern civilians toward the blue-clad unfortunates. In summer 1864, General Winder recommended, given the overcrowding at Camp Sumter, that another POW facility be built. In early August authorities chose a site near Millen, Georgia (seventy miles northwest of Savannah). During the next two months, a tall wooden stockade was built that enclosed forty-two acres, a space so large (Andersonville had twenty-six)

---

[4] Peggy Robbins, "Prisoners" in Patricia L. Faust, ed., *Historical Times Illustrated Encyclopedia of the Civil War* (New York: Harper & Row, 1986), 604.

[5] Futch, *Andersonville Prison*, 21; Arch Fredric Blakey, *General John H. Winder, C.S.A.* (Gainesville: University of Florida Press, 1990), 189; Jerrold Northrop Moore, *Confederate Commissary General: Lucius Bellinger Northrop and the Subsistence Bureau of the Southern Army* (Shippensburg, PA: White Mane Publishing Co., 1996), 289.

that Winder believed it was "the largest prison in the world." It came to be called Camp Lawton.

The first Northern POWs arrived in the second week of October; eventually Camp Lawton would hold 10,300 prisoners. The facility had barely gotten underway, however, when it had to be evacuated; Sherman and his army were marching toward it. Lawton was emptied by November 22, about the time Sherman's troops were entering Milledgeville, eighty miles to the northwest.

Frances's tale of her sister feeding Union prisoners being marched back to Camp Sumter is a touching one. When Lawton was abandoned, Confederates sent sick captives to Savannah for exchange ("releasing, without equivalent, 15,000 sick and wounded, and actually forcing them, as a free gift, upon the unwilling hospitality of their own government," in the words of the journalist). The rest were taken by train south to a holding camp near Blackshear, Georgia. Toward the end of the war, twenty-five hundred of these latter were hauled by train across south Georgia to Thomasville. Many of them were then marched northward back to Andersonville, despite their pitiable condition.[6] Their route would have taken them through Albany, perhaps past Pine Bluff; hence sister Cora's story of bringing out vegetables and dairy goods for the hungry fellows, and the Ohio veteran's postwar letter of gratitude to her.

4. Fanny declares that Union prisoners at Camp Sumter received the same measure of rations as Southern fighting men, and some evidence supports her. In May 1864, a Confederate officer inspected the camp and reported that rations were "the same as those issued to Confederate soldiers in the field." Still, insufficient rations, shortage of utensils and of wood for cooking remained severe problems throughout the existence of the prison.

---

[6] William Marvel, *Andersonville: The Last Depot* (Chapel Hill: University of North Carolina Press, 1994), 222; Derden, *Camp Lawton*, 155, 195.

Dr. Futch, the historian of Andersonville, is on the mark in declaring "many Southern apologists maintain that the prisoners received the same rations as the guards."[7] Eliza Andrews was one of them.

5. As for the number of guards at Andersonville—"never more than 1,200 or 1,500, and these were drawn from the State Reserves"— Miss Andrews was well informed. The number of guards stayed about the same throughout spring and summer 1864, even as the number of inmates grew: 1,193 [guards] to 13,218 [prisoners]on May 1; 1,462 to 23,120 on June 18; and 1,551 to 29,998 July 20–31. Most of these were indeed Georgia Reserves, "as raw as troops can be," General Winder complained in late June. (The Georgia Reserve Force, created in spring 1864, comprised males seventeen to eighteen years old and forty-five to fifty years old. Four regiments of Reserves were stationed at Andersonville. Fanny was also right in stating that many of these were unfit for field duty.)[8]

At the same time, she rather overstated the threat of an uprising by the inmates. Tall timbers formed a wall fifteen feet high, atop which at distances were sentry boxes for guards who kept watch on the crowded prisoners below them. Fifteen feet into the stockade was a wooden railing called "the dead line"; guards shot without warning any Yankee who crossed this line, even inadvertently.[9] More important, a well-constructed earthwork, with artillery that could sweep the entire stockade, had been built off the southwest corner of the stockade. That was only one of six more batteries placed around the prison, whose inmates were well aware of the canister and shrapnel that could be fired at them if they rose up.[10]

---

[7] Futch, *Andersonville Prison*, 7, 21.

[8] Futch, *Andersonville Prison*, 20, 31, 73, 77, 79; William R. Scaife and William Harris Bragg, *Joe Brown's Pets: The Georgia Militia 1861–1865* (Macon: Mercer University Press, 2004), 213.

[9] Robert S. Davis, *Ghosts and Shadows of Andersonville: Essays on the Secret Social Histories of America's Deadliest Prison* (Macon: Mercer University Press, 2006), 12.

[10] Marvel, *Last Depot*, 152.

Still, the young woman—who worried about "the consequences of turning loose so large a body of men, naturally incensed and made desperate by suffering, to incite the negroes and ravage the country, while there were only women and children and old men left on the plantations to meet their fury"—was the same Fanny Andrews who fretted about Yankee raiders descending upon Andersonville to free their comrades. She writes of

> an expedition sent out from Sherman under Gen. Kilpatrick, having for its object the destruction of the Stockade at Andersonville, and release of the prisoners to wreak their vengeance on the people whom they believed to be responsible for their sufferings. The success of this movement was frustrated only by the incessant rains of that stormy winter, which flooded the intervening country so that it was impossible for even the best equipped cavalry to pass, and thus averted what might have been the greatest tragedy of the war.

Except that it didn't happen; in early January 1865 Sherman and his army were in and around Savannah, 180 miles east of Andersonville. The commanding general was at the time planning to lead his forces into South Carolina, not back across Georgia. And on January 11, 1865, when Fanny wrote of "perpetual alarms of Yankee raiders," Brig. Gen. Judson Kilpatrick, in charge of Sherman's cavalry, was overseeing a parade review of his troopers in the streets of Savannah.[11]

But fear wields a heavy cudgel, as one reads in the pages of *The War-Time Journal*. Throughout January one sees trepidation and excoriation of Yankees virtually drip across its pages, even amidst expressions of sympathy for the poor souls still suffering at Camp Sumter. Fanny Andrews was experiencing what many Southerners did.

---

[11] Derek Smith, *Civil War Savannah* (Savannah: Frederic C. Beil, 1997), 221–31; John F. Marszalek, *Sherman: A Soldier's Passion for Order* (New York: Free Press, 1993), 317–18; Samuel J. Martin, *Kill-Cavalry: The Life of Union General Hugh Judson Kilpatrick* (Mechanicsburg, PA: Stackpole Books, 2000), 208.

Wartime emotions can be complex indeed, as one further sees in the ensuing journal extracts.

Jan. 11, Wednesday.—I am just getting well of measles, and a rough time I had of it. Measles is no such small affair after all, especially when aggravated by perpetual alarms of Yankee raiders. For the last week we have lived in a state of incessant fear. All sort of rumors come up the road and down it, and we never know what to believe. Mett and I have received repeated letters from home urging our immediate return, but of course it was impossible to travel while I was sick in bed, and even now I am not strong enough to undertake that terrible journey across the burnt country again. While I was ill, home was the one thought that haunted my brain, and if I ever do get back, I hope I will have sense enough to stay there. I don't think I ever suffered so much before in all my life, and dread of the Yankees raised my fever to such a pitch that I got no rest by night or day. I used to feel very brave about Yankees, but since I have passed over Sherman's track and seen what devastation they make, I am so afraid of them that I believe I should drop down dead if one of the wretches should come into my presence.[12] I would rather face them anywhere than here in South-West Georgia, for the horrors of the stockade have so enraged them that they will have no mercy on this country, though they have brought it all on themselves, the cruel monsters, by refusing to exchange prisoners. But it is horrible, and a blot on the fair name of our Confederacy. Mr. Robert Bacon says he has accurate information that on the first of December, 1864, there were 13,010 graves at Andersonville.[13]

---

[12] This passage is quoted in Mary Ellen Snodgrass, *Encyclopedia of Southern Literature* (Santa Barbara, CA: ABC-CLIO, 1997), 50.

[13] Several months after the war, Clara Barton, the Massachusetts humanitarian, led a group of three dozen workmen to mark the graves of Union soldiers who had died at Andersonville and had been buried in the prison cemetery. The expedition counted 12,920 graves (Steve Davis, "Monumentation and the National Cemetery at Andersonville," *Blue & Gray* 3/3 [December 1985–January 1986]: 48–49).

It is a dreadful record. I shuddered as I passed the place on the cars, with its tall gibbet full of horrible suggestiveness before the gate, and its seething mass of humanity inside, like a swarm of blue flies crawling over a grave. It is said that the prisoners have organized their own code of laws among themselves, and have established courts of justice before which they try offenders, and that they sometimes condemn one of their number to death.[14] It is horrible to think of, but what can we poor Confederates do? The Yankees won't exchange prisoners, and our own soldiers in the field don't fare much better than these poor creatures. Everybody is sorry for them, and wouldn't keep them here a day if the government at Washington didn't force them on us. And yet they lay all the blame on us. Gen. Sherman told Mr. Cuyler that he did not intend to leave so much as a blade of grass in South-West Georgia, and Dr. Janes told sister that he (Sherman) said he would be obliged to send a formidable raid here in order to satisfy the clamors of his army, though he himself, the fiend Sherman, dreaded it on account of the horrors that would be committed. What Sherman dreads must indeed be fearful. They say his soldiers have sworn that they will spare neither man, woman nor child in all South-West Georgia. It is only a matter of time, I suppose, when all this will be done. It begins to look as if the Yankees can do whatever they please and go everywhere they wish—except to heaven; I do fervently pray the good Lord to give us rest from them there.

While I was at my worst, Mrs. Lawton came out with her brother-in-law, Mr. George Lawton, and Dr. Richardson, Medical

---

[14] During summer 1864, a number of prisoners began robbing their comrades, even in broad daylight. The inmates organized and, with General Winder's permission, hunted down some seventy-five "raiders," as they had come to be called. An internal court found dozens guilty and sentenced them to have to run a gauntlet of their comrades, who beat them with clubs and sticks. Six ringleaders were sentenced to death. On July 11, 1864, they were hanged on makeshift gallows constructed inside the stockade (Stephanie Steinhorst and Chris Barr, *The Prison Camp at Andersonville* [Fort Washington, PA: Eastern National, 2014], 22).

Director of Bragg's army,[15] to make sister a visit. The doctor came into my room and prescribed for me and did me more good by his cheerful talk than by his prescription. He told me not to think about the Yankees, and said that he would come and carry me away himself before I should fall into their hands. His medicine nearly killed me. It was a big dose of opium and whisky, that drove me stark crazy, but when I came to myself I felt much better. Dr. Janes was my regular physician and had the merit of not giving much medicine, but he frightened me horribly with his rumors about Yankee raiders. We are safe from them for the present, at any rate, I hope; the swamps of the Altamaha are so flooded that it would take an army of Tritons to get over them now.

Jan. 12, Thursday.—The rest of them out visiting again all the morning, leaving me to enjoy life with Mrs. Meals and Hannah More. The Edwin Bacons and Merrill Callaway and his bride were invited to spend the evening with us and I found it rather dull. I am just sick enough to be a bore to myself and everybody else. Merrill has married Katy Furlow, of Americus, and she says that soon after my journey home last spring she met my young Charlestonian, and that he went into raptures over me, and said he never was so delighted with anybody in his life, so it seems that attraction was mutual. I have a letter from Tolie; she is living in Montgomery, supremely happy, of course, as a bride should be. She was sadly disappointed at my absence from the wedding. The city is very gay, she says, and everybody inquiring about me and wanting me to come. If I wasn't afraid the Yankees might cut me off from home and sister, too, I would pick up and go now. Yankee, Yankee, is the one detestable word always ringing in Southern ears. If all the words of hatred in every language under

---

[15] Dr. Tobias Gibson Richardson (1827–1892) practiced surgery in New Orleans before the war. As a Confederate, he became medical-inspector of the Army of Tennessee. After the war, he returned to New Orleans. He was elected president of the American Medical Association in 1877 (Joseph Jones, "Roster of the Medical Officers of the Army of Tennessee," *Southern Historical Society Papers* 22 [1894]: 251–52).

heaven were lumped together into one huge epithet of detestation, they could not tell how I hate Yankees. They thwart all my plans, murder my friends, and make my life miserable.

Jan. 13th, Friday.—Col. Blake, a refugee from Mississippi, and his sister-in-law, Miss Connor, dined with us. While the gentlemen lingered over their wine after dinner, we ladies sat in the parlor making cigarettes for them.[16] The evening was spent at cards, which bored me a little, for I hate cards; they are good for nothing but to entertain stupid visitors with, and Col. Blake and Miss Connor do not belong in that category. Mett says she don't like the old colonel because he is too pompous, but that amuses me,—and then, he is such a gentleman.

The newspapers bring accounts of terrible floods all over the country. Three bridges are washed away on the Montgomery & West Point R.R., so that settles the question of going to Montgomery for the present. Our fears about the Yankees are quieted, too, there being none this side of the Altamaha, and the swamps impassable.

Jan. 16, Monday.—Sister has come back, bringing little Mrs. Sims with her. Metta and I are to spend next week in Albany with Mrs. Sims, if we are not all water-bound in the meantime, at Pine Bluff. The floods are subsiding up the country, but the waters are raging down here. Flint River is out of its banks, the low grounds are overflowed, and the backwater has formed a lake between the negro quarter and the house, that reaches to within a few yards of the door. So much the better for us, as Kilpatrick and his raiders can never make their way through all these floods.

Sister is greatly troubled about a difficulty two of her negroes, Jimboy and Alfred, have gotten into. They are implicated with some others who are accused of stealing leather and attacking a white man. Alfred is a great, big, horrid-looking creature, more like an orang-outang than a man, though they say he is one of the most peaceable and humble negroes on the plantation,

---

[16] Cigarettes date back to Central America centuries ago, but the French coined the term ("little cigar") in the 1830s. Their use became widespread in Europe after the Crimean War (1853–1856).

and Jimboy has never been known to get into any mischief before. I hope there is some mistake, though the negroes are getting very unruly since the Yankees are so near.

Jan. 19, Thursday.—About noon a cavalryman stopped at the door and asked for dinner. As we eat late, and the man was in too big a hurry to wait, sister sent him a cold lunch out in the entry. It was raining very hard, and the poor fellow was thoroughly drenched, so after he had eaten, sister invited him to come into the parlor and dry himself. It came out, in the course of conversation, that he was from our own part of Georgia, and knew a number of good old Wilkes County families. He was on his way to the Altamaha, he said, and promised to do his best to keep the raiders from getting to us.

Jan. 22.—The rains returned with double fury in the night and continued all day. If "the stars in their courses fought against Sisera,"[17] it looks as if the heavens are doing as much for us against Kilpatrick and his raiders. There was no service at St. Paul's, so Mrs. Sims kept Metta and me in the line of duty by reading aloud High Church books to us. They were very dull, so I didn't hurt myself listening. After dinner we read the Church service and sang hymns until relieved by a call from our old friend, Capt. Hobbs.

Jan. 25, Wednesday.—Dined at Judge Vason's, where there was a large company. He is very hospitable and his house is always full of people. Albert Bacon came in from Gum Pond and called in the afternoon, bringing letters, and the letters brought permission to remain in South-West Georgia as long as we please, the panic about Kilpatrick having died out. I would like to be at home now, if the journey were not such a hard one. Garnett and Mrs. Elzey are both there, and Mary Day is constantly expected. I have not seen Garnett for nearly three years. He has resigned his position on Gen. Gardiner's staff,[18] and is going to take command of a battalion of "galvanized Yankees," with the

---

[17] The phrase comes from Judges 5:20. Sisera commanded a Canaanite army defeated by the Israelites.

[18] "Gen. Gardiner" was Confederate brigadier general William M. Gardner.

rank of Lieutenant-Colonel.[19] I don't like the scheme. I have no faith in Yankees of any sort, especially these miserable turncoats that are ready to sell themselves to either side. There isn't gold enough in existence to galvanize one of them into a respectable Confederate.

Jan. 27, Friday.—While going our rounds in the morning, we found a very important person in Peter Louis, a paroled Yankee prisoner, in the employ of Capt. Bonham. The captain keeps him out of the stockade, feeds and clothes him, and in return, reaps the benefit of his skill. Peter is a French Yankee,[20] a shoemaker by trade, and makes as beautiful shoes as I ever saw imported from France. My heart quite softened towards him when I saw his handiwork, and little Miss Sims was so overcome that she gave him a huge slice of her Confederate fruit cake. I talked French with him, which pleased him greatly, and Mett and I engaged him to make us each a pair of shoes. I will feel like a lady once more, with good shoes on my feet. I expect the poor Yank is glad to get away from Anderson on any terms. Although matters have improved somewhat with the cool weather, the tales that are told of the conditions there last summer are appalling.

---

[19] "Galvanized Yankees," according to the authority on the subject, were "former soldiers of the Confederate States of America…[who] accepted the blue uniform of the United States Army in exchange for freedom from prison pens…. Sent to the Western frontier…they soon found a new foe, the Plains Indians" (D. Alexander Brown, *The Galvanized Yankees* [Urbana: University of Illinois Press, 1963], 1). The terms got mixed up during the war, however, as here Miss Andrews clearly refers to her brother taking over *galvanized Confederates*—Union soldiers, probably imprisoned at Camp Sumter, agreeing to don the Confederate gray to try to save their lives this late in the war. The process made metallurgic sense, as the process of galvanizing involved covering blue steel with dull gray zinc (Brown, *Galvanized Yankees*, 121–22; Marvel, *Last Depot*, 300n.7).

[20] [Miss Andrews's note:]

Everybody that fought in the Union army was classed by us as a Yankee, whether Southern Union men, foreigners, or negroes; hence the expressions "Irish Yankee," "Dutch Yankee," "black Yankee," etc., in contradistinction to the Simon-pure native product, "the Yankee" *par excellence.*

Mrs. Brisbane heard all about it from Father Hamilton, a Roman Catholic priest from Macon who has been working like a good Samaritan in those dens of filth and misery. It is a shame to us Protestants that we have let a Roman Catholic get so far ahead of us in this work of charity and mercy. Mrs. Brisbane says Father Hamilton told her that during the summer the wretched prisoners burrowed in the ground like moles to protect themselves from the sun.[21] It was not safe to give them material to build shanties as they might use it for clubs to overcome the guard. These underground huts, he said, were alive with vermin and stank like charnel houses.[22] Many of the prisoners were stark naked, having not so much as a shirt to their backs.[23] He told a pitiful story of a Pole who had no garment but a shirt, and to make it cover him the better, he put his legs into the sleeves and tied the tail round his neck. The others guyed him so on his appearance,

---

[21] In May 1864, a Catholic priest from Macon, the Rev. William John Hamilton, visited Andersonville, wishing particularly to minister to the many Catholics believed to be among the prison population. Father Hamilton, an Irishman, spent three days in the crowded stockade, with the complete cooperation of Captain Wirz, himself a Catholic.

[22] Although forest stood all around the stockade, prison authorities never gave inmates enough wood to build huts or shanties, much less build barracks for them. "Many prisoners burrowed in the ground for shelter," Futch writes, "running the risk of suffocation from cave-ins, and of course their quarters became waterholes when heavy rains fell" (*Andersonville Prison*, 31). During Wirz's trial in fall 1865, Hamilton remembered, "I would frequently have to creep on my hands and knees into the holes that the men had burrowed in the ground and stretch myself out along side of them to hear their confessions" (*Andersonville Prison*, 59–60; Marvel, *Last Depot*, 140; Davis, *Ghosts and Shadows of Andersonville*, 129–31).

[23] Father Hamilton testified, "I saw a great many men perfectly nude; they seemed to have lost all regard for delicacy, shame, morality or anything else," (Davis, *Ghosts and Shadows*, 12). Futch adds "Prisoners who needed clothing would expect no help from their captors, for the Confederacy could not clothe its own men in the field. Consequently many prisoners suffered from lack of both shelter and clothing. Indeed, some had no clothing at all" (Futch, *Andersonville Prison*, 31–32).

and the poor wretch was so disheartened by suffering, that one day he deliberately stepped over the deadline and stood there till the guard was forced to shoot him. But what I can't understand is that a Pole, of all people in the world, should come over here and try to take away our liberty when his own country is in the hands of oppressors. One would think that the Poles, of all nations in the world, ought to sympathize with a people fighting for their liberties. Father Hamilton said that at one time the prisoners died at the rate of 150 a day,[24] and he saw some of them die on the ground without a rag to lie on or a garment to cover them. Dysentery was the most fatal disease, and as they lay on the ground in their own excrements, the smell was so horrible that the good father says he was often obliged to rush from their presence to get a breath of pure air.[25] It is dreadful. My heart aches for the poor wretches, Yankees though they are, and I am afraid God will suffer some terrible retribution to fall upon us for letting such things happen. If the Yankees ever should come to South-West Georgia, and go to Anderson and see the graves there, God have mercy on the land! And yet, what can we do? The Yankees themselves are really more to blame than we, for they won't exchange these prisoners, and our poor, hard-pressed Confederacy has not the means to provide for them, when our own soldiers are starving in the field. Oh, what a horrible thing war is when stripped of all its "pomp and circumstance"!

---

[24] Father Hamilton was a bit high. August 23 was the single-highest day of deaths at Camp Sumter, when 127 inmates perished (Futch, *Andersonville Prison*, 44; "Consolidated return for the C.S. military prison, Camp Sumter…for the week ending August 28, 1864," *OR*, ser. 2, vol. 7, 518).

[25] Diarrhea and dysentery were indeed the leading causes of death among Andersonville prisoners; in the six months from March 1 to September 1, 1864, they accounted for 58.7 percent of inmates' deaths—3,530 of them (Futch, *Andersonville Prison*, 107).

February 1865

In early February Frances recorded in her diary all the preparations that she, Mett, Cora, and neighbors were making for a theatrical program being staged for entertainment. "We spent the evening at Maj. Edwin Bacon's, rehearsing for tableaux and theatricals," she wrote on the February 2, "and I never enjoyed an evening more…. After the rehearsal came a display of costumes and a busy devising of dresses, which interested me very much. I do love pretty clothes, and it has been my fate to live in these hard war times, when one can have so little."

Because she loved pretty clothes—as a lot of women do—given the lack of sewing materials in the Confederacy, the wartime Georgia girl exercised imagination and creativity in making and repairing her wardrobe. In "Dress under Difficulties," her article published in *Godey's Lady's Book* in 1866, she describes the art of sartorial improvisation:

> How we patched, and pieced, and ripped, and altered; how we cut, and turned, and twisted; how we made one new dress out of two old ones; how we squeezed new waists out of single breadths taken from skirts which could ill spare a single fold; how we worked and strained to find out new fashion, and then worked and strained still harder to adopt them—all these things form chapters in the lives of most of us, which will not be easily forgotten.[1]

When Fanny succeeded at this art form, she was quite pleased. In the middle of February, a party was held in Albany which, to judge by the journalist's notice of everyone's costumery, must have been quite

---

[1] Elzey Hay, "Dress under Difficulties," in S. Kittell Rushing, ed., *Journal of a Georgia Woman, 1870–1872* (Knoxville: University of Tennessee Press, 2002), 75.

fancy indeed. But as with much of *The War-Journal*, Miss Andrews's writing led back to the Yankees, in this case "their horrid blockade."

> Metta was the belle, par excellence, but Miss Pyncheon and I were not very far behind, and I think I was ahead of them all in my dress. Miss Pyncheon wore a white puffed Tarleton, with pearls and white flowers. The dress, though beautiful, was not becoming because the one fault of her fine, aristocratic face is want of color. A little rouge and sepia would improve her greatly, if a nice girl could make up her mind to use them. Mett wore white Suisse with festoon flounces, over my old blue Florence silk skirt, the flounces, like charity, covering a multitude of faults. She was a long way the prettiest one in the room, though her hair is too short to be done up stylishly. But my dress was a masterpiece [sic!] though patched up, like everybody else's, out of old finery that would have been cast off years ago, but for the blockade. I wore a white barred organdy with a black lace flounce round the bottom that completely hid the rents made at dances in Montgomery last winter, and a wide black lace bow and ends in the back, to match the flounce. Handsome lace will make almost anything look respectable, and I thank my stars there was a good deal of it in the family before the Yankees shut us off by their horrid blockade. My waist was of light puffed blonde, very fluffy, made out of the skirt I wore at Henry's wedding, and trimmed round the neck and sleeves with ruchings edged with narrow black lace. My hair was frizzed in front, with a cluster of white hyacinths surmounting the top row of curls, and a beautifully embroidered butterfly Aunt Sallie had made for me half-hidden among them, as if seeking its way to the flowers. My train was very long, but I pinned it up like a tunic, over a billowy flounced muslin petticoat, while dancing.

On February 10, Fanny and Mett took the train to Americus, thirty miles to the north, to visit their cousin Dr. Bolling Pope, a physician in practice there. The two sisters were shopping downtown when they encountered Cousin Bolling. In this extract, Fanny remarks on the fine dresses still able to be worn by "a brand new bride from beyond the blockade"—meaning Memphis, which had been under Federal occupation for two and a half years, and whose citizens could now trade in Northern goods. She also reflects on her red hair, Yankee manners, and the kind of men she likes.

We had gone only a few steps when we saw him coming toward us. His first words were the announcement that he was married! I couldn't believe him at first, and thought he was joking. Then he insisted that we should go home with him and see our new cousin. We felt doubtful about displaying our patched up Confederate traveling suits before a brand new bride from beyond the blockade, with trunk loads of new things, but curiosity got the better of us, and so we agreed to go home with him. He is occupying Col. Maxwell's house while the family are on the plantation in Lee county. When we reached the house with Cousin Bolling, Mrs. Pope—or "Cousin Bessie," as she says we must call her now, made us feel easy by sending for us to come to her bedroom, as there was no fire in the parlor, and she would not make company of us. She was a Mrs. Ayres, before her marriage to Cousin Bolling, a young widow from Memphis, Tenn., and very prominent in society there. She is quite handsome, and, having just come from beyond the lines, her beautiful dresses were a revelation to us dowdy Confederates, and made me feel like a plucked peacock. Her hair was arranged in three rolls over the top of the head, on each side of the part, in the style called, "cats, rats, and mice," on account of the different size of the rolls, the top one being the largest. It was very stylish. I wish my hair was long enough to dress that way, for I am getting very tired of frizzes; they are so much trouble, and always will come out in wet weather. We were so much interested that we stayed at Cousin Bolling's too long and had to run nearly all the way back to the depot in order to catch our train. On the cars I met the very last man I would have expected to see in this part of the world—my Boston friend, Mr. Adams. He said he was on his way to take charge of a Presbyterian church in Eufaula, Ala. He had on a broadcloth coat and a stovepipe hat, which are so unlike anything

worn by our Confederate men that I felt uncomfortably conspicuous while he was with me. I am almost ashamed, nowadays, to
be seen with any man not in uniform, though Mr. Adams, being
a Northern man and a minister, could not, of course, be expected
to go into the army. I believe he is sincere in his Southern sympathies, but his Yankee manners and lingo "sorter riles" me, as the
darkies say, in spite of reason and common sense. He talked religion all the way to Smithville, and parted with some pretty sentiment about the "sunbeam I had thrown across his path." I don't
enjoy that sort of talk from men; I like dash and flash and fire in
talk, as in action.

In her upbringing, social status, and outlook, Eliza Frances Andrews was a Southern belle. This comes through in her deprecation of
poor White folks (called "crackers") in the area of Pine Bluff. Cora's
husband, Troup Butler, had an invalid sister, Mrs. Julia Meals, living
with the family during the war. Fanny described her as "a pious widow
of ample means which it was her chief ambition in life to spend in
doing good." As attestation, Julia planned to organize a Sunday school
at Pine Bluff for the children of the poor Whites living nearby.

Mrs. Meals asked me to go with her in the afternoon to visit some
of the cracker people in our neighborhood and try to collect their
children into a Sunday school which the dear, pious little soul proposed to open at Pine Bluff after the manner of Hannah More.[2]
At one place, where the parents were away from home, the children ran away from us in a fright, and hid behind their cabin. I
went after them, and capturing one little boy, soon made friends
with him, and got him to bring the others to me. I was surprised
to find the wife of our nearest cracker neighbor, who lived just
beyond the lime sink, in a cabin that Brother Troup wouldn't put
one of his negroes into, a remarkably handsome woman, in spite
of the dirt and ignorance in which she lives. Her features are as

---

[2] Hannah More (1745–1833) was an English philanthropist and writer on
religious and ethical topics. She and her sister Martha also founded schools in the
area of Somerset, in southwest England.

regular and delicate as those of a Grecian statue, and her hair of a rich old mahogany color that I suppose an artist would call Titian red. It was so abundant that she could hardly keep it tucked up on her head. She was dirty and unkempt, and her clothing hardly met the requirements of decency, but all that could not conceal her uncommon beauty. I would give half I am worth for her flashing black eyes. We found that her oldest child is thirteen years old, and has never been inside a church, though Mt. Enon is only three miles away. I can't understand what makes these people live so. The father owns 600 acres of good pine land, and if there was anything in him, ought to make a good living for his family.

Fanny was enjoying herself at Pine Bluff, especially with the new season approaching. "Spring is so beautiful," she beamed under date of February 2; "I don't wonder the spring poet breaks loose then." But he would have to be a Confederate poet: "our 'piney woods' don't enjoy a very poetical reputation, but at this season they are the most beautiful place in the world to me." A bit later in her journal she rhapsodizes, "if I had my choice of all the climates I know anything about, to live in, I would choose the region between Macon and Thomasville."

Though Frances liked southwest Georgia, writing, "Father says that this is the best place for us now that Kilpatrick's raiders are out of the way," she was also getting homesick. Here, as written on February 16:

We found Mrs. Julia Butler at Mrs. Sims's, straight from Washington, with letters for us, and plenty of news. I feel anxious to get back now, since Washington is going to be such a center of interest. If the Yanks take Augusta, it will become the headquarters of the department. Mrs. Butler says a train of 300 wagons runs between there and Abbeville, and they are surveying a railroad route.[3] Several regiments are stationed there and the town is

---

[3] Abbeville, South Carolina, is forty miles northeast of Washington. The department referred to was the Confederate District of Georgia. In early 1865,

alive with army officers and government officials. How strange all
this seems for dear, quiet little Washington! It must be delightful
there, with all those nice army officers. I am going back home as
soon as I can decently change my mind. I have been at the rear
all during the war, and now that I have a chance, I want to go to
the front. I wish I could be here and there, too, at the same time.

The thought of "quiet little Washington" coming alive with army
officers and political figures seemed more than a little stirring to our
journalist. "One good thing the war has done among many evils," she
wrote about this time, "it has brought us into contact with so many
pleasant people we should never have known otherwise. I know it
much be charming to have all those nice army officers around."

They write us that little Washington has gotten to be the great
thoroughfare of the Confederacy now, since Sherman has cut the
South Carolina R.R. and the only line of communication between
Virginia and this part of the country, from which the army draws
its supplies, is through there and Abbeville. This was the old stage
route before there were any railroads, and our first "rebel" president traveled over it in returning from his Southern tour nearly
three-quarters of a century ago, when he spent a night with Col.
Alison in Washington.[4] It was a different thing being a rebel in
those days and now. I wonder the Yankees don't remember they
were rebels once, themselves.

Lt. Gen. Daniel H. Hill commanded it from his headquarters in Augusta (Hal
Bridges, *Lee's Maverick General: Daniel Harvey Hill* [New York: McGraw-Hill,
1961], 271–72). During the war, Federals never attempted to capture the city,
second-largest in Georgia.

[4] During April–June 1791, President Washington visited cities in Virginia,
the Carolinas, and Georgia. He had previously traveled through the North, in
keeping with his decision to see every state in the Union.

March 1865

"Gen. Elzey and staff are at our house, and the town is full of people that I want to see," Frances Andrews entered in her journal on March 1. It was evident that her and Metta's time at Pine Bluff would soon come to an end.

Fanny, ever resourceful, was good at finding pleasure in life's little turns. In this case (entry of March 8), it was about undergarments.

> Cousin Bessie lent me one of her fine embroidered linen nightgowns, and I was so overpowered at having on a decent piece of underclothing after the coarse Macon Mills homespun I have been wearing for the last two years, that I could hardly go to sleep. I stood before the glass and looked at myself after I was undressed just to see how nice it was to have on a respectable undergarment once more. I can stand patched-up dresses, and even take a pride in wearing Confederate homespun, where it is done open and above board, but I can't help feeling vulgar and common in coarse underclothes. Cousin Bessie has brought quantities of beautiful things from beyond the blockade, that make us poor Rebs look like ragamuffins beside her. She has crossed the lines by special permit, and will be obliged to return to Memphis by the 2d of April, when her pass will be out. It seems funny for a white woman to have to get a pass to see her husband, just like the negro men here do when their wives live on another plantation. The times have brought some strange upturnings.

On March 8, 1865, it was apparent to those who viewed the war realistically that the South was losing, and that the end was near. General Lee's army was trapped in the Petersburg trenches as Grant's huge army maneuvered to capture the Confederate capital at Richmond. The South's second largest army had been shattered in the battle of Nashville. Sherman's hordes were marching into North Carolina, having ravaged a wide swath of South Carolina. Abraham Lincoln had just begun his second term as the North's president, pledged to prosecute the war to Union victory.

"Cousin Bolling is awfully blue about the war, and it does begin to look as if our poor little Confederacy was about on its last legs," Miss Andrews acknowledged on March 8. "But I am so accustomed to all sorts of vicissitudes that I try not to let thoughts of the inevitable disturb me." Then, in a remarkable admission for a resolute Rebel, she added, "The time to be blue was five years ago, before we went into it."

Worse, rumor had it that the Yankees were a hundred miles from Pine Bluff. That same day, March 8, "we met Mr. Wheaton and Maj. Daniel on our way to the depot, and they told us that a dispatch had just been received stating that the Yanks have landed at St. Mark's and are marching on Tallahassee." St. Marks is a coastal town on the Florida panhandle, just two dozen miles south of Tallahassee. "We first heard they were 4,000 strong, but before we reached the depot, their numbers had swelled to 15,000." Most of this was untrue. On March 4, 1865, Northern vessels landed a thousand troops near St. Marks. Marching inland, the Federals were turned back two days later by hastily assembled Confederates in a short fight.

On March 11 our journalist recorded, "the latest news is that the Yankees have whipped our forces at Tallahassee, but…communication [is] so uncertain that one never knows what to believe." This also was patently incorrect—but Miss Andrews was right in blaming uncertain communication links that could give rise to sensational rumor.[1]

The journalist's entry for Friday, March 10, began simply, "A day of public fasting and prayer for our poor country." Fanny did not elaborate, as she did not have to. Southerners were made very aware through newspapers that nine times during the war President Davis

---

[1] John E. Johns, *Florida During the Civil War* (Gainesville: University of Florida Press, 1963), 203–205; Tracy J. Revels, *Florida's Civil War: Terrible Sacrifices* (Macon: Mercer University Press, 2016), 160.

had issued proclamations setting days for nationwide fasting and prayer. The last of these was March 10, 1865.[2]

Even in those dark days, Fanny Andrews could brighten over fashion.

> *March 13, Monday.*—Mett, Mecca, and I took a long drive to look at some new muslin dress goods that we heard a countryman down towards Camilla had for sale.[3] They were very cheap—only twenty dollars a yard. Mett and I each bought a dress and would have got more if Mrs. Settles, the man's wife, would have sold them. How they came to let these two go so cheap I can't imagine. I felt as if I were cheating the woman when I paid her 500 dollars in Confederate money for 20 yards of fairly good lawn. We stopped at Gum Pond on the way back and paid a visit. Albert Bacon gave me a beautiful red-bird that he shot for me to trim my hat with.

In stark contrast were the tattered Southern soldiers Fanny saw during an outing a week later: "These are unceremonious times," she admitted, "when social distinctions are forgotten and the raggedest rebel that tramps the road in his country's service is entitled to more honor than a king."

---

[2] Harry S. Stout, *Upon the Altar of the Nation: A Moral History of the Civil War* (New York: Viking, 2006), 432–33.

[3] Mecca Joyner's father, after the family home in Atlanta had been burned in Sherman's fires, bought an old hotel in Cuthbert "for his family to refuge in," as Miss Andrews notes in her journal entry of April 4, 1865.

April 1865

Snuff-topped flowers? Dead rats in capes? Yankees at Thomasville?

The end was approaching, as everyone knew. So how better to face grim reality than with a few practical jokes?

April 1, Saturday.—There was fooling and counter fooling between Pine Bluff and Gum Pond all day. Jim Chiles and Albert Bacon began it by sending us a beautiful bouquet over which they had sprinkled snuff. We returned the box that held the flowers, filled with dead rats dressed up in capes and mob caps like little old women. Then Albert tried to frighten us by sending a panicky note saying a dispatch had just been received from Thomasville that the Yankees were devastating the country round there, and heading for Andersonville. We pretended to believe it, and sister wrote back as if in great alarm, inquiring further particulars.

Albert got his father to answer with a made-up story that he and Wallace had both gone to help fight the raiders at Thomasville. They must have thought us fools indeed, to believe that the enemy could come all the way from Tallahassee or Savannah to Thomasville, without our hearing a word of it till they got there, but we pretended to swallow it all, and got sister to write back that Metta and I were packing our trunks and would leave for Albany immediately, so as to take the first train for Macon; and to give color to the story, she sent word for Tommy, who was spending the day with Loring Bacon, to come home and tell his aunties good-by. They were caught with their own bait, and Albert and Jimmy, fearing they had carried the joke too far, came galloping over at full speed to prevent our setting out. We saw them coming across the field, and Mett and I hid ourselves, while sister met them with a doleful countenance, pretending that we had already gone and that she was frightened out of her wits. She had rubbed her eyes to make them look as if she had been crying, and the children and servants, too, had been instructed to pretend to be in a great flurry. When the jokers confessed their trick, she pretended to be so hurt and angry that they were in dismay, thinking they had really driven us off, though all the while we were locked in our own room, peeping through the cracks, listening to it all, and ready to burst with laughter. They had mounted their horses and declared that they would go after us and fetch us back, if they had to ride all the way to Albany, when old uncle Setley spoiled out whole plot by laughing and yawping so that he excited their suspicion. They got down from their horses and began to look for wheel tracks on the ground, and at last Jim, who missed his calling in not being a detective, went and peeped in the carriage-house and saw the carriage standing there in its place. This convinced him that we had not gone to Albany, but where were we? Then began the most exciting game of hide-and-seek I ever played. Such a jumping in and out of windows, crawling under beds and sliding into corners, was never done before. The children and servants, all but old fool Setley, acted their parts well, but Jimmy was not to be foiled. They bid sister good-by several times and rode away as if they were going home, then suddenly returned in the hope of taking us by surprise. At last, after dark, we thought they were off for good, and went in to supper, taking the precaution, however, to bar the front door and draw the dining-room curtains. But we had hardly begun to eat when Jimmy burst into the room, exclaiming:

"Howdy do, Miss Fanny; you made a short trip to Albany."

We all jumped up from the table and began to bombard him with hot biscuits and muffins and whatever else we could lay hands on. Then Mr. Bacon came in, a truce was declared, and we sat down and ate supper—or what was left of it—together.

There was one matter, though, about which there could be no joking: enslaved African Americans, the folk Southerners liked to call "servants," were about to be emancipated from centuries of bondage. The difficulty with which White Southerners had in facing this revolutionary prospect is suggested in this passage of Fanny's journal, under date of April 1, 1865:

Mett says she wouldn't care much if they could all be set free—but what on earth could we do with them, even if we wanted to free them ourselves? And to have a gang of meddlesome Yankees come down here and take them away from us by force—I would never submit to that, not even if slavery were as bad as they pretend. I think the best thing to do, if the Confederacy were to gain its independence, would be to make a law confiscating the negroes of any man who was cruel to them, and allowing them to choose their own master. Of course they would choose the good men, and this would make it to everybody's interest to treat them properly.

Such imaginings as here displayed by our journalist are beside the point, especially her rumination on "if the Confederacy were to gain its independence." It was the first week of April 1865, and even a fierce rebel could sense the war's outcome: "the Yankees may have put an end to our glorious old plantation life forever."

After dinner on Sunday, April 2, Frances and Metta were preparing to take leave of Pine Bluff and southwest Georgia for their return home. The two sisters gave their farewells to relatives, friends…and the slaves.

I went to the quarter after dinner and told the negroes good-by. Poor things, I may never see any of them again, and even if I do, everything will be different. We all went to bed crying, sister, the children, and servants. Farewells are serious things in these times, when one never knows where or under what circumstances friends will meet again. I wish there was some way of getting to one place without leaving another where you want to be at the same time; some fourth dimension possibility, by which we might double our personality.

Chapter 3 in *The War-Journal* is titled "A Race with the Enemy," and it covers April 3–21, when Frances and Metta made their way back across Georgia, from Pine Bluff to Haywood. At its beginning, Andrews tells us, "the war was virtually over when we left our sister, though we did not know it." Indeed, one sees in this chapter only the dribs and drabs of tumultuous war news that the two sisters encountered in the several weeks of the Confederacy's final collapse.

At least their return trip would be easier. Although Union soldiers had wrecked much railroad track south of Atlanta, the line to Macon had been repaired. On April 3, Fanny wrote in her journal that once they reached Macon, they could travel by train to Atlanta, and from there eastward. "Mr. George Hull writes that the Georgia R.R. will be open for travel by the last of this month," referring to the west-east line connecting Atlanta to Augusta. This meant that the travelers could take the cars from Atlanta to their stop-off point at Camak, just twenty miles south of Haywood and home.[1]

On April 3, Fanny and Mett left Pine Bluff in a carriage or wagon, heading for Albany. ("The ride to Albany was very unpleasant," the journal notes; "the sun scorching hot, the glare of the sun blinding.") Then it was on the cars to Smithville, a couple of dozen miles farther north. For a leg of this trip, they were accompanied by Julia Meals, their good friend. At Smithville they took the train westward to Cuthbert, maybe twenty miles from the Alabama line. This was off course to a journey heading generally to the northeast, but as Mr. Hull predicted that the Georgia Railroad would not open till the end of the month, "our visits to Cuthbert and Macon will just fill in the interval for Mett and me," Fanny reasoned. "We can then go home by way of Atlanta."

At Smithville, just before they boarded their train, the Andrews sisters saw a thousand Federal prisoners being hauled past them on a

---

[1] On March 28, 1865, the *Atlanta Daily Intelligencer* announced that the first train in from Macon had arrived the previous evening. The Georgia Railroad was also in operation, serving Atlanta and Augusta, by May 1 (Franklin M. Garrett, "The Phoenix Begins to Rise: The *Atlanta Daily Intelligencer* Announces the Return of the Railroads," *Atlanta History* 37/4 [Winter 1994]: 7–8).

George P. Hull was the superintendent of the Atlanta & West Point Railroad, which ran southwest to the Chattahoochee River (Davis, *What the Yankees Did to Us*, 58). Sherman's soldiers had wrecked a considerable stretch of it in late August 1864; it was back at work by March 7, 1865 (Garrett, "Phoenix," 6).

train; they were the last POWs being kept at Andersonville. At the start of April, Captain Wirz still had several thousand prisoners in his stockade. By the first week of April a heavy Union mounted column was pushing through Alabama, heading east, and Wirz worried that it could be heading his way. So Confederate authorities arranged for his remaining POWs to be borne all the way to Jacksonville, Florida. There the Federal commander agreed to receive them—for Wirz it was not so much an exchange as a way of getting these last prisoners off his hands. Something like this had not been done before on such a scale— the deliberate freeing of enemy prisoners—so Fanny at first thought they were to be exchanged. But in a note she corrected herself: "This was a mistake. The Confederacy having now practically collapsed, and the government being unable to care for them any longer, the prisoners remaining in the stockade were sent to Jacksonville, where the Federals were in possession, and literally forced back as a free gift on their friends."

Fanny and other young ladies were standing rail-side at Smithville depot, carrying their lunch baskets. Nearby teenage Confederate guards reacted to the fetching females by firing their weapons overhead. As their cars crept past, the Yankees inside got caught up as well and blew kisses at the women. Our journalist describes the scene:

> Our guard fired a salute as they passed, and some of the prisoners had the impudence to kiss their hands at us—but what better could be expected of the foreign riff-raff that make up the bulk of the Yankee army? If they had not been prisoners I would have felt like they ought to have a lesson in manners, for insulting us, but as it was, I couldn't find it in my heart to be angry. They were half-naked, and such a poor, miserable, starved-looking set of wretches that we couldn't help feeling sorry for them in spite of their wicked war against our country, and threw what was left of our lunch at them, as their train rattled by, thinking it would feed two or three of them, at least. But our aim was bad, and it fell short, so the poor creatures didn't get it, and if any of them

noticed, I expect they thought we were only "d—d rebel women" throwing our waste in their faces to insult them.[2]

Still, Fanny wished them good riddance; their departure from a climate "that seems to be so unfriendly to them" would probably have been welcomed by the Yankees anyway.

The short rail ride to Cuthbert allowed Miss Andrews to look out of the car window and once more savor the Southern landscape.

The railroad from Smithville to Cuthbert runs into the "oaky woods" beyond Smithville, which are more broken and undulating than the pine flats, and the swamps are larger and more beautiful on account of the greater variety of vegetation. They are a huge mosaic, at this season, of wild azaleas, Atamasco lilies, yellow jessamine, and a hundred other brilliant flowers. My taste may be very perverted, but to my mind there is no natural scenery in the world so beautiful as a big Southern swamp in springtime. It has its beauty in winter, too, with the somber cypress, the stately magnolias, the silvery bays, and the jungle of shrubs and vines, gay with the red berries of holly and winter smilax.

Even with the Confederacy dying, Southern social life could go on. In Cuthbert, Fanny and Mett were invited to a wedding. Mett went, and came back cooing over the bride's dress, "which is a great credit to the taste and ingenuity of our Southern girls in patching up pretty things out of all sorts of odds and ends," Fanny observed. Our journalist, though, had run out of resources; "my one new dress isn't made up yet, and everything else I have is too frazzled out to wear." So she stayed in her hotel room, with the quiet satisfaction of having adhered to Lent in not joining the wedding frivolity.

The sisters were enjoying themselves at Cuthbert. Indeed, they even planned to continue their journey into southeast Alabama, but on April 5 Fanny learned that Yankee raiders had captured Selma—which was true. Union Brig. Gen. James Wilson was leading a mounted force

---

[2] Marvel describes this incident in *The Last Depot*, 236.

through the now-hollow Confederacy ("nothing but the march of victorious generals to take possession of a conquered country," as Miss Andrews sniffed contemptuously).[3]

More bad news came the next day, April 6, when everyone learned that Richmond, the capital of the Confederacy, had finally fallen. Since the preceding June, Robert E. Lee's Army of Northern Virginia had been forced into siege fortifications protecting Petersburg, the vital railroad junction twenty miles south of Richmond. The South Side Railroad into Petersburg was the last supply line for Lee's army and the citizenry of the capital. Everyone knew that when the railroad was cut, Lee's Petersburg lines would have to be abandoned and the capital exposed. This occurred on April 1, when Federal troops won a victory in the battle of Five Forks and a massive Northern assault broke Lee's lines early the next day. President Davis was at church when a note was handed him, stating that he must evacuate the capital as fast as he could. Confederate authorities did so, and Union troops marched in on April 3.[4]

Lee managed to extricate his army—now reduced to some twenty-nine thousand infantry—from the Petersburg lines and start a desperate march to the west.[5] "Everybody feels very blue," Frances recorded on April 6, "but not disposed to give up as long as we have Lee."

The very next day, though, brought word that Montgomery had fallen—the ninth Southern state capital captured so far in the war.[6] "The war is closing in upon us from all sides," Fanny lamented.

---

[3] James Pickett Jones, *Yankee Blitzkrieg: Wilson's Raid through Alabama and Georgia* (Athens: University of Georgia Press, 1976), 89–92.

[4] Jeffry D. Wert, "Petersburg Campaign" in Patricia L. Faust, ed., *Historical Times Illustrated Encyclopedia of the Civil War* (New York: Harper & Row, 1986), 577–79.

[5] Douglas Southall Freeman, *R. E. Lee: A Biography*, 4 vols. (New York: Charles Scribner's Sons, 1934–35), 4:58.

[6] Federal capture of Southern state capitals began with Nashville, February 1862; then Baton Rouge (May 1862); Jackson (May 1863); Little Rock (September 1863); Milledgeville (November 1864); Columbia (February 1865);

At Cuthbert, cousin Bolling, the physician, had charge of an army hospital (he specialized in ophthalmology). On Sunday, April 9, as she wrote, Fanny "went to worship with a little band of Episcopalians, mostly refugees, who meet every Sunday in a schoolhouse. Services were conducted by an old schoolteacher, a Mr. George, who doubled on the Sabbath as a priest. There is something very touching in the unrewarded labor of this good man, grown gray in the service of his God."

More touching still were all the frail and maimed soldiers from Dr. Bolling's and other nearby hospitals.

> They came, some limping on crutches, some with scarred and mangled faces, some with empty sleeves, nearly all with poor, emaciated bodies, telling their mute tale of sickness and suffering, weariness and heartache. I saw one poor lame fellow leading a blind one, who held on to his crutch. Another had a blind comrade hanging upon one arm while an empty sleeve dangled where the other ought to be. I have seen men since I came here with both eyes shot out, men with both arms off, and one poor fellow with both arms and a leg gone. What can our country ever do to repay such sacrifice? And yet, it is astonishing to see how cheerful these brave fellows are, especially Cousin Bolling's patients, who laughingly dub themselves "The Blind Brigade."

One of the Cuthbert army hospitals had been named for Gen. John B. Hood, the former commander of the Army of Tennessee. On the evening of April 10, Fanny, Mett and a group of their friends who also enjoyed singing—"the tableaux club"—had gathered at the Joyners' residence for a rehearsal. Afterward the club serenaded a couple of houses when "somebody said it would be a good idea to go and cheer up the soldiers in the Hood Hospital, which was but a block or two away, with some war songs."

Raleigh (April 1865); Richmond (April 1865); and Montgomery (April 1865). Only Tallahassee and Austin remained.

The poor fellows were so delighted when they heard us that all who were able, dressed themselves and came out on the ter-races, while others crowded to the windows and balconies. They sent a shower of roses down on us, and threw with them slips of paper with the names of the songs they wished to hear. We gave them first:

"Cheer, boys, cheer, we march away to battle," which pleased them so much that they called for it a second time.[7] Then someone struck up *"Vive l'Amour,"* and Mett gave an impromptu couplet:

"Here's to the boys in Confederate gray, *Vive la compagnie,*
Who never their country nor sweethearts betray, *Vive,* etc."

---

[7] Henry Russell's song "Cheer, Boys, Cheer" was published in Nashville and Memphis in 1861 (E. Lawrence Abel, *Singing the New Nation: How Music Shaped the Confederacy, 1861–1865* [Mechanicsburg, PA: Stackpole Books, 2000], 300n.54). The song was also called "The Song of Southern Boys," and the cho-rus, which the patients at Hood Hospital knew, ran "Cheer, boys, cheer, for country, mother country, / Cheer, boys, cheer, the willing strong right hand / Cheer, boys, cheer, there's wealth for honest labor / Cheer, boys, cheer, for the new and happy land!" (E. Lawrence Abel, *Confederate Sheet Music* [Jefferson, NC: McFarland & Company, 2004], 38–39).

T. Conn Bryan tells the story of the Cuthbert hospital singers in *Con-federate Georgia* (Athens: University of Georgia Press, 1953), 196.

"Cheer, Boys, Cheer" is unknown today, but it remained popular for years after the war. As reported in *Confederate Veteran*, in the 1890s, during the dedication of a Confederate monument in Owensboro, Kentucky, the main or-ator for the event referred to Southern soldiers: "Through the vista of years we see them again as they struggle in their icy trenches or charge through the 'un-trodden snow' at Fort Donelson; again we hear them singing, 'Cheer, boys, cheer, we'll march away to battle,' as they lead the charge of Albert Sidney Johnston's army through Grant's camps at Shiloh." At this point, *Veteran* editor S. A. Cun-ningham inserted, "[Just here a group of well-trained voices arose suddenly upon the platform and sang that old-time thrilling war song, and the innovation gave renewed interest to the splendid address.]" ("Confederate Monument at Owens-boro," *Confederate Veteran* 8/9 [September 1900]: 388–89).

While the soldiers were clapping and shouting the chorus, two good lines popped into my head, and when the noise had subsided a little, I sang:

"Here's a toast to the boys who go limping on crutches,
Vive la compagnie,
They have saved our land from the enemies' clutches,
Vive, etc."

I waved my hand at a group of brave fellows leaning on crutches, as I finished, and a regular rebel yell went up from the hospital grounds. Flowers were rained down from the windows, and I never was so delighted in my life—to think that my little knack of stringing rhymes together had served some good purpose for once. The soldiers clapped and shouted and rattled their crutches together, and one big fellow standing near me threw up his battered old war hat, and cried out:

"Bully for you! Give us some more!" and then I added:

"Here's death to the men who wear Federal blue,
They are cowardly, cruel, perfidious, untrue," etc.

But after all, it looks as if the wretches are going to bring death, or slavery that is worse than death, to us. We may sing and try to put on a brave face, but alas! who can tell what the end of it all is to be?

The next day, one of the attending physicians at Hood Hospital congratulated Fanny on her impromptu ditty.

Dr. Boyd says that my little rhyme about the boys on crutches did the sick soldiers more good than all his medicines. Some poor fellows who had hardly noticed anything for a week, he says, laughed and clapped their hands like happy children, as they lay on the beds and listened. He says they have been talking about it ever since.

On the 13th, the tableaux club convened again, and this time someone suggested that the troupe serenade the soldiers in the Hill Hospital, "as it would seem like slighting them to pass them by after serenading the others."

But they knew we were coming and so things didn't go off with the warmth and naturalness of our other visit. They had prepared an entertainment for us, and brought us some lemonade made with brown sugar and citric acid. It was dreadful stuff, but the dear fellows were giving us the best they had, and, I am afraid, depriving themselves of supplies they needed for their own use. While we were drinking, somebody led off with a verse of the "Confederate Toast" and then looked at me, and I added one that I felt half-ashamed of because I had made it up before hand and felt like an impostor, but couldn't help it when I knew beforehand what was coming:

"Here's to the Southern rebel, drink it down;
Here's to the Southern rebel, drink it down;
Here's to the Southern rebel,
May his enemies go to the—"

I came to a sudden stop at the last word and the soldiers, with a laugh and a yell, took up the chorus and carried it through. Then we amused ourselves for some time answering each other with couplets, good, bad, and indifferent—mostly indifferent. My parting one was:

"Hurrah for the soldiers who stay on the Hill;
They have fought, they have suffered, they are full of pluck still."

Full of pluck, Eliza Frances Andrews, our Confederate heroine, may still have been in these dark days of a waning cause, but it was enough just to stay one step ahead of the Yankees. On Saturday, April 15, came a rumor that Federal raiders were heading for Eufaula, in southeast Alabama (twenty-five miles to the west of Cuthbert). But someone seemingly better informed predicted that the enemy raiders were heading for Columbus, Georgia (fifty miles to the north of where the Andrews sisters were at the time). Fanny complained about all the "Yankee panics" she had experienced in the past few months, so she was not much disturbed by this one. If the Yankees were riding for Columbus, Fanny and Mett would elude them. Early on the morning of April 17, the two women, in company of former Confederate brigadier general Robert Toombs and his daughters, boarded the Southwestern R. R. train from Cuthbert to Macon, which they reached by nightfall. The two female Confederates had indeed eluded the enemy; Wilson's raiders that day were entering Columbus, Georgia, eighty miles west of Macon, after routing Southern forces in a sharp battle.[8]

> *April 17, Monday.* Up early, to be ready for the train at seven.... All sorts of wild rumors were flying, among them that fighting had already begun at Columbus.... The excitement was intense all along the route. At every little station crowds were gathered to hear the news, and at many places we found a report had gone out that both our train and yesterday's had been captured. The excitement increased as we approached Fort Valley, where the Muscogee road (from Columbus) joins the Southwestern, and many of the passengers predicted that we should be captured there. At the next station below Fort Valley, our fears regarding the fate of Columbus were confirmed by a soldier on the platform, who shouted out as the train slowed down, "Columbus gone up the spout!" Nobody was surprised, and all were eager to hear particulars. I was glad to learn that our poor little handful of Confederates had made a brave fight before surrendering. The city was not given up till nine last night, when the Yankees slipped over the railroad bridge and got in before our men, who were defending the other bridge, knew anything about it. We had not enough to watch both bridges, and it seemed more likely the attack would be made by the dirt road. Then everybody blundered in the dark, fighting pretty much at random. If a man met someone he did not know, he asked whether he was a Yank or Reb, and if the answer did not suit his views he fired. At last everybody became afraid to tell who or what they were.

Miss Andrews's sources—probably Columbians who had fled their city—got the story right. Wilson's raiders approached Columbus

---

[8] Charles A. Misulia, *Columbus Georgia 1865: The Last True Battle of the Civil War* (Tuscaloosa: University of Alabama Press, 2010), 183.

from the west. The city's defenders, too few to guard both major bridges across the Chattahoochee River, took up planking on the southernmost one and prepared to defend the other. Federals attacked the Confederate fortified line on the Alabama side and broke it. The Southerners fled across the bridge into Columbus. Wilson's forces pursued, capturing the city and about a thousand Confederates; some six hundred escaped, fleeing eastward.[9]

> It was thought that our forces had retired towards Opelika. When we reached Fort Valley the excitement was at fever heat. Train upon train of cars was there, all the rolling stock of the Muscogee Road having been run out of Columbus to keep it from being captured, and the cars were filled with refugees and their goods. It was pitiful to see them, especially the little children, driven from the homes by the frozen-hearted Northern Vandals, but they were all brave and cheerful, laughing good-naturedly instead of grumbling over their hardships. People have gotten so used to these sort of things that they have learned to bear them with philosophy. Soldiers who had made their escape after the fight, without surrendering, were camped about everywhere, looking tired and hungry, and more disheartened than the women and children. Poor fellows, they have seen the terrors of war nearer at hand than we.

Approaching Macon that afternoon, "I saw some poor little fortifications thrown up along the line of the South-Western, with a handful of men guarding them, and that is the only preparation for defense I have seen. We are told that the city is to be defended, but if that is so, the Lord only knows where the men are to come from."

The train chugged into the city and Fanny was getting off when on the loading platform whom should she see but her oldest brother, Fred, who had last been with her during part of the sisters' December trek from Washington to Albany. Fred helped his sisters get their baggage from the depot to the Lanier House on Mulberry Street, where

---

[9] Jones, *Yankee Blitzkrieg*, 134-39; *Misulia, Columbus 1865*, 159-66.

they would stay till boarding time for the morning train to Atlanta. The transport process was made harder because there was rumor afoot that Macon would be evacuated before the Yankee raiders approached. Government officials were taking all horses to remove their stores.

> Mulberry Street, in front of the Lanier House, is filled with officers and men rushing to and fro, and everything and everybody seems to be in the wildest excitement. In the hotel parlor, when I came from Lily's, whom should I find but Mr. Adams, our little Yankee preacher! I used to like him, but now I hate to look at him just because he is a Yankee. What is it, I wonder, that makes them so different from us, even when they mean to be good Southerners! You can't even make one of them look like us, not if you were to dress him up in a full suit of Georgia jeans. I used to have some Christian feeling towards Yankees, but now that they have invaded our country and killed so many of our men and desecrated so many homes, I can't believe that when Christ said "Love your enemies," he meant Yankees. Of course I don't want their souls to be lost, for that would be wicked, but as they are not being punished in this world, I don't see how else they are going to get their deserts.

The next morning, April 18, amid continued panic that the Yankees were coming, it seemed as if everyone in Macon wanted to board the train for Atlanta. "There was such a crowd waiting at the depot that we could hardly push our way through," Fanny wrote. She, Mett, and two friends were lucky to get adjoining seats in the ladies' car. They were also relieved when Fred got their luggage aboard. The train was so crowded that some passengers had to leave their bags behind; "some decided to stay with their trunks; they contained all that some poor refugees had left them." "The Yankees were expected before night," Fanny recorded, but in this Dame Rumour would be proven wrong. The advance of Wilson's column did not approach the city till the 20th, when the Confederate commander, Maj. Gen. Howell Cobb, surrendered it.

"There was a terrible rush on all the outgoing trains," our journalist continues.

Ours had on board a quantity of government specie and the assets of four banks, besides private property, aggregating all together, it was said, more than seventeen million dollars—and there were somewhere in the neighborhood of 1,000 passengers. People who could not get inside were hanging on wherever they could find a sticking place; the aisles and platforms down to the last step were full of people clinging on like bees swarming round the doors of a hive. It took two engines to pull us up the heavy grade around Vineville, and we were more than an hour behind time, in starting, at that. Meanwhile, all sort of rumors were flying. One had it that the road was cut at Jonesborough, then, at Barnesville, and finally that a large force of the enemy was at Thomaston advancing toward the road with a view to capturing our train. I never saw such wild excitement in my life. Many people left the cars at the last moment before we steamed out, preferring to be caught in Macon rather than captured on the road, but their places were rapidly filled by more adventurous spirits. A party of refugees from Columbus were seated near us, and they seemed nearly crazed with excitement. Mary Elizabeth Rutherford, who was always a great scatter-brain when I knew her at school, was among them, and she jumped up on the seat, tore down her back hair and went into regular hysterics at the idea of falling into the hands of the Yankees. Such antics would have been natural enough in the beginning of the war, when we were new to these experiences, but now that we are all old soldiers, and used to raids and vicissitudes, people ought to know how to face them quietly. Of course it would have been dreadful to be captured and have our baggage rifled and lose all your clothes, but if the Yankees had actually caught us, I don't think I would have gone crazy over it. So many sensational reports kept coming in that I finally lost patience and felt like saying something cross to everybody that brought me a fresh bit of news. Before we left Macon, Mr. Edward Shepherd gave me the worst fright I almost ever had, by telling me that my trunk and Jenny Toombs's had been thrown out of the baggage car and were lying on the track, but this proved to be a false alarm, like so many others. Then somebody came in and reported that the superintendent of the road had a dispatch in his hand at that moment, stating that the enemy was already in Barnesville. The statement seemed so authoritative that Fred went to Gen. Mackall himself, and was advised by him to continue his journey, as no official notice had been received of the cutting the road.[10] At last, to the great relief of us all, the train steamed out of Macon and traveled along in peace till it reached Goggins's Station four miles from Barnesville, where it was stopped by some country people who said that the down train from Atlanta had been captured and the Yankees were just five miles from Barnesville waiting for us. A council was held by the railroad officials and some of the army officers on board, at which it was decided that the freight we were carrying was too valuable to be risked, although the news was not very reliable, having been brought in by two schoolboys. There was danger also, it was suggested, that a raiding party might mistake such a very long and crowded train, where the men were nearly all forced out on the platforms, for a movement of troops and fire into us. I confess to being pretty badly scared by this possibility, but the women on board seemed to have worked off their excitement by this time, and we all kept quiet and behaved ourselves very creditably. While the council was still in session, fresh reports came in confirming those already brought, and we put back to Macon, without standing on the order of our going. Helen Swift, a friend of the Toombses, who had joined us at Macon, lives only fifteen miles from the place where we turned back. She was bitterly disappointed, and I don't blame her for nearly crying her eyes out. Mr. Adams undertook to administer spiritual

---

[10] William Whann Mackall, 1817–91, had served as the Confederate Army of Tennessee's chief of staff from January to September 1864. For the next nine months he served in an undefined capacity (Richard M. McMurry, "William Whann Mackall" in William C. Davis, ed., *The Confederate Generals*, 6 vols (Harrisburg, PA: National Historical Society, 1991), vol. 4 126–27.

consolation, but I don't think Helen was very spiritually-minded towards Yankees just at that time.

Excited crowds were waiting at all the stations as we went back, and the news we brought increased the ferment tenfold. The general impression seems to be that the Yanks are advancing upon Macon in three columns, and that they will reach the city by tomorrow or next day, at latest. We came back to the Lanier House, and Fred hopes to get us out by way of Milledgeville, before they arrive. When our train got back to Macon, the men on board had gradually dropped off on the way, so that I don't suppose there were more than 200 or 300 remaining of all that had gone out in the morning. The demoralization is complete. We are whipped, there is no doubt about it. Everybody feels it, and there is no use for the men to try to fight any longer, though none of us like to say so.

The train's return to Macon had been caused by rumors of Yankees ahead, which proved false. "Just before we reached Macon," Miss Andrews noted, "the down train, which had been reported captured, overtook us at a siding, with the tantalizing news that we might have got through to Atlanta if we had gone straight on." More depressing still was the desolate appearance of a city in the throes of abandonment and evacuation.

There was an immense crowd at the depot on our return, and when I saw what a wild commotion the approach of the Yankees created, I lost all hope and gave up our cause as doomed. We made a brave fight but the odds against us were too great. The spell of invincibility has left us and gone over to the heavy battalions of the enemy. As I drove along from the station to the hotel, I could see that preparations were being made to evacuate the city. Government stores were piled up in the streets and all the horses and wagons that could be pressed into service were being hastily loaded in the effort to remove them. The rush of men had disappeared from Mulberry St. No more gay uniforms, no more prancing horses, but only a few ragged foot soldiers with wallets and knapsacks on, ready to march—Heaven knows where. Gen. Elzey and staff left early in the morning to take up their new quarters either in Augusta or Washington, and if we had only known it, we might have gone out with them.[11] I took a walk on the streets while waiting to get my room at the hotel, and found everything in the wildest confusion. The houses were closed, and doleful little groups were clustered about the street corners discussing the situation. All the intoxicating liquors that could be found in the stores, warehouses, and barrooms, had been seized by the authorities and emptied on the ground. In some places the streets smelt like a distillery, and I saw men, boys, and negroes down on their knees lapping it up from the gutter like dogs. Little children were staggering about in a state of beastly intoxication. I think there can be no more dreary spectacle in the world than a city on the eve of evacuation, unless it is one that has already fallen into the hands of the enemy.

Frances Andrews's despondency deepened during her walk through the Macon streets when she heard someone say that General Lee had surrendered his army. The rumor was correct. In a weeklong march west from Petersburg, Lee looked vainly for government supply trains at depots to feed his hungry men, and struggled to stay ahead of Grant's pursuing forces. Several rearguard battles were fought, as at Sailors Creek on April 6, but when two days later Confederate cavalry reported that sizable bodies of Union troops blocked the roads ahead, Lee knew he had to capitulate. The memorable rites were performed at Appomattox Court House on April 9.[12]

---

[11] Maj. Gen. Arnold Elzey had been a friend of the Andrews family before the war. In its closing months, he held an unspecified post at Augusta (John M. Otey to Elzey, Augusta, March 23, 1865, *OR*, vol. 49, pt. 2, 116). Miss Andrews's observations on the chaos in Macon are quoted in Richard W. Iobst, *Civil War Macon* (Macon: Mercer University Press, 1999), 385–88.

[12] James I. Robertson, "Appomattox Campaign" in Patricia L. Faust, ed., *Historical Times Illustrated Encyclopedia of the Civil War* (New York: Harper & Row, 1986), 20–21.

Our journalist did not know these details, of course, but just the rumor wrecked her spirits. "I returned with a heavy heart, for while out I heard fresh rumors of Lee's surrender. No one seems to doubt it, and everybody feels ready to give up hope. 'It is useless to struggle longer,' seems to be the common cry, and the poor wounded men go hobbling about the streets with despair on their faces. There is a new pathos in a crutch or an empty sleeve, now, that we know it was all for nothing." Back at Lanier House, a small group gathered. "We tried to keep up our spirits by singing some of the favorite war songs," she sadly wrote, "but they seemed more like dirges now, and we gave up and went to our rooms."

With the Macon-Atlanta railroad still so treacherous, the pilgrims decided instead to board the train from Macon to Milledgeville on the morning of April 19. This one, too, proved to be chaotic and crushed by citizens seeking escape; word spread that Confederate forces had finally given up the city the evening before. The sisters got on the cars, though; Fanny noticed that "nearly all our companions on yesterday's wild-goose chase towards Atlanta were aboard." When they reached Milledgeville, they were offered a carriage ride to the hotel by none other than Gov. Joseph E. Brown, who had been on the train to the capital.

Apparently, Fanny had been a previous guest of "that awful Milledgeville Hotel," and this encounter proved at least as ugly as her earlier unhappy stays.

> We had engaged a large room with two beds so that we girls could all be together, but when we entered, our hearts sank, accustomed as we are to war-time fare. There was no slop-tub, wash basin, pitcher nor towels, and the walls on each side of the beds were black with tobacco spit. The fireplace was a dump heap that was enough to turn the stomach of a pig, and over the mantel some former occupant had inscribed this caution: "One bed has lice in it, the other fleas, and both bugs; chimney smokes; better change."

Prompted by curiosity I turned down the cover of one bed, and started such a stampede among the bugs that we all made for the door as fast as our feet would carry us and ordered another room, which, however, did not prove much better. Our next step was to make a foray for water and towels. The only water supply we could find was in a big washtub at the head of the stairs, where everybody stopped to drink, those who had no cups stooping down and lapping it up with their hands, or dipping in their heads. There was but one chambermaid to the whole establishment, and she was as hard to catch as the Irishman's flea. Both Fred and Mr. Toombs were off, hunting for conveyances, so we had to shift for ourselves. We tried to ring a bell that hung in the passage, but Sherman's angels had cut the cord. A young captain who was watching our maneuvers, advised us to cry "Fire!" as the surest way of getting water brought. Just at this time, Fred's boy, Arch, came up and we made him shovel some of the dirt out of our room and bring up fresh water in a broken pitcher we found there. After making ourselves as decent as circumstances would permit, we went down to the dining-room. There was literally nothing on the table but some broken crockery, the remains of Sherman's little tea-party, but one of the black waiters promised to get us a nice dinner if we would "jest have de patience to deviate back to de parlor" and wait a little while, till he could get it ready. He was so polite and plausible that we "deviated," and after more than half an hour, went back to the dining-room, where we exercised our patience for another half-hour, when, at last, he came bustling in with some ham and eggs and raw corn bread. I looked about on my plate for a clean spot on which to deposit my share, and, finding none, dabbed it down at random, and went for it, dirt and all, for I was desperately hungry.

During their stopover in Milledgeville, Fanny and Mett had the opportunity to visit the state capitol, which had been defaced by Sherman's men five months before. With a small group of acquaintances, our journalist saw it all: "We went into the capitol with them and saw the destruction the Yankees had made. The building was shockingly defaced, like everything else in Milledgeville. There don't seem to be a clean or a whole thing left in the town."

Fortunately, brother Fred found "a man with a miserable little wagon and two scrubby mules hid out in the woods" who agreed to take the Andrews sisters from Milledgeville to Mayfield (two dozen miles south of Washington) for twenty-five hundred dollars. We may assume they were Confederate dollars, in which case the countryman was either stoically patriotic or magnanimously philanthropic as he gave away his services for free, paid in the worthless currency of a collapsed government ("nobody wants to take Confederate money," Fanny observed; "the rumors about Lee's surrender, together with the panicky state of affairs at home, have sent our depreciated currency rolling down hill with accelerated velocity"). There was something else: the countryman asked Fred, still an officer in the Confederate artillery, if he could secure an order that would exempt his mule team from being impressed by military officials. Lieutenant Andrews complied. "About eight o'clock in the morning our wagon was at the door and we bade a joyous farewell to Milledgeville," Fanny entered in her journal for Thursday, April 20. "Fred and Arch had to walk, the wretched team being hardly able to carry Mett and me and the trunks."

Fanny guessed that the wagon master was earning a hundred dollars per mile for the trek from Milledgeville to Mayfield (quite off the mark, for the distance was less than forty miles). But the cross-country trek involved something vastly more, a peril of incalculable dimension, at least to us, Eliza Frances Andrews's readers:

After the first few miles we were so tired that we took off our hats and lay down in the wagon to take a nap. When we waked we found that both hats and a basket containing all our toilet articles, had jolted out and been lost. So many people had passed us that Fred said it was no use to try to get them back, but I made Arch take one of the mules out of the wagon and go back to look for them, and, as much to my surprise as delight, he recovered the basket. I was so glad to see it that I forgot to grieve over the hats. Besides my brush and tooth-brush, it contained all the leaves of my journal that I have written since leaving home last winter, which I had torn out of the book on the stampede from Macon, fearing my trunk might be lost. What a mess there would be if it had been found by some of the people I have been writing about!

What a mess, indeed. The possibility that *The War-Time Journal of a Georgia Girl*, at least its first part, from December 1864 through April 1865, might have been lost on a middle Georgia country road leads one to speculate as to whether the twenty-four-year-old, upon her return home amidst turbulent times, would have recomposed her journal. But thanks to her persistence—and Arch's good luck—we have Fanny's observations in their original form—a providential gift to Southern literature.

From their wagon, as they passed back through the "Burnt Country," the pilgrims could see signs of repair and improvement. "The country," Fanny wrote on April 20, "seems to have pretty well recovered from the effects of Sherman's march, so far as appearances go; the fields are tilled and crops growing, but people are still short of provisions." Finding food and forage, though, was a challenge for our wayfarers; at Sparta, about halfway to Mayfield, "our sorry little team was too broken down to carry us any farther" that day. Fortunately, Fanny, Mett, Fred, and Arch were taken in for the night by a gentleman, "Mr. Harris," who had heard their names called, and who just happened to be a friend of Judge Andrews. Treated to a warm bath and sumptuous meal, Fanny actually began to feel recovered from "how dirty and draggled out" she had been earlier that day. Festivity failed after dinner, though, when the Harrises and their newfound guests attempted a postprandial songfest. "After supper we went into the parlor and had music," she wrote; "we tried tossing some of our old rebel songs, but the words stuck in our throats. Nobody could sing, and then Clara Harris played 'Dixie,' but it sounded like a dirge."

The pestiferous Yankees! "About two o'clock in the morning," Fanny continued, the whole town was roused by a courier who came in with news that the Yankees were in Putnam County, only twelve miles off. It is absurd for people to fly into a panic over every wild rumor that gets afloat, but I was glad the courier came, for three o'clock was the hour appointed for us to start, and I was sleeping so soundly that I am sure I would never have waked in time but for him.

Thanks to this early start, back on their rickety mule-hauled wagon the Andrews party reached Mayfield around 9 a.m. After an hour's wait, the travelers boarded the train that would take them back through Camak and on to Washington. Along the route that day, Friday, April 21, they received confirmation of General Lee's surrender in Virginia and news that General Johnston had reached an armistice with Sherman in North Carolina.

Alas, we all know only too well what that armistice means! It is all over with us now, and there is nothing to do but bow our heads in the dust and let the hateful conquerors trample us under their feet. There is a complete revulsion in public feeling. No more talk now about fighting to the last ditch; the last ditch has already been reached; no more talk about help from France and England, but all about emigration to Mexico and Brazil. We are irretrievably ruined, past the power of France and England to save us now. Europe has quietly folded her hands and beheld a noble nation perish. God grant that she may yet have cause to repent her cowardice and folly in suffering this monstrous power that has crushed us to roll on unchecked. We fought nobly and fell bravely, overwhelmed by numbers and resources, with never a hand held out to save us.[13] I hate all the world when I think of

---

[13] With this phrase, Miss Andrews is alertly adapting one of the most familiar phrases in the Lost Cause Myth, General Lee's words in his General Orders No. 9, his farewell address to the Army of Northern Virginia after its surrender at Appomattox: "After four years of arduous service marked by unsurpassed courage and fortitude the Army of Northern Virginia has been compelled to yield to overwhelming numbers and resources." After Col. Charles Marshall of the

it. I am crushed and bowed down to the earth, in sorrow, but not in shame. No! I am more of a rebel to-day than ever I was when things looked brightest for the Confederacy.

Such was our defiant Rebel's response to defeat. Frances Andrews was, on the other hand, genuinely mournful upon hearing at the Camak depot that Lincoln had been assassinated.

Some fools laughed and applauded, but wise people looked grave and held their peace. It is a terrible blow to the South, for it places that vulgar renegade, Andy Johnson, in power, and will give the Yankees an excuse for charging us with a crime which was in reality only the deed of an irresponsible madman. Our papers ought to reprobate it universally.

Finally, from onboard the train came the first glimpses of Washington. "When the old town clock came into view, a shout of joy went up from us returning wanderers," Fanny recorded. But the "quiet little village we had left sleeping in the winter sunshine five months ago" had morphed into a bustling town filled with Confederate soldiers and government wagon trains. Washington was situated on one of the major roads linking Georgia with the Carolinas and Virginia. Paroled Southern soldiers, on horseback and foot, were pouring through the town. Washington also became a military center, or at least a way station for the men making their slow way home.[14] "The whole world seems to be moving on Washington now," our journalist opined. "An average

---

general's staff presented a draft, Lee deleted a paragraph he viewed as a bit too partisan and changed a few words (Freeman, *Lee*, 4:149–50, 154). The final text is so iconic as to be included in Thomas Daniel Young, Floyd C. Watkins, and Richard Croom Beatty, eds., *The Literature of the South* (Glenview, IL: Scott, Foresman and Company, 1968 [1952]), 137.

[14] Robert M. Willingham Jr., *The History of Wilkes County, Georgia* (Washington: Wilkes Publishing Company, 2002), 180. Willingham quotes Miss Andrews's diary entry of April 21, 1865 ("Surely this old home of ours is the choicest spot of all the world," *History of Wilkes County*, 187).

of 2,000 rations are issued daily, and over 15,000 men are said to have passed through already, since it became a military post, though the return of the paroled men has as yet hardly begun." The war might have been lost, but its end was, at least to judge from our journalist's viewpoint, a gradual series of events still unfolding.

An overjoyed Garnett Andrews greeted his daughters at the depot, along with the rest of the family, and even the dog Toby, "frisking and barking for joy." Judge Andrews had opened Haywood to so many friends and relatives that the house, spacious as it was, teemed with folk (Fanny had to give up her bedroom and bunk with Mett). Moreover, the family opened the grounds of its estate as camping areas for soldiers. General Elzey and his staff arrived in Washington on April 23. The general and his wife found quarters in the old Georgia Bank building downtown, thanks to Dr. J. J. Robertson, its overseer; his officers pitched camp nearby.

> *April 24, Monday.* —The shattered remains of Lee's army are beginning to arrive. There is an endless stream passing between the transportation office and the depot, and trains are going and coming at all hours. The soldiers bring all sorts of rumors and keep us stirred up in a state of never-ending excitement. Our avenue leads from the principal street on which they pass, and great numbers stop to rest in the grove. Emily is kept busy cooking rations for them, and pinched as we are ourselves for supplies, it is impossible to refuse anything to the men that have been fighting for us. Even when they don't ask for anything the poor fellows look so tired and hungry that we feel tempted to give them everything we have. Two nice-looking officers came to the kitchen door this afternoon while I was in there making some sorghum cakes to send to Gen. Elzey's camp. They then walked slowly through the back yard, and seemed reluctant to tear themselves away from such a sweet, beautiful place. Nearly everybody that passes the street gate stops and looks up the avenue, and I know they can't help thinking what a beautiful place it is. The Cherokee rose hedge is white with blooms. It is glorious. A great many of the soldiers camp in the grove, with Col. Weems

[the Confederate commander of the post[15]] has located a public camping-ground for them further out of town. The officers often ask for a night's lodging, but our house is always so full of friends who have a nearer claim, that a great many have to be refused. It hurts my conscience ever to turn off a Confederate soldier on any account, but we are so overwhelmed with company—friends and people bringing letters of introduction—that the house, big as it is, will hardly hold us all, and members of the family have to pack together like sardines.

April 25, Tuesday. Maj. Hall, one of Gen. Elzey's staff, has been taken with typhoid fever, so father sent out to the camp and told them to bring him to our house, but Mrs. Robertson had a spare room at the bank and took him there where he can be better cared for than in our house, that is full as an ant-hill already. I went round to the bank after breakfast to see Mrs. Elzey and inquire about him. The square is so crowded with soldiers and government wagons that it is not easy to make way through it. It is especially difficult around the government offices, where the poor, ragged, starved, and dirty remnants of Lee's heroic army are gathered day and night. The sidewalk along there is alive with vermin, and some people say they have seen lice crawling along on the walls of the houses. Poor fellows, this is worse than facing Yankee bullets. These men were, most of them, born gentlemen, and there could be no more pitiful evidence of the hardships they have suffered than the lack of means to free themselves from these disgusting creatures. Even dirt and rags can be heroic, sometimes. At the spring in our grove, where the soldiers come in great numbers to wash their faces, and sometimes, their clothes, lice have been seen crawling in the grass, so that we are afraid to walk there. Little Washington is now, perhaps, the most important military post in our poor, doomed Confederacy. The naval and medical departments have been moved here—what there is left of them. Soon all this will give place to Yankee barracks, and our dear old Confederate gray will be seen

---

[15] Col. Walter Weems, provost-in-charge at Washington (Willingham, *History of Wilkes County*, 180). The bracketed note is Miss Andrews's.

no more. The men are all talking about going to Mexico and Brazil; if all emigrate who say they are going to, we shall have a nation made up of women, negroes, and Yankees.

Washington had indeed become an important way station in the hegira of the Confederate "government" following its evacuation of Richmond. In late April, Captain William H. Parker had established temporary headquarters in Washington for the Confederate Naval Department, whose officials had fled the capital. Parker had served as superintendent and commandant of the Confederate Naval Academy in Richmond. When the government was preparing to abandon the capital, he was directed with 150 midshipmen to take charge of the Confederate Treasury Department's holdings; he was told they consisted of a half-million dollars in gold and silver (though he never saw it). The crates were loaded on one of the trains leaving Richmond for Danville, 125 miles to the southwest; the president; his wife, Varina; and cabinet officers took off in another one. From there, the trains passed through Greensboro, then Charlotte, North Carolina, and on to Chester, South Carolina, where the railway service ended. Parker and his precious cargo then were packed onto wagons and proceeded to Abbeville. From there it was another forty miles to Washington, which he reached around April 17. There he spent a day or so before departing to Augusta. Parker and his midshipmen returned to Washington on April 23, staying there for several days more. "The navy department has been ordered away from here," Fanny entered into her journal on April 27.

...and Washington would seem a very queer location for a navy that had any real existence. Capt. Parker sent Lieut. Peck this morning with a letter to father and seven great boxes full of papers and instruments belonging to the department, which he requested father to take care of. Father had them stored in the cellar, the only place where he could find a vacant spot, and so now, about all that is left of the Confederate Navy is here in our house, and we laugh and tell father, that he, the staunchest Union man in Georgia, is head of the Confederate Navy.

Miss Andrews's mention of the C.S. Medical Department so-journing to "Little Washington" is harder to document, although one may surmise that, like the C.S. Navy, there was not much of a C.S. Medical Department left in late April 1865. Most of its files had been destroyed in the fires that consumed downtown Richmond at the time of the Confederate evacuation.[16]

Our journalist's statement that "the men are all talking about going to Mexico and Brazil" is revealing. The number of Southerners who sought to escape Yankee occupation of the postwar South has not been established, but an estimate includes the twenty-nine hundred who came to Brazil from 1867 to 1871. Emperor Dom Pedro welcomed the immigrants; during the war, Brazil had offered help to the Confederacy in various diplomatic ways (it was also a slaveholding nation until a few decades after the Americans' war). Descendants of these migrant Southerners remain in Brazil, bearing the name *Confederados*. Emperor Maximilian of Mexico also favored postwar colonization, to the point of appointing ex-Confederate naval leader Matthew Fontaine Maury his commissioner of colonization and former general John B. Magruder chief of a land office. Ex-Confederates accordingly founded a number of colonies in Mexico after the war, chiefly at Carlota, seventy miles west of Vera Cruz, but also in Chihuahua and Coahuila, at Saltillo and near Tampico. Frances Andrews's documentation of colonization talk among her townsfolk as early as April 1865 adds further documentation to a fascinating story.[17]

---

[16] Willingham, *History of Wilkes County*, 187; R. Thomas Campbell, *Academy on the James: The Confederate Naval School* (Shippensburg, PA: Burd Street Press, 1998), 17, 135–38, 142–47; William H. Parker, "The Gold and Silver in the Confederate States Treasury," *Southern Historical Society Papers* 21 (1893): 305–309; Glenna R. Schroeder-Lein, "Samuel Preston Moore" in Richard N. Current, ed., *Encyclopedia of the Confederacy*, 4 vols. (New York: Simon & Schuster, 1993), 3:1077.

[17] Eugene C. Harter, *The Lost Colony of the Confederacy* (Jackson: University Press of Mississippi, 1985), 12; Andrew Rolle, *The Lost Cause: The Confederate Exodus to Mexico* (Norman: University of Oklahoma Press, 1965), 91–92, 208–

Resuming social life with family and friends in Washington was pleasant and rewarding, but the inescapable talk of defeat and apprehension for the future intensified Fanny's sorrow.

> Everybody is cast down and humiliated, and we are all waiting in suspense to know what our cruel masters will do with us. Think of a vulgar plebeian like Andy Johnson, and that odious Yankee crew at Washington, lording it over Southern gentlemen![18] I suppose that we shall be subjected to every indignity that hatred and malice can heap upon us. Till it comes, "Let us eat, drink and be merry, for to-morrow we die." Only, we have almost nothing to eat, and to drink, and still less to be merry about.

The sight of all those worn-out soldiers in and around Washington was further cause for despondency. On April 26, General Elzey and his staff hosted a picnic in a pretty grove outside of town. "Our amusements were cards, fishing in the creek, rambling about through the woods, and sitting in little circles on the grass, talking about what

---

209 (Rolle quotes the Andrews *Journal*, 9); Cyrus B. Dawsey and James M. Dawsey, *The Confederados: Old South Immigrants in Brazil* (Tuscaloosa: University of Alabama Press, 1995), 15–17.

[18] Like many Southerners, Fanny Andrews worried about how the victorious North would treat the conquered South. Even before the war was over, President Lincoln began laying out proposals whereby Confederate states could be readmitted to the Union. His "Ten Percent Plan" posited that in any Southern state where the number of citizens who had been loyal to the Union reached ten percent, they could organize a new state government. "That odious Yankee crew at Washington" Miss Andrews refers to were the Radical Republicans, such as Ohio senator Benjamin Wade and Pennsylvania congressman Thaddeus Stevens, who firmly opposed Lincoln's leniency. After he assumed the presidency on April 15, 1865, Vice President Andrew Johnson set a course for Reconstruction that followed Lincoln's but pitted him against the Radical wing of the Republican Party. In calling Andrew Johnson a "vulgar plebeian," Fanny was referring to his background in Tennessee: childhood poverty, little schooling, and work as a tailor's apprentice. Such a man would draw the scorn of an educated and polished Southern lady (Eric Foner, *A Short History of Reconstruction* [New York: Harper & Row, 1990], 16–17, 28–29, 82–83, 104).

we are going to do under the new order of things," our journalist remarked.

...down in the bottom of our hearts we felt that there is likely to
be little occasion for laughter in the end. The drive home was rather hot and dusty, and our enjoyment was damped by the sight
of the poor soldiers that we met, trundling along the road; they
looked so weary and ragged and travel-stained. Many of them,
overcome with fatigue, were lying down to rest on the bare
ground by the roadside. I felt ashamed of myself for riding when
they had to walk. These are the straggling remnants of those
splendid armies that have been for four years a terror to the
North, the glory of the South, and the wonder of the world. Alas,
alas!

The presence of so many Southern soldiers prompted Fanny to
further muse about and ponder the failed cause as she did here, in her
entry for Friday, April 28:

Emily was kept so busy all day cooking rations for soldiers that
she hardly had time for anything else, and I was so sorry for the
poor fellows that no matter what I happened to have in my hand,
if a soldier came up and looked wistfully at it, I couldn't help giving it to him. Some of them, as they talked to me about the surrender, would break down and cry like children. I took all the lard
and eggs mother had left out for Emily to cook with and gave to
them, because I could not bear to see them eating heavy old bis-
cuit made of nothing but flour and water. In this way a good part
of our supper was disposed of before we sat down to it, but nobody grudged the loss. In spite of his being such a strong Union
man, and his bitter opposition to secession, father never refuses
anything to the soldiers. I blame the secession politicians myself,
but the cause for which my brothers risked their lives, the cause
for which so many noble Southerners have bled and died, and for
which such terrible sacrifices have been made, is dear to my
heart, right or wrong. The more misfortunes overwhelm my poor
country, the more I love it; the more the Yankees triumph, the
worse I hate them, wretches! I would rather be wrong with men

like Lee and Davis, than right with a lot of miserable oppressors like Stanton and Thad Stevens.[19] The wrong of disrupting the old Union was nothing to the wrongs that are being done for its restoration.

In the early afternoon of Sunday, April 30, Frances Andrews returned from church—like many Southerners of the upper crust, she was an Episcopalian. "When I came in from the church in the afternoon, I found Burton Harrison, Mr. Davis's private secretary, among our guests."

How the Confederate president's aide came to Little Washington is a good story. Even before he got Lee's fateful telegram of April 2, Jefferson Davis began taking steps in anticipation of Richmond having to be evacuated. On March 29, he sent his wife, Varina; their four children; Varina's sister Maggie; and two servants—all under the guardianship of Burton Harrison—out of the city on a train headed for North Carolina. Ominously, before sending Varina off, the president gave her a pistol. The country was sinking into chaos, and Jeff worried about lawless groups roaming the land. "You can at least, if

---

[19] Edwin M. Stanton (1814–1869) became Lincoln's secretary of war in January 1862. He continued in this position under President Johnson, whose approach to Reconstruction Stanton opposed. Because of this and other tensions, Congress in 1867 passed the Tenure of Office Act, which forbade the president from removing Cabinet members without Senate consent. When, in February 1868, Johnson fired Stanton anyway, the House voted (with unanimous Republican support) to impeach him for violating the Tenure Act. In the Senate trial, mid-May 1868, thirty-five senators voted to convict—one short of the necessary two-thirds majority. Johnson served out his term, to March 1869. Stanton submitted his resignation as secretary of war within days of Johnson's acquittal.

Thaddeus Stevens (1792–1868) was the Pennsylvania congressman who during Reconstruction led Republican radicals in the House. Like Stanton, he opposed President Johnson's policies and argued for his removal (Frank L. Byrne, "Edwin McMasters Stanton," and Hans L. Trefousse, "Thaddeus Stevens," in John T. Hubbell and James W. Geary, eds., *Biographical Dictionary of the Union: Northern in Leaders of the Civil War* [Westport, CT: Greenwood Press, 1995], 499–500, 506–507).

reduced to the last extremity," he warned, "force your assailants to kill you," as he showed her how to load, aim, and fire the weapon.

Mrs. Davis's entourage traveled through Danville to Charlotte, where a furnished house had been arranged. On April 8, Captain Parker, the naval officer heading for Washington, persuaded Varina, Burton Harrison, and the children to accompany him farther south through Chester, Newberry, and Abbeville. The party had made its way to Washington when Miss Andrews encountered Harrison on April 30.[20] Fanny wrote about it in her journal.

> He came in with Mrs. Davis, who is being entertained at Dr. Ficklen's.[21] Nobody knows where the President is, but I hope he is far west of this by now. All sorts of ridiculous rumors are afloat concerning him; one, that he passed through town yesterday hid in a box marked "specie," might better begin with an *h*. Others, equally reliable, appoint every day in a week for his arrival in Washington with a bodyguard of 1,000 men, but I am sure he has better sense than to travel in such a conspicuous way. Mr. Harrison probably knows more about his whereabouts than anybody else, but of course we ask no questions. Mrs. Davis herself says that she has no idea where he is, which is the only wise thing for her to say. The poor woman is in a deplorable condition—no home, no money, and her husband a fugitive. She says she sold her plate in Richmond, and in the stampede from that place, the money, all but fifty dollars, was left behind. I am very sorry for her, but we are all reduced to poverty, and the most we can do is for those of us who have homes to open our doors to the rest.

---

[20] William J. Cooper Jr., *Jefferson Davis, American* (New York: Alfred A. Knopf, 2000), 522; Varina Davis, *Jefferson Davis, Ex-President of the Confederate States of America: A Memoir*, 2 vols. (Baltimore: Nautical & Aviation Publishing Company of America, 1990 [1890]), 2:577–78; Parker, "Confederate States Treasury," 306.

[21] Dr. Fielding Ficklen was a longtime resident of Washington, living in a fine home on S. Alexander Street (Willingham, *History of Wilkes County*, 180).

Jefferson Davis and five cabinet members (War Secretary John C. Breckinridge stayed behind for a few days) pulled out of Richmond by train around 11 p.m. on April 2. The next afternoon, the officials reached Danville, where they spent a week. By two criteria, Danville thus became the third Confederate capital, albeit a very brief one. The president held a meeting of his cabinet: Judah P. Benjamin (secretary of state), George A. Trenholm (treasurer), George Davis (attorney general), Stephen R. Mallory (Navy) and John H. Reagan (postmaster general). He issued a proclamation to the people of his country. Painfully acknowledging the occupation of the capital by the enemy, Davis nonetheless tried to cheer up the citizenry: "Let us not then despond, my countrymen, but, relying on the never failing mercies and protecting care of our God, let us meet the foe with fresh defiance, with unconquered and unconquerable hearts."

The president and his followers departed Danville by train during the night of April 11–12, steaming into Greensboro, North Carolina, the next afternoon. After a couple of days there, they moved by wagons—Federals had cut the rail line—to Charlotte, spending another week there, during which time several more mounted brigades joined the presidential caravan. Then it was on to Abbeville, though it took a week to get there. Miss Andrews was incorrect in assuming that the president would avoid the sight of a large, mounted escort. William J. Cooper, one of Davis's biographers, remarks, "only the presence of an escort of some 3,000 cavalrymen indicated that their horses and wagons constituted anything more than another small caravan of people displaced by the war." But rumor of approaching Federals led Davis to dismiss most of his escort and to press on in a nighttime march to Washington, which he reached in the late morning of May 3.[22]

---

[22] Michael C. Hardy, *The Capitals of the Confederacy: A History* (Charleston: History Press, 2015), 7–8, 74; Cooper, *Jefferson Davis*, 523–31; *Reminiscences of General Basil W. Duke* (West Jefferson, OH: Genesis Publishing Co., 1997 [1911]), 465; Frank E. Vandiver, *Their Tattered Flags: The Epic of the Confederacy* (New York: Harper's Magazine Press, 1970), 302.

"About noon the town was thrown into the wildest excitement by the arrival of President Davis," Fanny wrote in her journal that day. The Confederate States government was collapsing, but the ability of its chief executive to throw a town into wild excitement in early May 1865 attests to Southerners' reluctance to accept defeat in their war for independence—as we shall see in the ensuing pages of Miss Andrews's diary.

May 1865

Eliza Frances Andrews's *War-Time Journal* illustrates the uncertain and delayed transmission of news across the shrinking Confederacy in the last few months of the war. Fanny heard of the fall of Richmond on April 6 (Confederates evacuated on the second; Federals marched in the next day). She first heard of Lee's surrender on April 19; the rumor was confirmed the next day (the capitulation at Appomattox had occurred on April 9).

Official records for the Army of Northern Virginia show that 28,312 officers and men were paroled.[1] At the time of Lee's surrender, Sherman's army had reached Raleigh while Gen. Joseph E. Johnston's forces were concentrated near Hillsboro, thirty-five or forty miles to the northwest; Johnston commanded troops numbering approximately twenty thousand. On April 17, he and General Sherman initiated surrender discussions. Not long into the negotiations, Sherman and Johnston began to consider the surrender of all remaining Confederate troops, even those outside Johnston's area of command. On April 18, the two commanders signed an agreement to that effect. When it reached Washington, though, President Johnson ruled that Sherman had overreached his authority and nullified the compact. Sherman learned of this and on April 24 notified Johnston that the armistice they had arranged would be revoked in a few days. Under these strictures, the two generals on met again on April 26 at their same site, the Bennett place near Durham, and this time drew up a surrender document that applied only to Johnston's troops. Because his authority extended into South Carolina and Georgia, Johnston surrendered 39,012 officers and men—considerably more than Lee had given over to Grant in Virginia.[2]

---

[1] Douglas Southall Freeman, *Lee's Lieutenants: A Study in Command*, 3 vols. (New York: Charles Scribner's Sons, 1942–44), 3:768.

[2] Craig L. Symonds, *Joseph E. Johnston: A Civil War Biography* (New York: W. W. Norton & Company, 1992), 344; "Tabular statement of officers and men

It was on Monday, May 1, that our journalist learned of these developments: "Men were coming in all day, with busy faces, to see Mr. Harrison, and one of them brought news of Johnston's surrender, but Mr. Harrison didn't tell anyone about it except father, and the rest of us were left in ignorance till afternoon when Fred came back, with the news from Augusta."

But a war winding down still held danger for the Andrews family and their neighbors in Washington. Rumors persisted of the pestiferous Yankees, as Fanny recorded on May 1.

> While we were at dinner, a brother of Mrs. Davis came in and called for Mr. Harrison, and after a hurried interview with him, Mr. Harrison came back into the dining-room and said it had been decided that Mrs. Davis would leave tomorrow. Delicacy forbade our asking any questions, but I suppose they were alarmed by some of the numerous reports that are always flying about the approach of the Yankees. Mother called on Mrs. Davis this afternoon, and she really believes they are on their way here and may arrive at any moment.

The Yankees really weren't. On April 23, Union brigadier general James Wilson, at Macon, learned that Jefferson Davis had been seen at Charlotte, apparently heading for Georgia. On April 27, Wilson sent a small mounted force toward Augusta, but in the first week of May he kept the bulk of his command in middle Georgia in the belief that

---

of the Confederate Army paroled at Greensborough, N.C., and other points, in accordance with the military convention of April 26, 1865," *OR*, vol. 47, pt. 1, 1066. There were two more sizable capitulations. On May 4 at Citronelle, Alabama, forty miles north of Mobile, Gen. Richard Taylor surrendered some 40,000 men, including "deserters, draft evaders, chronic absentees, reserve forces and militiamen" in his department, according to biographer Michael T. Parrish (*Richard Taylor: Soldier Prince of Dixie* [Chapel Hill: University of North Carolina Press, 1992], 441). On May 26, Confederate generals at New Orleans surrendered troops in the Trans-Mississippi theater (Joseph H. Parks, *General Edmund Kirby Smith C.S.A.* [Baton Rouge: Louisiana State University Press, 1954], 477–78).

Davis and his entourage were moving toward the southwest part of the state. Unaware of this, Mrs. Davis, her family, Harrison, and an escort now increased by some paroled soldiers left Washington on May 2, heading southwest. (Our journalist recorded, "Mr. Harrison left this morning, with a Godspeed from all the family and prayers for the safety of the honored fugitives committed to his charge.") News of Johnston's surrender of most of the troops in Georgia caused Harrison to suggest a rerouting; they would head south between Macon and Augusta, ultimately for Florida, possibly toward the coast looking for a ship out to sea. Before she left, Varina wrote a letter to her husband, then at Abbeville (it reached the president that same day). In it she expressed hope to reach Pensacola, "and take a ship or what else I can." As it turned out, the pilgrims encountered no Federals before the president and his wife reunited east of Macon.[3]

It wasn't just the Yankees that posed threats to the citizenry of Wilkes County; it could be the very Confederate soldiers for whom Fanny Andrews so often expressed admiration.

> The conduct of a Texas regiment in the streets this afternoon gave us a sample of the chaos and general demoralization that may be expected to follow the breaking up of our government. They raised a riot about their rations, in which they were joined by all the disorderly elements among both soldiers and citizens. First they plundered the Commissary Department, and then turned loose on the quartermaster's stores. Paper, pens, buttons, tape, cloth—everything in the building—was seized and

---

[3] Jones, *Yankee Blitzkrieg*, 170, 172; Varina Davis, *Jefferson Davis*, 2:616–19; A. J. Hanna, *Flight into Oblivion* (Richmond: Johnson Publishing Company, 1938), 94; Burton N. Harrison to Jefferson Davis, May 2, 1865 in Dunbar Rowland, ed., *Jefferson Davis, Constitutionalist: His Letters, Papers and Speeches*, 10 vols. (Jackson: Mississippi Department of Archives and History, 1923), 5:587–88; Hudson Strode, *Jefferson Davis: Tragic Hero: The Last Twenty-five Years 1864–1889* (New York: Harcourt, Brace & World, 1964), 209; Herman Hattaway and Richard E. Beringer, *Jefferson Davis, Confederate President* (Lawrence: University Press of Kansas, 2002), 421.

strewn about on the ground. Negroes and children joined the mob and grabbed what they could of the plunder. Col. Weems's provost guard refused to interfere, saying they were too good soldiers to fire on their comrades, and so the plundering went on unopposed. Nobody seemed to care much, as we all know the Yankees will get it in the end, any way, if our men don't. I was at Miss Maria Randolph's when the disturbance began, but by keeping to the back streets I avoided the worst of the row, though I encountered a number of stragglers, running away with their booty. The soldiers were very generous with their "confiscated" goods, giving away paper, pens, tape, &c., to anybody they happened to meet. One of them poked a handful of pen staves at me; another, staggering under an armful of stationery, threw me a ream of paper, saying: "There, take that and write to your sweetheart on it." I took no notice of any of them, but hurried on home as fast as I could, all the way meeting negroes, children, and men loaded with plunder. When I reached home I found some of our own servants with their arms full of thread, paper, and pens, which they offered to me, and some of them gave me several reams of paper. I carried them to father, and he collected all the other booty he could find, intending to return it to headquarters, but he was told that there is no one to receive it, no place to send it to—in fact, there seemed to be no longer any headquarters nor any other semblance of authority. Father saved one box of bacon for Col. Weems by hauling it away in his wagon and concealing it in his smokehouse. All of Johnston's army and the greater portion of Lee's are still to pass through, and since the rioters have destroyed so much of the forage and provisions intended for their use, there will be great difficulty in feeding them. They did not stop at food, but helped themselves to all the horses and mules they needed. A band of them made a raid on Gen. Elzey's camp and took nine of his mules. They excused themselves by saying that all government stores will be seized by the Yankees in a few days, any way, if left alone, and our own soldiers might as well get the good of them while they can. This would be true, if there were not so many others yet to come who ought to have their share.

Miss Andrews was right in calling the looting a sample of the chaos and demoralization that might be expected to follow the dissolution of governmental authority; at least one historian has linked the mayhem in Washington to news of Joe Johnston's surrender.[4] The disturbances continued the next day, May 2.

> The disorders begun by the Texans yesterday were continued to-day, every fresh band that arrived from the front falling into the way of their predecessors. They have been pillaging the ordnance stores at the depot, in which they were followed by negroes, boys, and mean white men. I don't see what people are thinking about to let ammunition fall into the hand of the negroes, but everybody is demoralized and reckless and nobody seems to care about anything any more. A number of paroled men came into our grove where they sat under the trees to empty the cartridges they had seized. Confederate money is of no more use now than so much waste paper, but by filling their canteens with powder they can trade it off along the road for provisions. They scattered lead and cartridges all over the ground. Marshall went out after they left and picked up enough to last him for years. The balls do not fit his gun, but he can remold them and draw the powder out of the cartridges to shoot with. I am uneasy at having so much explosive material in the house, especially when I consider the careless manner in which we have to live.

Misbehavior could come in all forms, big and small, as Fanny observed on the third of May.

> We had an instance of ill-behavior at our house last night—the first and only one that has occurred among the hundreds—thousands, I might say, that have stopped at our door. Our back yard and kitchen were filled all day with parties of soldiers coming to get their rations cooked, or to ask for something to eat. Mother kept two servants hard at work, cooking for them. While we were

---

[4] Michael B. Ballard, *A Long Shadow: Jefferson Davis and the Final Days of the Confederacy* (Jackson: University Press of Mississippi, 1986), 12.

at supper, a squad of a dozen or more cavalrymen rode up and asked for a meal. Every seat at the table was filled, and some of the family waiting because there was no room for us, so mother told mammy to set a table for them on the front piazza, and serve them with such as we had ourselves—which was nothing to brag on, I must own. They were so incensed at not being invited into the house that mammy says they cursed her and said Judge Andrews was a d—d old aristocrat, and deserved to have his house burned down. I suppose they were drunk, or stragglers from some of the conscript regiments enrolled after the flower of our armies had been decimated in the great battles.

The soldiers' riot of May 1–2 did not dampen the social atmosphere that so intrigued Frances Andrews, as she makes abundantly clear in her diary on May 2.

There is so much company and so much to do that even the servants hardly have time to eat. I never lived in such excitement and confusion in my life. Thousands of people pass through Washington every day, and our house is like a free hotel; father welcomes everybody as long as there is a square foot of vacant space under his roof. Meeting all these pleasant people is the one compensation of this dismal time, and I don't know how I shall exist when they have all gone their ways, and we settle down in the mournful quiet of subjugation. Besides the old friends that are turning up every day, there is a continual stream of new faces crossing my path, and I make some pleasant acquaintances or form some new friendship every day. The sad part of it is that the most of them I will probably never meet again, and if I should, where, and how? What will they be? What will I be? These are portentous questions in such a time as this…. Some of our friends pass on without stopping to see us because they say they are too ragged and dirty to show themselves. Poor fellows! If they only knew how honorable rags and dirt are now, in our eyes, when endured in the service of their country, they would not be ashamed of them. The son of the richest man in New Orleans trudged through the other day, with no coat to his back, no shoes on his feet. The town is full of celebrities, and many poor fugitives, whose necks are in danger, meet here to concert plans for escape, and I put it in my prayers every night that they may be successful. Gen. Wigfall started for the West some days ago, but his mules were stolen, and he had to return. He is frantic, they say, with rage and disappointment. Gen. Toombs left to-night, but old Governor Brown, it is said, has determined not to desert his post. I am glad he has done something to deserve respect, and hope he may get off yet, as soon as the Yankees appoint a military governor. Clement Clay is believed to be well on his way to the Trans-Mississippi, the Land of Promise now, or rather the City of Refuge from which it is hoped a door of escape may be found to Mexico or Cuba.

Not all was gaiety at Haywood, however. Garnett, a lieutenant colonel in the army, had not yet come home from North Carolina. On April 30, General Elzey came to announce that Fanny's older brother had been wounded in fighting at Salisbury. A bit more news came the next day, a report that Miss Andrews frankly found "apocryphal," but worthy of a reward anyway.

Our back yard and kitchen have been filled all day, as usual, with soldiers waiting to have their rations cooked. One of them, who had a wounded arm, came into the house to have it dressed, and said that he was at Salisbury when Garnett was shot and saw him fall. He told some miraculous stories about the valorous deeds of "the colonel," and although they were so exaggerated that I set them down as apocryphal, I gave him a piece of cake, notwithstanding, to pay for telling them.

Earlier in the year Eliza's brother Garnett had taken charge of a unit of "galvanized Confederates"—turncoat Yankee prisoners who agreed to fight for the South—dignified by the name of "2nd Foreign Battalion," with the rank of lieutenant colonel. He took his command into North Carolina, where he became part of a force being organized by Brig. Gen. William M. Gardner. On April 12, Gardner's several thousand troops engaged Union cavalry near Salisbury, a hundred miles west of Raleigh, and were thoroughly whipped. Two and a half weeks later, word arrived at Haywood concerning the battle and Garnett's role in it.

> *April 30, Sunday.*—We were all standing under the ash tree by the fountain after breakfast, watching the antics of a squirrel up in the branches, when Gen. Elzey and Touch [name by which the general's son, Arnold, a lad of fourteen, was known among his friends] came to tell us that Garnett was wounded in the fight at Salisbury, N.C. Mr. Saile brought the news from Augusta, but could give no particulars except that his wound was not considered dangerous, and that his galvanized Yanks behaved badly, as anybody might have known they would. A little later the mail brought a letter from Gen. Gardiner, his commanding officer, entirely relieving our fears for his personal safety. He is a prisoner, but will soon be paroled.[5]

Then came the heartening word on May 2 that Garnett was at Abbeville, just forty miles away.

> We had a larger company to dinner to-day than usual, but no one that specially interested me. In the afternoon came a poor soldier from Abbeville, with a message from Garnett that he was there, waiting for father to send the carriage to bring him home. He sat on the soft grass before the door, and we fed him on sorghum cake and milk, the only things we had to offer. I am glad the cows have not been emancipated, for the soldiers always beg for milk; I never saw one that was not eager for it at any time. After the soldier, Ed Napier came in, who was a captain in Garnett's

---

[5] William C. Davis, "William Montgomery Gardner" in Davis, ed., *The Confederate General*, 6 vols. (Harrisburg: National Historical Society, 1991), 2:163. In his 1960 edition of *The War-Time Journal*, Professor King did not note the journalist's misspelling of General Gardner's name, but in his index listed the officer as "Gardner, Gen. William M. (corrected)." The bracketed note about Arnold Elzey Jr. is Miss Andrews's.

battalion and was taken prisoner with him. He says that Garnett covered himself with glory; even the Yankees spoke of his gallantry and admired him.

Fred, the oldest of Judge Andrews's three sons, had come home, so the next day he set out to fetch his brother. Conveyance and transportation, however, were at risk because of all the horse-thievery going on.

May 3, Wednesday.—Fred started for Abbeville in the carriage to bring Garnett home. We hear now that the Yankees are in Abbeville, and, if so, I am afraid they will take the horses away and then I don't know how Garnett will get home. They are father's carriage horses, and we would be in a sad plight with no way to ride. Our cavalry are playing havoc with stock all through the country. The Texans are especially noted in this respect. They have so far to go that the temptation is greater in their case. There is hardly a planter in Wilkes County who has not lost one or more of his working animals since they began to pass through. They seize horses, even when they are already well-mounted, and trade them off. They broke into Mr. Ben Bowdre's stable and took possession of his carriage horses, and helped themselves to two from the buggies of quiet citizens on the square. Almost everybody I know has had horses stolen or violently taken from him. I was walking with Dr. Sale in the street yesterday evening, and a soldier passed us leading a mule, while the rightful owner followed after, wasting breath in useless remonstrances. As they passed us, the soldier called out: "A man that's going to Texas must have a mule to ride, don't you think so, lady?" I made no answer, Dr. Sale gave a doubtful assent. It is astonishing what a demoralizing influence association with horses seems to exercise over the human race. Put a man on horseback and his next idea is to play the bully or to steal something.

The fear of somebody stealing one's horse led to a funny incident at Haywood on the morning of May 3. Capt. Henry Irwin, Mrs.

Elzey's brother, had come to stay with the Andrews family the week before.

> We had a good laugh on Capt. Irwin this morning. He is counting on the sale of his horse for money to carry him home, and seems to imagine that every man in a cavalry uniform is a horse thief bent on capturing his little nag. A Capt. Morton, of the cavalry, called here after breakfast, with a letter of introduction from friends, and our dear little captain immediately ran out bareheaded, to stand guard over his charger. I don't know which laughed most when the situation was explained.

Laughter, it is well known, can be good therapy, even in rough times. Such was the case in Fanny's entry from May 3: "Capt. Palfrey and Capt. Swett, of Gen. Elzey's staff, called later to bid us good-by," she wrote. "They had no money, but each was provided with a card of buttons with which they count on buying a meal or two on the way. Cousin Liza added to their store a paper of pins and Cora another card of buttons. We laughed very much at this new kind of currency."

Upon sober thought, Southerners' situation in summer 1865 was anything but laughable. In her entry of May 2, the learned Frances Andrews referred to an event in English history, the Monmouth Rebellion, an effort to overthrow King James II in 1685. After its failure, the rebels were tried in courts ("assizes") at Winchester, leading to the execution of several hundred. The Monmouth rebels had been notoriously brutalized by soldiers commanded by Col. Piercy Kirke, whose men ironically wore lamb-like badges.

> The most terrible part of the war is now to come, the "Bloody Assizes." "Kirke's Lambs," in the shape of Yankee troopers, are closing in upon us; our own disbanded armies, ragged, starving, hopeless, reckless, are roaming about without order or leaders, making their way to their far-off homes as best they can. The props that held society up are broken. Everything is in a state of disorganization and tumult. We have no currency, no law save the primitive code that might makes right. We are in a transition

state from war to subjugation, and it is far worse than was the transition from peace to war. The suspense and anxiety in which we live are terrible.[6]

Suspense and anxiety, however, were put aside as Washingtonians buzzed over the Confederate president riding into town. With him by now was just one cabinet member out of the original six. Attorney General George Davis had resigned on April 26. Shortly afterward, George Trenholm, the treasurer, resigned, citing poor health. On May 3, as the entourage crossed the Savannah River, perhaps a score of miles from Washington, Judah Benjamin had set out on his own, heading for Florida. War Secretary Breckinridge had stayed behind to direct the disbandment of cavalry. The day before they rode into Washington, Navy Secretary Mallory also composed his letter of resignation; he intended to travel by rail to join his family in west central Georgia. That left only Postmaster Reagan, but Davis had other company with him as well, including three aides: Cols. William Preston Johnston (son of Gen. Albert Sidney), John Taylor Wood (former naval commander) and Frank R. Lubbock (ex-governor of Texas). In addition were Davis's servant Robert and Col. Charles E. Thorburn, who had joined the party at Greensboro with another servant. Much of the cavalry had been paid and sent off, but apparently other horsemen were riding along; as Miss Andrews observed, "the fact that they are all going in the same direction to their homes is the only thing that keeps them together."[7]

---

[6] This passage is quoted by Wiley Sword in *Southern Invincibility: A History of the Confederate Heart* (New York: St. Martin's Press, 1999), 337.

[7] Hardy, *Capitals*, 98; Rembert W. Patrick, *Jefferson Davis and his Cabinet* (Baton Rouge: Louisiana State University Press, 1944), 352; Robert Douthat Meade, *Judah P. Benjamin: Confederate Statesman* (New York: Oxford University Press, 1943), 318; Cooper, *Jefferson Davis*, 531–32; Rodman L. Underwood, *Stephen Russell Mallory: A Biography of the Confederate Navy Secretary and United States Senator* (Jefferson, NC: McFarland & Company, 2005), 176; Royce Gordon Shingleton, *John Taylor Wood: Sea Ghost of the Confederacy* (Athens:

In her journal entry of May 3, we see Fanny writing not only about the president, but also General Elzey, Dr. John and Mrs. Mary Robertson, Capt. Henry Irwin, and Colonel Thorburn. But all eyes were on Jefferson Davis.

> He rode into town ahead of his escort, and as he was passing by the bank, where the Elzeys board, the general and several other gentlemen were sitting on the front porch, and the instant they recognized him they took off their hats and received him with every mark of respect due the president of a brave people. When he reined in his horse, all the staff who were present advanced to hold the reins and assist him to dismount, while Dr. and Mrs. Robertson hastened to offer the hospitality of their home.[8] About forty of his immediate personal friends and attendants were with him, and they were all half-starved, having tasted nothing for twenty-four hours. Capt. Irwin came running home in great haste to ask mother to send them something to eat, as it was reported the Yankees were approaching the town from two opposite directions closing in upon the President, and it was necessary to send him off at once. There was not so much as a crust of bread in our house, everything available having been given to soldiers. There was some bread in the kitchen that had just been baked for a party of soldiers, but they were willing to wait, and I begged some milk from Aunt Sallie, and by adding to these our own

---

University of Georgia Press, 1979), 154; Burton N. Harrison, "Extracts from a Narrative" in Rowland, ed., *Jefferson Davis, Constitutionalist*, 7:10.

[8] Dr. John J. Robertson was one of Washington's prominent citizens. He and Robert Toombs had represented Wilkes County at Georgia's secession convention in January 1861. He was an elder of the Washington Presbyterian Church and president of the board of trustees for the Female Seminary. In the last year of the war General Elzey and his family resided at both Judge Andrews's and Dr. Robertson's homes. For the one night he spent in Washington, Jefferson Davis stayed with John and Mary Robertson (Willingham, *History of Wilkes County*, 139, 144–45, 157, 181). The Robertsons occupied a spacious apartment above the Bank of Georgia on the north side of the town square (Strode, *Jefferson Davis: Tragic Hero*, 212; Willingham, *History of Wilkes County*, 180).

dinner as soon as Emily could finish cooking it, we contrived to get together a very respectable lunch. We had just sent it off when the president's escort came in, followed by couriers who brought the comforting assurance that it was a false alarm about the enemy being so near. By this time the president's arrival had become generally known, and people began flocking to see him; but he went to bed almost as soon as he got into the house, and Mrs. Elzey would not let him be waked. One of his friends, Col. Thorburne, came to our house and went right to bed and slept fourteen hours on a stretch. The party are all worn out and half-dead for sleep. They travel mostly at night, and have been in the saddle for three nights in succession. Mrs. Elzey says that Mr. Davis does not seem to have been aware of the real danger of his situation until he came to Washington, where some of his friends gave him a serious talk, and advised him to travel with more secrecy and dispatch than he has been using.

Jefferson Davis spent less than twenty-four hours in Washington, from noon on May 3 to ten in the morning of the next day. During this time, he held his last meeting with the only cabinet officers remaining, Mallory and Reagan. (Breckinridge would not arrive until after Davis had left town.) The president's last official act was the appointment of Capt. Micajah H. Clark as acting treasurer of the Confederate government, which still laid claim to several hundred thousand dollars. The presence at Washington of so much precious metal worried Fanny. Captain Parker and his cadets, to whom the money had originally been entrusted, had returned to Abbeville from Washington around April 28 and had stored the treasure in a warehouse. A few days later Parker was told to hand over the money to Brig. Gen. Basil Duke (whose cavalry brigade had joined the caravan at Charlotte) and to disband his company of midshipmen. Parker did so, proud that his young sailors had guarded the Confederate Treasury for thirty days.[9]

---

[9] Willingham, *History of Wilkes County*, 181; Hardy, *Capitals*, 102; Parker, "Confederate States Treasury," 309.

Throughout his travels, Parker had been accompanied by John F. Wheless, paymaster for the C.S. Navy and by Judge William W. Crump, who at Richmond had served as assistant treasurer and guardian of Virginia bank funds that had been packed in with the national gold and silver.[10] Crump's fretting over his charge rubbed off on our journalist, as we see in her entry of May 3:

> Judge Crump is back too, with his Confederate treasury, containing, it is said, three hundred thousand dollars in specie. He is staying at our house, but the treasure is thought to be stored in the vault at the bank. It will hardly be necessary for him to leave the country, but his friends advise him to keep in the shade for a time. If the Yankees once get scent of money, they will be sure to ferret it out. They have already begun their reign of terror in Richmond, by arresting many of the prominent citizens. Judge Crump is in a state of distraction about his poor little wandering exchequer, which seems to stand an even chance between the Scylla and Charybdis of Yankee cupidity. I wish it could be divided among the men whose necks are in danger, to assist them in getting out of the country, but I don't suppose one of them would touch it. Anything would be preferable to letting the Yankees get it.

That Frances Andrews was conversant in Greek mythology should not surprise us. Down through the ages "caught between Scylla and Charybdis" has meant being stuck between two decidedly unpleasant options—in the original myth, having to skirt the Strait of Messina (between Italy and Sicily). On opposite sides of the strait were a vicious six-headed monster (Scylla) and a dangerous whirlpool (Charybdis).

As it turned out, Fanny would get her wish (not letting the Yankees get the Confederate treasure): Acting Treasurer Clark later prepared a detailed report of how a third of a million dollars had been disbursed.

---

[10] Willingham, *History of Wilkes County*, 175.

Amount of gold and silver coin and silver bullion in the Confederate Treasury when the treasure train left Danville, April 6, 1865, about
$327,000.00

Paid to soldiers in Greensboro, about $39,000.00

Removed from the treasure train at Greensboro and taken with the President and Cabinet; separated from Davis near Sandersville, Georgia, May 6, and sent on to Florida $35,000.00

Paid to Maj. E. C. White near Savannah River to pay escorting officers and troops about $26 each, about $108,000.00

Paid to Major R. J. Moses for soldiers' provisions in Washington and Augusta, about $40,000.00

Paid to John C. Breckinridge, for transmission to the Trans-Mississippi Department $1,000.00

Paid to James A. Semple, a bonded officer of the Navy, who, with an assistant agreed to take it, concealed under the false bottom of a carriage, to Charleston or Savannah and then ship it to a Confederate agent in Bermuda, Nassau, or Liverpool, or some other foreign port for the account of the Confederate Government, about $86,000.00

Paid to Colonels Johnston, Lubbock, Thorburn, and Wood, $1,510 each (taken by Federals except amounts carried by Wood and Lubbock)
$6,040.00

Paid Captain Given Campbell for scouts $300.00

Paid Acting Secretary of the Treasure Reagan (taken by Federals)
$3,500.00

Paid to midshipmen and other naval guards of the treasure train
$1,500.00

Paid to Lieutenant Bradford for the marines	$300.00
Paid for miscellaneous expenses	$6,360.00
Total expenditures, about	$327,000.00[11]

Capital fallen, armies surrendered, government collapsed, treasury exhausted, president in flight: such was the Confederate States of America two hundred weeks after the first gun had been fired at Fort Sumter. Yet some Southerners remained defiant. Capt. Shaler Smith and a Lieutenant Hallam, both Kentuckians, were among the dinner guests at Haywood on Wednesday evening, the third. Fanny noted that they weren't heading home, though, but across the Mississippi, where some Confederates hoped to carry on the war. "They still believe the battle of Southern independence will be fought out there and won," she recorded; "if faith as a grain of mustard seed can move mountains, what ought not faith like this to accomplish!"[12]

There was the fact that the chief ordnance officer of the Confederate army was now a boyish second lieutenant.

> Mr. Hallam is a high-spirited young fellow, and reminds me of the way we all used to talk and feel at the beginning of the war. I believe he thinks he could fight the whole Yankee nation now, single-handed, and whip them, too. He is hardly more than a boy, and only a second lieutenant, yet, as he gravely informed me, is now the chief ordnance officer of the Confederate army. He was taken prisoner and made his escape without being paroled, and since the surrender of Lee's and Johnston's armies, he really is, it seems, the ranking ordnance officer in the poor little remnant that is still fixing its hope on the Trans-Mississippi.

Jefferson Davis, however, remained the focus of public attention in Little Washington. "The people of the village sent so many good

---

[11] Hanna, *Flight into Oblivion*, 90–92.
[12] The reference is to Matthew 17:20, "faith like a mustard seed."

things for the president to eat," she wrote on May 4, "that an ogre couldn't have devoured them all." Judge Andrews and Fanny's sister Cora (who had come up from Albany to spend the summer) paid a call on Davis that morning. "Father says his manner was so calm and dignified that he could not help admiring the man," she commented. Jefferson Davis was doing a good job in facing facts, for early on May 4 he had finally decided finally to admit that his government was gone, as he declared in a conference with John Reagan and a few other officers. "It is all over," Quartermaster General A. R. Lawton, one of the attendees, said afterward; "the Confederate Government is dissolved." Someone observed the irony of the dissolution of the administration occurring in a town named Washington, declaring that "Providence had the most inscrutable way of exhibiting His purposes."

Word must have gotten out that the president had decided to leave town and continue his flight amid rumors that Wilson's Union cavalry was out looking for him. People wandered outside the bank building in hopes of getting one last glimpse of the Confederate president. After his conference—the last one of his cabinet—Davis walked across the street to the town square and said a few words to the Reverend Henry Tupper, the local Baptist minister. On hand was Frank Vizetelly, artist for the *London Illustrated News* who had joined the Davis party. The president had decided to shrink his escort to just ten men, his three aides and a few others. Around 10 a.m. he began to say goodbye to the officers of his guard. There were signs of sorrow all around; the Englishman observed of Davis, "with tears in his eyes he begged the men to seek their own safety and leave him to his fate." (For the first time Davis's servant Robert saw his master crying.) The artist drew a picture of the scene, the downcast Davis with hat in hand.[13] Frances wrote of the scene, under date of May 4:

---

[13] Willingham, *History of Wilkes County*, 181; Cooper, *Jefferson Davis*, 533; Ballard, *Long Shadow*, 132–33; Strode, *Jefferson Davis: Tragic Hero*, 215; Jefferson Davis, *The Rise and Fall of the Confederate Government*, 2 vols. (New York: Da Capo Press, 1990 [1881]), 2:589.

> Crowds of people flocked to see him, and nearly all were melted
> to tears. Gen. Elzey pretended to have dust in his eyes and Mrs.
> Elzey blubbered outright, exclaiming all the while, in her impul-
> sive way: "Oh, I am such a fool to be crying, but I can't help it!"
> When she was telling me about it afterwards, she said she could
> not stay in the room with him yesterday evening, because she
> couldn't help crying, and she was ashamed for the people who
> called to see her looking so ugly, with her eyes and nose red.

By the time the last farewell had been bade, Davis's small escort had
impatiently headed out already, leaving the president and a lone companion to mount up and ride away.

Secretary Breckinridge entered Washington a little later; "as a result," states the general's biographer, "only Reagan and Breckinridge
remained of the Confederate government."[14] Our journalist notes that
"Gen. Breckinridge is called the handsomest man in the Confederate
army." At age forty-five, the former U.S. congressman, vice president
and senator, now C.S. major general and secretary of war, possessed
striking blue eyes and sported a flowing moustache. The Kentuckian
impressed onlookers as much by his gentlemanly charm as by his appearance.

Quite the opposite pertained to another Confederate general who
had also arrived in town: Braxton Bragg, commander of the Army of
Tennessee till he resigned after his disastrous defeat at Missionary
Ridge, but who finished out the war as President Davis's military ad-
viser. Bragg had ridden with the Davis entourage for a while in South
Carolina. Now in Washington, he decidedly failed to impress Frances
Andrews. If Breckinridge was the South's handsomest general, "Bragg
might be called the ugliest." ("I saw him at Mrs. Vickers's, where he is
staying and he looks like an old porcupine.")

---

[14] William C. Davis, *Breckinridge Statesman Soldier Symbol* (Baton Rouge:
Louisiana State University Press, 1974), 522.

Yet she wrote approvingly of Bragg's reputation as a disciplinarian of his troops.[15]

> I never was a special admirer of his, though it would be a good thing if some of his stringent views about discipline could be put into effect just now—if discipline were possible among men without a leader, without a country, without a hope. The army is practically disbanded, and citizens, as well as soldiers, thoroughly demoralized. It has gotten to be pretty much a game of grab with us all; every man for himself and the Devil (or the Yankees, which amounts to the same thing) take the hindmost. Nearly all government teams have been seized and driven out of town by irresponsible parties—indeed, there seems to be nobody responsible for anything any longer. Gen. Elzey's two ambulances were taken last night, so that Capt. Palfrey and Capt. Swett are left in the lurch, and will have to make their way home by boat and rail, or afoot, as best they can.

There was much to see and to write about—Frances Andrews's journal entry for May 4 runs for more than seven printed pages: "large numbers of cavalrymen passed through town during the day"; General Breckinridge disbursed some more specie to the men ("Mr. Hallam called in the afternoon, and…showed me ninety dollars in gold…. I don't see what better could be done with the money than to pay it all out to the soldiers of the Confederacy before the Yankees gobble it up"). This was the same day, too, that Fred brought Garnett home from the war. "Garnett looks very thin and pale," she observed; "the saber cuts on his head are nearly healed, but the wound in his shoulder is still very panful. His fingers are partially paralyzed from it, but I hope not permanently." At least he was home, yet Garnett's wound was slow to heal. On May 12, she entered in her journal, "Poor Garnett is

---

[15] Earl J. Hess, *Braxton Bragg: The Most Hated Man in the Confederacy* (Chapel Hill: University of North Carolina Press, 2016), 248–49; Judith Lee Hallock, *Braxton Bragg and Confederate Defeat, Volume Two* (Tuscaloosa: University of Alabama Press, 1991), 32.

suffering very much from his arm. He is confined to bed, threatened with fever, and we can't get proper food for him." At the same time, she proudly wrote, "Gen. Elzey heard one Yankee soldier say to another yesterday, as he was walking behind them on the street, in passing our house: 'Garnett Andrews gave one of our men the hell of a saber cut the other day, at Salisbury.' I am glad he gave them something so good to remember him by."

Just enjoying a good meal could be something worth writing about.

> Aunt Sallie invited Mr. Habersham Adams, her pastor, and his wife, to dinner, and Cousin Liza, Mary Day, Cora, Metta, and me, to help them eat it. She had such a dinner as good old Methodist ladies know how to get up for their preachers, though where all the good things came from, Heaven only knows. She must have been hoarding them for months. We ate as only hungry Rebs can, that have been half-starved for weeks, and expect to starve the rest of our days. We have no kind of meat in our house but ham and bacon, and have to eat hominy instead of rice, at dinner. Sometimes we get a few vegetables out of the garden, but everything has been so stripped to feed the soldiers, that we never have enough to spread a respectable meal before the large number of guests, expected and unexpected, who sit down to our table every day. In spite of all we can do, there is a look of scantiness about the table that makes people afraid to eat as much as they want—and dreadful things we have to give them, at that! Cornfield peas have been our staple diet for the last ten days. Mother has them cooked in every variety of style she ever heard of, but they are cornfield peas still. All this would have been horribly mortifying a year or two ago, but everybody knows how it is now, and I am glad to have even cornfield peas to share with the soldiers.

Speaking of sharing with soldiers, "Three cavalry officers ate dinner at the house while we were at Aunt Sallie's." Fanny wasn't there, but "Mother says they were evidently gentlemen, but they were so ragged and dirty that she thought the poor fellows did not like to give their names. They didn't introduce themselves, and she didn't ask who they were."

The sacking of C.S. ordnance stores in Washington that Miss Andrews had written about on May 2 ("they scattered lead and cartridges all over the ground") prompted further comment:

> Boys and negroes and sportsmen are taking advantage of the ammunition scattered broadcast by the pillaging of the ordnance stores, to indulge in fireworks of every description, and there is so much shooting going on all around town that we wouldn't know it if a battle were being fought. Capt. Irwin came near being killed this afternoon by a stray minie ball shot by some careless person. The R. R. depot is in danger of being blown up by the quantities of gunpowder scattered about there, mixed up with percussion caps. Fred says that when he came up from Augusta the other day, the railroad between here and Barnett was strewn with loose cartridges and empty canteens that the soldiers had thrown out of the car windows.

Amidst this turbulence on Thursday, May 4, France Andrews reflected on her journal-writing.

> I have so little time for writing that I make a dreadful mess of these pages. I can hardly ever write fifteen minutes at a time without interruption. Sometimes I break off in the middle of a sentence and do not return to it for hours, and so I am apt to get everything into a jumble. And the worst of it is, we are living in such a state of hurry and excitement that half the time I don't know whether I am telling the truth or not. Mother says that she will have to turn the library into a bedroom if we continue to have so much company, and then I shall have no quiet place to go to, and still less time to myself. It seems that the more I have to say, the less time I have to say it in. From breakfast till midnight I am engaged nearly all the time with company, so that the history of each day has to be written mostly in the spare moments I can

steal before breakfast on the next, and sometimes I can only scratch down a few lines to be written out at length whenever I can find the time. I have been keeping this diary for so long and through so many difficulties and interruptions that it would be like losing an old friend if I were to discontinue it. I can tell it what I can say to no one else, not even to Metta.

May 5, Friday.—It has come at last—what we have been dreading and expecting so long—what had caused so many panics and false alarms—but it is no false alarm this time; the Yankees are actually in Washington.

Indeed they were. Union general Wilson had sent out bodies of troops looking for Jeff Davis. By the time the president left Little Washington, some 13,000 Federal horsemen were spread across Middle and South Georgia. Brig. Gen. Emory Upton, commanding one of Wilson's divisions, led his troops into Augusta on May 3.[16]

He was soon sending out detachments to nearby towns. Our journalist recorded the experience.

Before we were out of bed a courier came in with news that Kirke—name of ill omen—was only seven miles from town, plundering and devastating the country. Father hid the silver and what little coin he had in the house, but no other precautions were taken. They have cried "wolf" so often that we didn't pay much attention to it, and besides, what could we do, anyway? After dinner we all went to our rooms as usual, and I sat down to write. Presently some one knocked at my door and said: "The Yankees have come, and are camped in Will Pope's grove." I paid no attention and went on quietly with my writing. Later, I dressed and went down to the library, where Dr. Cromwell was waiting for me, and asked me to go with him to call on Annie Pope. We found the streets deserted; not a soldier, not a straggler did we see. The silence of death reigned where a few hours ago all was stir and bustle—and it is the death of our liberty. After the

---

[16] Edward G. Longacre, *Grant's Cavalryman: The Life and Wars of General James H. Wilson* (Mechanicsburg, PA: Stackpole Books, 1996 [1972]), 220, 222.

excitement of the last few days, the stillness was painful, oppressive. I thought of Chateaubriand's famous passage: "Lorsque dans le silence de l'abjection" &c.[17] News of the odious arrival seems to have spread like a secret pestilence through the country, and travelers avoid the tainted spot. I suppose the returning soldiers flank us, for I have seen none on the streets to-day, and none have called at our house. The troops that are here came from Athens. There are about sixty-five men, and fifteen negroes, under the command of a Major Wilcox. They say that they come for peace, to protect us from our own lawless cavalry—to *protect* us, indeed! with their negro troops, runaways from our own plantations! I would rather be skinned and eaten by wild beasts than beholden to *them* for protection. As they were marching through town, a big buck negro leading a raw-boned jade is said to have made a conspicuous figure in the procession. Respectable people were shut up in their houses, but the little street urchins immediately began to sing, when they saw the big Black Sancho and his Rosinante:

"Yankee Doodle went to town and stole a little pony;
He stuck a feather in his cap and called him Macaroni."

They followed the Yanks nearly to their camping ground at the Mineral Spring, singing and jeering at the negroes, and strange to say, the Yankees did not offer to molest them. I have not laid eyes on one of the creatures myself, and they say they do not intend to come into town unless to put down disturbances—the sweet, peaceful lambs! They never sacked Columbia; they never burnt Atlanta; they never left a black trail of ruin and desolation through the whole length of our dear old Georgia! No, not they! I wonder how long this sugar and honey policy is to continue. They deceive no one with their Puritanical hypocrisy, bringing our own runaway negroes here to protect us. Next thing they will have a negro garrison in the town for our benefit.

---

[17] More evidence of our journalist's erudition: Francois-Rene de Chateaubriand (1768–1848) translated Tacitus' *Annals*. From the French: "when in the silence of abjection, the only sounds that can be heard are the chains of slaves and the voice of the collaborator, when everything trembles before the tyrant."

Fanny Andrews was seeing her first Yankees—"about sixty-five white men, and fifteen negroes, under the command of a Major Wilcox"—but it was upon the uniformed African Americans that she focused her attention. In July 1862, the U.S. Congress had passed an act authorizing President Lincoln to enlist persons of African descent for "any military or naval service for which they may be found competent." Lincoln was slow to act, though, and the North did not begin to organize regiments of Black soldiers for another year. One such unit, the 54th Massachusetts, took part in the Federals' pillage of Darien, Georgia, in June 1863. In Savannah after Sherman's departure there remained a Union garrison, which was augmented in March 1865 by three regiments of United States Colored Troops.[18]

So some Georgians had seen Black men in blue uniforms before, just not Frances Andrews.

Her contempt for Federals' "bringing our own runaway negroes here to protect us" is understandable, but the presence of Black soldiers among Union occupation forces made sense. Southerners—White and Black—knew that with Confederate defeat, slavery was gone, or soon would be. How the two races would work out a new social order remained to be seen. In the meantime, as one historian has written, "African American soldiers could act as a buffer between the white and black populace, assisting former slaves in the transition from slavery to freedom while protecting them from retaliation by whites."[19]

Just as important, and equally uncertain, was how ex-Confederates would handle conquest and subjugation in the post-Appomattox

---

[18] James M. McPherson, *Ordeal by Fire: The Civil War and Reconstruction* (New York: McGraw-Hill, 1992 [1982]), 347–48; Dudley Taylor Cornish, *The Sable Arm: Negro Troops in the Union Army, 1861–1865* (New York: W. W. Norton & Company, 1966 [1956]), 148–49; Alexander A. Lawrence, *A Present for Mr. Lincoln: The Story of Savannah from Secession to Sherman* (Savannah: Oglethorpe Press, 1997 [1961]), 240.

[19] Robert J. Zalimas, Jr., "A Disturbance in the City: Black and White Soldiers in Postwar Charleston" in John David Smith, ed., *Black Soldiers in Blue: African American Troops in the Civil War Era* (Chapel Hill: University of North Carolina Press, 2002), 363–64.

South. Here, too, our journalist appears as a rebellious spitfire. When Georgia seceded in January 1861, Fanny and her sister Cora had secretly sewn a "Bonnie Blue Flag" that across the South was waved in celebration of secession; their father, an opponent of disunion, would have disapproved. "It consisted of a large five-pointed star, the emblem of States' Rights, and was made of White domestic on a field of blue," Fanny recalled. Now, with Union troops in town, she feared having to look at the Yankees' Stars and Stripes—actually, she worried about what the Confederate soldiers still milling through Washington would do if they saw it.

> Their odious old flag has not yet been raised in the village, and I pray God they will have the grace to spare us that insult, at least until Johnston's army has all passed through. The soldiers will soon return to their old route of travel, and there is no telling what our boys might be tempted to do at the sight of that emblem of tyranny on the old courthouse steeple, where once floated the "lone star banner" that Cora and I made with our own hands—the first rebel flag that was ever raised in Washington. Henry brought us the cloth, and we made it on the sly in Cora's room at night, hustling it under the bed, if a footstep came near, for fear father or mother might catch us and put a stop to our work. It would break my heart to see the emblem of our slavery floating in its place.

Others felt the same way. When the Yankees were said to be nearing town, in the dark of night some veterans of the Irvin Artillery crept up to "our old liberty pole," cut it down and carried it off. "It was a sad night's work," Fanny admitted, "but there was no other way to save it from desecration."

If May 5 was the day the Yankees came, May 6 was a day for getting used to them. "Reenforcements have joined Wilcox, and large numbers of Stoneman's and Wilson's cavalry are passing through on their way to Augusta," Miss Andrews recorded. From his headquarters at Macon, General Wilson was serving as military governor of Georgia.

Maj. Gen. George Stoneman was commanding at Knoxville, Tennessee, but some of his mounted troops were in Georgia searching for Jeff Davis (who was captured on May 10 near Irwinville, eighty miles south of Macon).[20]

In Washington, residents were treated to the awkward sight of Federal and Confederate soldiers riding past each other: "about noon, two brigades of our cavalry passed going west, and at the same time a body of Yankees went by going east."

There were several companies of negroes among them, and their hateful old striped rag was floating in triumph over their heads. Cousin Liza turned her back on it, Cora shook her fist at it, and I was so enraged that I said I wished the wind would tear it to flinders and roll it in the dirt till it was black all over, as the colors of such a crew ought to be. Then father took me by the shoulder and said that if I didn't change my way of talking about the flag of my country he would send me to my room and keep me there a week. We had never known anything but peace and security and protection under that flag, he said, as long as we remained true to it. I wanted to ask him what sort of peace and protection the people along Sherman's line of march had found under it, but I didn't dare. Father don't often say much, but when he does flare up like that, we all know we have got to hold our tongues or get out of the way. It made me think of that night when Georgia seceded. What would father have done if he had known that our secession flag was made in his house? It pinches my conscience, sometimes, when I think about it. What a dreadful thing it is for a household to be so divided in politics as we are! Father sticks to the Union through thick and thin, and mother sticks to father, though I believe she is more than half a rebel at heart, on account of the boys. Fred and Garnett are good Confederates, but too considerate of father to say much, while all the rest of us are red-hot Rebs. Garnett is the coolest head in the family, and Henry the hottest. I used to sympathize with father myself, in the beginning,

---

[20] Longacre, *Grant's Cavalryman*, 224; Ballard, *Long Shadow*, 140–42.

for it did seem a pity to break up a great nation about a parcel of African savages, if we had known any other way to protect our rights; but now, since the Yankees have treated us so abominably, burning and plundering our country and bringing a gang of negro soldiers to insult us, I don't see how anybody can tolerate the sight of their odious flag again.

Aside from the symbolic insults Miss Andrews felt from the new Yankee conquerors, the blackguards were using their occupational authority to continue the very "plundering [of] our country" that Fanny so hated. Haywood was located in the northwest section of Washington, a good distance north of Broad Street, so the Andrews family could not see the "plunder with which the wretches, both black and white, were loaded,"

but Cousin Mary Cooper, who lives right on the street, opposite our gate, told us that she saw one white man with a silver cake basket tied to the pommel of his saddle, and nearly all of them had stolen articles dangling from the front of their saddles, or slung on in bags behind. And yet, they blame us for not respecting their flag, when we see it again for the first time in four years, floating over scenes like this!

Then there were the verbal insults.

A large body of the brigands are camped back of Aunty's meadow, and have actually thrown the dear old lady, who was never known to speak a cross word to anybody, into a rage, by their insolence. Capt. Hudson had almost to kick one of them out of the house before he could get him to move, and the rascal cried out, as he went down the steps: "I thought you Rebs were all subjugated now, and I could go where I pleased." Another taunted her by saying: "You have got plenty of slaves to wait on you now, but you won't have them long."

The Yankee was right. Georgia's Black population numbered over 460,000. They were technically newly freed, but few knew how that freedom would look. "Of all the problems before the South and the Nation, the foremost," writes C. Mildred Thompson in *Reconstruction in Georgia*, "were the adaptation of the slave-driven negro to free labor, the adjustment of the land and planting system to new conditions, and the settlement of social relations between the two races living side by side when the old bond of master and slave was destroyed."[21] White planters and slaveowners such as Garnett Andrews confronted the basic question of how he and his family would now make a living. Fanny affirmed this in a terse, glum statement under date of May 4, speaking of her father: "he has lost not only his negroes, like everybody else, but his land, too."

Judge Andrews had plenty of company. "Gen. Yorke is with us now," Frances noted on May 6, referring to Confederate brigadier general Zebulon York. "He is a rough old fellow, but has a brave record, and wears an empty sleeve"—York had been wounded in his left arm, which had to be amputated. "They say he was the richest man in Louisiana 'before the deluge'—owned 30,000 acres of land and 900 negroes, besides plantations in Texas," she continued, and with good foundation: York and his business partner owned six plantations and 1,700 slaves, making York one of the richest men in Louisiana; "and now, he hasn't money enough to pay his way home."[22] "It is very hard on the West Point men," she added, "for they don't know anything but soldiering, and the army is closed to them: they have no career before them."

---

[21] William Harris Bragg, "Reconstruction" in John C. Inscoe, ed., *The Civil War in Georgia* (Athens: University of Georgia Press, 2011), 185; C. Mildred Thompson, *Reconstruction in Georgia; Economic, Social, Political 1865–1872* (Macon: Mercer University Press, 2017 [1915]), 42.

[22] Jack D. Welch, *Medical Histories of Confederate Generals* (Kent, OH: Kent State University Press, 1995), 241; Terry L. Jones, "Zebulon York" in William C. Davis, ed., *The Confederate General*, 6 vols. (Harrisburg, PA: National Historical Society, 1991), 6:167.

Fanny was a good hostess for visitors such as General York. "He is very fond of cigarettes, and I keep both him and Capt. Hudson supplied with them," she recorded. "The captain taught me how to roll them, and I have become so skilful that I can make them like we used to knit socks, without looking at what I am doing." When the General left Washington on May 7, he "went off with both pockets full of my cigarettes, and he laughingly assured me that he would think of me as long as they lasted."

At Haywood, however, camaraderie could be strained and levity somewhat pinched by what everyone was thinking.

> Gen. Elzey called after tea, and I failed to recognize him at first, because he had on a white jacket, and there is such a strange mixture of Yanks and Rebs in town that I am suspicious of every man who doesn't wear a gray coat. The moon was shining in my eyes and blinded me as I met the general at the head of the steps, and I kept a sour face, intended for a possible Yankee intruder, till he caught my hand and spoke; then we both laughed. Our laughter, however, was short-lived; we spent a miserable evening in the beautiful moonlight that we knew was shining on the ruin of our country. Capt. Irwin made heroic efforts to keep up his spirits and cheer the rest of us, but even he failed. Gen. Yorke, too, did his best to laugh at our miserable little jokes, and told some good stories of his own, but they fell flat, like the captain's. Judge Crump tried to talk of literature and art, but conversation flagged and always returned to the same miserable theme. Gen. Elzey said he wished that he had been killed in battle. He says that this is the most miserable day of his life, and he looked it.

In this atmosphere of resignation and defeat, ex-Confederate officers were taking private steps to salvage their pride. In her entry for May 6, our journalist noted that of the officers still in town, "some have already laid aside their uniforms and their military titles. They say they are not going to wait to be deprived of them at the command of a Yankee."

May 7, Sunday.—I went to the Baptist church and heard a good sermon from Mr. Tupper on the text: "For now we live by faith, and not by sight." There was not a word that could give the Yankees a handle against us, yet much that we poor rebels could draw comfort from. The congregation was very small, and I am told the same was the case at all the other churches, people not caring to have their devotions disturbed by the sight of the "abominations of desolation" in their holy places.

With this latter phrase Fanny Andrews was, of course, referring to Yankees. She was a good Episcopalian, but there was a reason she chose on this Sabbath to worship at the Reverend Henry Allen Tupper's Washington Baptist Church: the Episcopal Book of Common Prayer prescribed a prayer for the president of the United States. During the war, Southern priests changed this to a prayer for the Confederate president and sometimes got into trouble for this when Union officers walked in. With the end of the war, the old practice resumed, as our journalist observed: "now, the Yankees are denying us not only liberty of speech and of the press, but even of prayer, forcing the ministers in our Church to read the prayer for their old renegade of a president and those other odious persons 'in authority' at Washington. Well, as Bishop Elliott says," Frances added, alluding to Stephen Elliott, bishop of the Diocese of Georgia, "I don't know anybody that needs it more."

On May 2, two weeks after Lincoln's assassination, President Johnson authorized a $100,000 reward for Jefferson Davis's capture, linking him in some murky way to John Wilkes Booth's deed. Frances took note of this on May 7.

Since they have set a price on the head of our president, "immortal hate and study of revenge" have taken possession of my heart, and it don't make me love them or their detestable old flag any better because I have to keep my feelings pent up. Father won't let me say anything against the old flag in his presence, but he can't keep me from thinking and writing what I please. I believe I would burst sometimes, if I didn't have this safety-valve.[23]

The presence of the enemy in Washington only thickened our journalist's patriotic sentiments. Here (dated May 6):

I was walking on the street this afternoon with Mr. Dodd and a Lieut. Sale, from Ark., when we met three gorgeous Yankee officers, flaunting their smart new uniforms in the faces of our poor, shabby Rebs, but I would not even look their way till they had passed and couldn't see me. Oh, how I do love the dear old Confederate gray! My heart sickens to think that soon I shall have seen the last of it.... Some of our Confederates wear a dark, bluish-gray uniform which is difficult to distinguish from the Federal blue, and I live in constant fear of making a mistake. As a general thing our privates have no uniform but rags, poor fellows, but the officers sometimes puzzle me, unless they wear the Hungarian knot on their sleeves. It makes the letters, C.S.A., but one would not be apt to notice the monogram unless it was pointed out to him. It is a beautiful uniform, and I shall always love the colors, the gray and gold, for its sake—or rather for the sake of the men who wore it. There is a report that Confederate officers are going to be ordered to lay aside their uniforms. It will be a black day when this habit that we all love so well gives place to the badge of servitude. There is nothing in the history of nations to compare with the humiliations we Southerners have to endure.[24]

---

[23] Robert McElroy, *Jefferson Davis: The Unreal and the Real* (New York: Kraus Reprint Co., 1969 [1937]), 505–506. The quotation is from *Paradise Lost*: "What though the field be lost?/ All is not lost; th' unconquerable will,/And study of revenge, immortal hate,/And courage never to submit or yield."

[24] The sleeves of Confederate officers' frock coats were often decorated with gold braid shaped in an elegant design called an Austrian or Hungarian knot (Philip R. N. Katcher, *The Army of Northern Virginia* [London: Osprey Publishing, 1975], 8). They are pictured in Gordon L. Jones, *Confederate Odyssey: The George W. Wray Jr. Civil War Collection at the Atlanta History Center* (Athens: University of Georgia Press, 2014), 363, 367–69. The "dark, bluish-gray

And there were the Yankees' irritating "manners," as Fanny remarked, on Sunday the 7th: "When the first batch of Yankees entered Washington, one of them was heard to say: 'We have been hunting for this little mudhole the last six months.' No wonder they didn't succeed; it is anything but a mudhole now," referring both to the town's swollen population and the dry weather ("the streets are frightfully dusty").

Worse still was their thievery. When brother Fred returned from a short trip to Greensboro,

> he says the Yankees are plundering right and left around Athens. They ran a train off the track on the Athens Branch, and robbed the passengers. They have not given any trouble in Washington to-day, as the greater part of the cavalry that came to town on Saturday have passed on, and the garrison, or provost guard, or whatever the odious thing is called, are probably afraid to be too obstreperous while so many Confederate troops are about. They have taken up their quarters in the courthouse now, but have not yet raised their old flaring rag on the spot where our own brave boys placed the first rebel flag, that my own hands helped to make.

"Part of the regiment that plundered the train on the Athens Branch has been sent to Washington, and is behaving very badly," Fanny recorded in her journal. Also under date of May 8 was the story of Aunt Cornelia and her Federal guard.

> Aunt Cornelia's guard, too, refused to stay with her any longer because he was not invited to eat at the table with the family! Others of the company then went there and committed all sorts of depredations on the lot. They cursed Aunty and threatened to

---

uniform" Miss Andrews mentions was commonly associated with general officers. In North Carolina, for instance, a board of regulations in May 1861 called for gray frock coats for regimental officers, but coats "of dark blue cloth for General Officers and Officers of the General Staff" (Katcher, *Army of Northern Virginia*, 9).

burn the house down, and one of them drew a pistol on Mr. Hull for interfering, but promptly took to his heels when Mr. Hull returned the civility. He soon came back with several of his comrades and made such threats that Aunty sent to their commanding officer and asked for a guard, but received for answer that "they would guard her to hell." Capt. Hudson then went to the provost-marshal in command of the town, Capt. Lot Abraham, who sent a lieutenant with another guard.[25] Aunty complained to the lieutenant of the way she had been insulted, but he replied that the guard might stay or not, as he chose; that she had not treated the former one with proper consideration, and he would not compel another to stay in her house. Aunty was ready to choke with rage, she says, but dared not speak a word, and now the family have to purchase safety by having a horrid plebeian of a Yankee, who is fitter company for the negroes in the kitchen, sit at the table with them. The whole family are bursting with indignation, but dare not show it for fear of having their house burned over their heads. They spoke in whispers while telling me about it, and I was so angry that I felt as if I would like to run a knitting needle into the rascal, who sat lolling at his ease in an armchair on the piazza, looking as insolent as if he were the master of the house. It is said we are to have a negro garrison at Washington, and all sorts of horrible rumors are afloat. But we know nothing except what the tyrants choose that we shall.

It was in this mood that our journalist recorded her thoughts and feelings:

I sympathize with the spirit of that sturdy old heathen I have read about somewhere, who said to the priests who were trying to convert him, that he would rather stick to his own gods and go to

---

[25] Eliza Frances Andrews was correct: Capt. Lot Abraham, an officer in Emory Upton's division of Wilson's cavalry corps, was provost-marshal at Washington by the second week of May 1865. During his stay he paroled several thousand Confederates and claimed to have recovered $5,000 of "J. D.'s specie" (*OR*, vol. 49, pt. 2, 685, 702, 719, 788).

hell with his warrior ancestors, than sit down to feast in heaven with their little starveling band of Christians. That is the way I feel about Yankees; I would rather be wrong with Lee and his glorious army than right with a gang of fanatics that have come down here to plunder and oppress us in the name of liberty.

At least there were friends, visitors, and guests to help break the gloom. "Mrs. Elzey is like a gleam of sunshine on a rainy day," Fanny wrote; "she pitches into the Yankees with such vigor, and says such funny things about them, that even father has to laugh." And there was Henry Irwin, Ellen Elzey's brother, about whom Fanny wrote, "Capt. Irwin is a whole day of sunshine himself, but even his happy temper is so dimmed by sadness that his best jokes fall flat for want of the old spirit in telling them."

Back to the problem of money. When Zebulon York left Haywood on May 7, Fred agreed to accompany him at least to Garnett's plantation in Mississippi ("if anything is left there to look after," Fanny remarked). The next day, though, she entered this into her diary:

We shall all be too poor to travel, and too poor to extend the hospitality for which our Southern homes have been noted, any more. The pinch of want is making itself felt more severely every day, and we haven't the thought that we are suffering for our country that buoyed us up during the war. Men with thousands of Confederate money in their pockets cannot buy a pin. Father has a little specie which he was prudent enough to lay aside at the beginning of the war, but he has given a good deal of it to the boys at different times, when they were hard up, and the little that is left will have to be spent with the greatest care, to feed our family. I could not even pay postage on a letter if it were necessary to write one. I have serious notions of trying to sell cigarettes to the Yankees in order to get a little pocket money,—only, I could not bear the humiliation.[26]

---

[26] Robert Willingham quotes this passage in his *History of Wilkes County*, 192–93.

It's jolly well that our diarist loved seeing "the dear old Confederate gray," for she was seeing a lot of it in early May.

> Johnston's army is pouring in now. People are getting used to the presence of the Yankees, and Washington is a great thoroughfare for Confederates once more. Lee's men used up all the bread-stuffs in the commissariat, so the newcomers have to depend on private hospitality. The Yankees say they can't collect corn and flour to replace what was destroyed during the riots. They give out rations of meat, but nothing else, and it is pitiful to see the poor fellows going about the streets offering to exchange part of their scanty ration of bacon for bread. Numbers of them come to our door every day, begging for bread, and it almost makes me cry when a poor fellow sometimes pulls out a piece of rancid bacon from his haversack and offers it in pay. Mother will never take anything from a soldier, and we always share what little we have with them. It gives me more pleasure to feed the poor Rebs than to eat myself. I go out and talk with them frequently, while they are waiting to have their food cooked. This evening, two of them were sitting on the front steps talking over their troubles, and I heard one of them say: "If I kin just git back home to Sally once more, I won't care about nothin' else." He was young, I could see, through all the diet and grime on his face, so I suppose "Sally" was either his sweetheart, or the young bride he left when he went away to the war.

And yet she was saying goodbye to "numbers of them," as well.

> *May 8, Monday.* —We had a sad leave-taking at noon. Capt. Irwin, finding it impossible to get transportation to Norfolk by way of Savannah, decided last night that he would start for Virginia this morning with Judge Crump. He has no money to pay his way with, but like thousands of other poor Confederates, depends on his war horse to carry him through, and on Southern hospitality to feed and lodge him. He left his trunk, and Judge Crump his official papers, in father's care. Mother packed up a large quantity of provisions for them, and father gave them letters to friends of his

all along the route, though Georgia and Carolina, as far as his personal acquaintance extends. Our avenue is alive all the morning with Confederates riding back and forth to bid their old comrades good-by. The dear captain tried to keep up a brave heart, and rode off with a jest on his lips and moisture in his eyes, while as for us—we ladies all broke down and cried like children. The dear old Judge, too, seemed deeply moved at parting, and we could do nothing but cry, and nobody could say what we wanted to. Partings are doubly sad now, when the chances of meeting again are so few.

"Yankee perfidy" has long been a phrase of derision toward "those people," but it came on full display in Little Washington during the second week in May.

Johnston's men are coming through in full tide, and there is constant danger of a collision between them and the Yankees. There are four brigades of cavalry camped on the outskirts of town waiting to be paroled. Contrary to their agreement with Lee and Johnston, the Yankees now want to deprive these men of their horse and side arms, and refuse to parole them until they are dismounted and disarmed. Our men refuse to submit to such an indignity and vow they will kill every "d—d Yankee" in Washington rather than suffer such a perfidious beach of faith. Lot Abraham, or "Marse Lot," as we call him, seems to be a fairly good sort of a man for a Yankee, and disposed to behave as well as the higher powers will let him.

Fortunately, Captain Abraham and cool heads prevailed, for the issue of parole terms was quickly resolved, and in the Confederates' favor. Fanny exulted with this passage in her journal on May 10:

Our cavalry have won their point about the terms of surrender, and rode triumphantly out of town this afternoon, still retaining their side arms. There were 3,000 of them, and they made a sight worth looking at as they passed by our street gate. It is well the

Yanks gave up to them, for they said they were determined to fight again rather than yield, and our own returned volunteers were ready to help them.

Our journalist's disgust over the presence of Yankees in and about her home remained a staple of her confidential writing. She almost hoped that a fight would break out between them and the Confederates lingering about Washington.

[May 6] There is a brigade of Kentucky cavalry camped out in Mr. Wiley's grove, and some fear is felt of a collision between them and the Yankees. Some of them have already engaged in fist fights on their own account. I wish they would get into a general row, for I believe the Kentuckians would whip them. I am just exasperated enough to be reckless as to consequences.

[May 7] I wish our troops would get into a fracas with them and thrash them out of town.

[May 9] Our soldiers are likely to raise a row with them at any time, but it would do no good. Yesterday, they gave the garrison a scare by pretending to storm their quarters in the courthouse. They say the Yankees are very uneasy, and sing small whenever a big troop of our men arrive, though they grow very impertinent in the intervals.

Worse still was the presence of Black Federal soldiers among the garrison troops. "Think of a lot of negroes being brought here to play the master over us!" she exclaimed. As part of the Northern garrison at Washington was a regiment of Federal Cavalry made up of Tennessee Unionists, commanded by Lt. Col. Braziliah P. Stacy.[27] Among them were apparently some United States Colored Troops, as Miss Andrews mentioned on May 9. "While Gen. Stacy's men were camped out at the mineral spring, he made his headquarters at Mrs. James DuBose's house, and permitted his negro troops to have the freedom of the premises, even after Mrs. DuBose had appealed to him for protection," she

---

[27] *OR*, vol. 49, pt. 1, 325, 549.

wrote. "They go into people's kitchens and try to make the other negroes discontented and disobedient." Apparently, though, it was not working.

> The negroes, thus far, have behaved fairly well, except where they have been tampered with. Not one of father's has left us, and they are just as humble and obedient as ever. On Sunday, a good many runaways came in from the country but their loving brothers in blue sent them back—not from any regard to us or our institutions, but because they prefer to have their pets fed by their masters until their plans for emancipation are complete. They kept some of the likeliest of the men who went to them, as servants, and refused to give them up when the owners called for them.[28] Ben Harden, a giant of a country squire, exasperated at their refusal to restore one of his men, stepped in amongst them, collared the negro, and gave him a thrashing on the spot. There were so many Confederate soldiers on the square, watching the fracas, that the little handful of a garrison didn't venture to interfere, and he carried his negro off home unopposed.

Fanny had written on May 8, "I could not even pay postage on a letter if it were necessary to write one," with Confederate currency no longer of any value. On Wednesday, the 10th, a friend from Macon, Harry Day, brought letters from other folk in the area, as she noted in her journal, "since Confederate money and Confederate postage stamps have 'gone up'"—meaning up the spout, and not up in value—"most of us are too poor to indulge in corresponding with friends except by private hand, and besides, the mails are so uncertain that one does not feel safe in trusting them."[29] Several days later, on the 13th,

---

[28] "Likely" was a term commonly used by Southerners to refer to well-mannered or obedient slaves. As example, a leading slave mart in Atlanta, Crawford & Frazer, advertised for sale "a likely waiter" or "a likely maid servant" in the pages of the *Atlanta Daily Intelligencer* issue of April 15, 1863.

[29] "Gone up the spout" was a popular saying in the Confederacy's final days. As example, see J. Roderick Heller III and Carolynn Ayres Heller, eds., *The*

she added, "the Yankees have stopped our mails, or else the mails have stopped themselves. We get no papers, but thousands of wild rumors from every direction take their place and keep us stirred up all the time."

> We have had no mail at all for several days and rumor has it that the Augusta post office has been closed by order of the commanding officer, but nobody knows anything for certain. Our masters do not let us in to their plans, and we can only wait in suspense to see what they will do next.

Augusta, fifty miles away, was said not only to have had its post office closed, but also one of its prominent daily newspapers, the *Constitutionalist*, temporarily closed "because it uttered sentiments not approved by the conquerors," as Miss Andrews observed on May 10.[30] Such censorship was viewed harshly: "even father can't find any excuse for such doings," Frances acknowledged.

The list of Yankee abominations just grew and grew.

> The hardest to bear of all the humiliations yet put upon us, is the sight of Andy Johnson's proclamation offering rewards for the arrest of Jefferson Davis, Clement C. Clay, and Beverly Tucker, under pretense that they were implicated in the assassination of Abraham Lincoln. It is printed in huge letters on handbills and posted in ever public place in town.

After Lincoln's death, Washington officials jumped to the conclusion that Confederate agents in Canada, such as Clement C. Clay, had been involved with John Wilkes Booth's assassination plot.

Confederacy Is on Her Way up the Spout: Letters to South Carolina, 1861–1864 (Athens: University of Georgia Press, 1992).

[30] "In Augusta every editorial had to be submitted to the post commander for approval before publication, and for one fiery article the *Augusta Constitutionalist* was seized and a sentry put in the composing room" (Thompson, *Reconstruction in Georgia*, 142).

Accordingly, in the days following, Secretary of War Edwin M. Stanton had ordered the arrest of Jacob Thompson, George Sanders, and Beverly Tucker. William C. Cleary was added later. On May 2, President Johnson issued a proclamation declaring that "the atrocious murder of the Late Pres. Abraham Lincoln and the attempted assassination of Hon. W. H. Seward Secretary of State, were incited, concerted and procured by and between Jefferson Davis, Clement C. Clay, Beverley Tucker, George Sanders, W. C. Cleary, and other rebels and traitors." Rewards were set proportionately: $100,000 for Davis; $25,000 each for Thompson, Clay, Tucker and Sanders; and $10,000 for Cleary.[31]

Frances Andrews considered this "a flaming insult to every man, woman, and child in the village, as if they believed there was a traitor among us so base as to betray the victims of their malice, even if we knew where they were."

> If they had posted one of their lying accusations on our street gate, I would tear it down with my own hands, even if they sent me to jail for it. But I am sure that father would never permit his premises to be desecrated by such an infamy as that. It is the most villainous slander ever perpetrated, and is gotten up solely with a view to making criminals of political offenders so that foreign governments would be obliged to deliver them up if they should succeed in making their escape. Fortunately, the characters of the men they have chosen as scapegoats are so above suspicion as only to discredit the accusers themselves in the eyes of all decent people.

Clement Clay, representative from Alabama and Confederate representative in Canada, was a friend of Judge Andrews and had stayed at Haywood while Fanny and Mett were at Pine Bluff. She noted this

---

[31] Thomas Reed Turner, *Beware the People Weeping: Public Opinion and the Assassination of Abraham Lincoln* (Baton Rouge: Louisiana State University Press, 1982), 125, 127; William Hanchett, *The Lincoln Murder Conspiracies* (Urbana: University of Illinois Press, 1983), 64.

in her journal, adding, "and Jefferson Davis, our noble, unfortunate president—the accusation is simply a disgrace to those who make it."

Fortunately, the lingering presence of Confederate soldiers around Washington offered some emotional relief for Miss Andrews.

> Johnston's army is now in full sweep. The town is thronged with them from morn till night, and from night till morning. They camp in our grove by whole companies, but never do any mischief. I love to look out of my windows in the night and see their camp fires burning among the trees and their figures moving dimly in and out among the shadows, like protecting spirits. I love to lie awake and hear the sound of their voices talking and laughing over their hard experiences. Metta and I often go out to the gate after supper and sing the old rebel songs that we know will please them.

Fanny also enjoyed supposing that ex-Rebels hanging about created something of a threat to the Yankees in town. When she heard that the Federals had given in on the Southern veterans' demand to keep their horses and side arms, she recorded (May 10), "they say the little handful of a garrison were frightened all but out of their wits anyway, for our men could have eaten them up before they had time to send for reenforcements." Indeed, blue-clad reinforcements from Augusta arrived to bolster the occupying troops after some intoxicated Confederate cavalrymen picked a fight with some Yankees "and drove them all into the courthouse, wounding one man in the row."

"My brother Henry," wrote Miss Andrews, "who was about as hot-headed a fire-eater as could be found in the South," had served during the war as surgeon for several of Georgia's units.[32] On May 4 our journalist wrote that she didn't know where Henry was. A week

---

[32] "Fire-eater" was the term given to those Southerners who in the several decades before the war called for immediate secession from the Union. Examples are Robert Barnwell Rhett from South Carolina, Edmund Ruffin of Virginia, and the Texan Louis Wigfall (Eric H. Walther, *The Fire-Eaters* [Baton Rouge: Louisiana State University Press, 1992]).

later she joyfully recorded, "Henry reached home late in the afternoon." Unfortunately, he was "so ragged and dirty that none of us knew him till he spoke."

> He had not a change of clothes for three weeks, and his face was so dirty that he had to wash it before we could kiss him. He came all the way from Greensborough, N.C., on horseback, and when we asked him where he got his horse, he laughed and said that he bought a saddle for fifty cents in silver—his pay for three years' service—and kept on swapping till he found himself provided with a horse and full outfit. Garnett said he had better quit medicine and go to horse trading.... He is now ready to begin life anew with a broken-down old army horse as his sole stock in trade. Garnett has not even that much. The Yankees got his horse, and his boy Sidney, whom he left with Henry when he took to the field, disappeared—to enjoy the delights of freedom, I suppose.

Robert Augustus Toombs—Confederate secretary of state, brigadier general, and congressman—lived in an elegant mansion across Broad Street from the public square. On Thursday, May 11, the corpulent Toombs was in his sitting-room when Yankees marched through his front gate. Cora, Frances's sister, happened to be there "and saw it all," as our journalist noted.

> He divined their purpose and made his escape through the back door as they were entering the front, and I suppose he is safely concealed now in some country house. The intruders proceeded to search the dwelling, looking between mattresses and under bureaus, as if a man of Gen. Toombs's size could be hid like a paper doll![33] They then questioned the servants, but none of them

---

[33] Ulrich Bonnell Phillips cites Miss Andrews's *War-Journal* regarding this incident (*The Life of Robert Toombs* [New York: Burt Franklin, 1968 (1913)], 254). He also quotes (252–53) her observation of "the shattered remains of Lee's army" (journal, April 24) and "the wildest excitement" at President Davis's arrival (May 3).

would give the least information, though the Yankees arrested all the negro men and threatened to put them in jail. They asked old Aunt Betty where her master was, and she answered bluntly: "Ef I knowed, I wouldn't tell you." They then ordered her to cook dinner for them, but she turned her broad back on them, saying, "I won't do no sech thing; I'se a gwineter hep my missis pack up her clo'es." The servants were all very indignant at the manner in which they were ordered about, and declared that their own white folks had never spoken to them in "any sech a way." Mrs. Toombs's dinner was on the table and the family about to go into the dining-room when the intruders arrived, and they ate it all up besides ordering more to be cooked for them. They threatened to burn the house down if the general was not given up, and gave the family just two hours to move out. Gen. Gilmer, who was in the old army before the war, remonstrated with them, and they extended the time till ten o'clock at night, and kindly promised not to burn it at all if the general were delivered up to them in the meantime.[34] Mrs. Toombs straightened herself up and said: "Burn it then," and the family immediately began to move out. Neither Mrs. Toombs or Mrs. DuBose suffered the Yankees to see them shed a tear, though both are ready to die of grief, and Mrs. DuBose on the verge of her confinement, too. Everything is moved out of the house now, and Mrs. Toombs says she hopes it will be burned rather than used by the miserable plunderers and their negro companions. The family have found shelter with their relatives and distributed their valuables among their friends. The family pictures and some of the plate are stored in our house.

The despicable Yankees were under command of a captain named Saint—"and a precious saint he proved to be," as Fanny wrote mockingly. As it turned out, she recorded on the 12th, "the Saint and his

---

[34] Jeremy F. Gilmer, a West Pointer, earned a strong reputation as army engineer before the war. He served in this capacity for the Confederate army, rising in rank from captain to major general. In April 1865 he traveled with Breckinridge into Georgia, where he surrendered. He was paroled by Captain Abraham at Washington (*OR*, vol. 49, pt. 2, 685).

angels failed to burn Gen. Toombs's house, after all." Actually, the real saint proved to be Captain Lot Abraham. On May 12, he returned to Washington from Augusta with additional troops for his garrison "and immediately apologized to Mrs. Toombs for the insults to which she had been subjected, and said that orders for the raid upon her were given over his head and without his knowledge."

> He really seems to have the instincts of a gentleman, and I am afraid I shall be obliged to respect him a little, in spite of his uniform. Although considerably reenforced, his garrison seems to be still in wholesome fear of a conflict with our throngs of disbanded soldiers. A cavalryman went to the courthouse the other day and deliberately helped himself to a musket before their eyes, and they did not even remonstrate. Our cavalry are a reckless, unruly lot, yet I can't help admiring them because they are such red-hot rebels. It may be foolish, but somehow I like the spirit of those who refuse to repent, and who swear they would do it all over, if the thing were to be done again.

It was the little things Yankees did that so annoyed Frances Andrews. After a brisk conversation with her, one blue-clad abruptly turned and walked away, "without even touching his hat, as the most ignorant Confederate would have done." In another rencounter, "they called father 'old fellow' in a very insolent manner, that made me indignant."

There was, however, something more important, as Fanny recorded on the 13th.

> A favorite topic of conversation at this time is what we are going to do for a living. Mary Day has been working assiduously at paper cigarettes to sell the Yankees. I made some myself, with the same intention, but we both gave them all away to the poor Confederates as fast as we could roll them. It is dreadful to be so poor, but somehow, I can't suppress a forlorn hope that it won't last always, and that a time may come when we will laugh at all these troubles even more heartily than we do now. But although

we laugh, I sometimes feel in my heart more like crying, and I am afraid that father speaks the truth when he says that things are more likely to become worse than better.

"On my way to church I had a striking illustration of the difference between our old friends, and our new masters," Miss Andrews wrote on Sunday, May 14.

The streets were thronged with rebel soldiers, and in one part of my walk, I had to pass where a large number of them were gathered on the pavement, some sitting, some standing, some lying down, but as soon as I appeared, the way was instantly cleared for me, the men standing like a wall, on either side, with hats off, until I passed. A little farther on I came to a group of Yankees and negroes that filled up the sidewalk, but not one of them budged, and I had to flank them by going out into the dusty road. It is the first time in my life that I have ever had to give up the sidewalk to a man, much less to negroes! I was so indignant that I did not carry a devotional spirit to church.

For the people of Washington, Georgia—indeed, throughout the state—the emancipation promised by the Lincoln government and delivered by Union victory proved to be anything but sudden. "People are making no effort to detain their negroes now, for they have found out that they are free, and our power over them is gone," Frances recorded on May 14. Yet the uncertainty of freedom and the fears borne of an unprecedented societal transformation—again, for both races—caused many of the Andrews family servants to tarry about Haywood. "Our own servants have behaved very well thus far," observed our diarist. All the house help had stayed on; three field hands who had fallen into the Yankees' hands even drifted back to Haywood. At the same time, Cora's Black nurse, Caesar Ann, took off for Augusta "to try the sweets of freedom," as Fanny put it; "I suppose it is a mere question of time when we shall have to give them all up anyways, so it doesn't matter."

The Yankees themselves seemed uncertain of what to do. Sometimes they appropriated Black laborers to work for them; five of Judge Andrews's former slaves were thus pressed into labor—even "old Uncle Watson whom father himself never calls on to do anything except the lightest work about the place, and that only when he feels like it."[35] Sometimes Yankees provided runaways with conveyances for their exodus. "This morning," Frances wrote on the 14th, "they sent off several wagon-loads of runaways, and it is reported that Harrison and Alfred, two of father's men, have gone with them." At other times, garrison troops directed wayward servants back to their masters; "last week, Lot Abraham sent three of his white men to jail for tampering with 'slaves,' as they call them." These vagaries and variations, Fanny reckoned, were predictable from Whites unfamiliar with the workings of the South's peculiar institution. "They are very capricious in their treatment of negroes," the journalist remarked of Captain Abraham's soldiers, adding "as is usually the case with upstarts who are not used to having servants of their own."

At least there were some good Rebels still tarrying about Wilkes County. Thousands of Joe Johnston's veterans were still passing through Washington, but this would, of course, end at some time. "When the last one is gone, what desolation there will be," she lamented; "Johnston's army will soon have passed through, and then the Yankee garrison will feel free to treat us as it pleases."

As if the coffin of the Confederacy needed another nail, Frances entered into her journal entry of May 14 the news of Jefferson Davis's capture in South Georgia: "I walked in the grove after sunset and talked with the rebels who were camping there, and we mourned together over the capture of our beloved President." Mourning, indeed. "A settled gloom, deep and heavy, hangs over the whole land," Fanny wrote on May 15.

All hearts are in mourning for the fall of our country, and all minds rebellious against the wrongs and oppression to which our

---

[35] Dr. Thompson mentions this in *Reconstruction in Georgia*, 131.

cruel conquerors subject us. I don't believe this war is over yet. The Trans-Mississippi bubble has burst, but wait till the tyranny and arrogance of the United States engages them in a foreign war! Ah, we'll bide our time. That's what all the men say, and their eyes glow and their cheeks burn when they say it. Though the whole world has deserted us and left us to perish without even a pitying sigh at our miserable doom, and we hate the whole world for its cruelty, yet we hate the Yankees more, and they will find the South a volcano ready to burst beneath their feet whenever the justice of heaven hurls a thunderbolt at their heads. We are overwhelmed, overpowered, and trodden underfoot...but "immortal hate and study of revenge" lives, in the soul of every man.

By mid-May 1865, Southerners' hopes that the war might be continued beyond the Mississippi had indeed failed to come to pass. But for some, the idea of renewing the fight sometime, somewhere, appealed to our journalist. "The chief thought of our men now," she commented on May 16, "is how to embroil the United States either in foreign or internal commotions, so that we can rebel again." Two weeks later, though, came a somber realization:

Men look upon our cause as hopelessly lost, and all talk of the Trans-Mississippi and another revolution has ceased. Within the last three weeks the aspect of affairs has changed more than three years in ordinary times could have changed it. It is impossible to write intelligibly even about what is passing under one's eyes, for what is true to-day may be false to-morrow.

A people "overwhelmed, overpowered, and trodden underfoot" could only dread what was yet to come after Confederate defeat. "Father says that if a man were to sit down and write a programme for reducing the country to the very worst condition it could possibly be in," Fanny remarked on May 15, "his imagination could not invent anything half so bad as the misery that is likely to come upon us."

Even the Black folk were in for a surprise. Fanny wrote, also on May 15, "The cities and the towns are already becoming overcrowded with runaway negroes. In Augusta they are clamoring for food, which the Yankees refuse to give, and their masters, having once been deserted by them, refuse to take them back." The freed people thus had nowhere to go. "Even in our little town the streets are so full of idle negroes and bluecoats that ladies scarcely even venture out."

With the economy disrupted, many were suffering. Word came from the Athens area that "the Yankees have committed such depredations there that the whole country is destitute and the people desperate. The poor are clamoring for bread, and many of them have taken to 'bushwhacking' as their only means of living." Under the circumstances, bushwhacking—taking what one wanted under force of arms—could be seen as a necessary imperative. Referring to "our men," she wrote,

> They all say that if the Yankees had given us any sort of tolerable terms they would submit quietly, though unwillingly, to the inevitable; but if they carry out the abominable programme of which flying rumors reach us, extermination itself will be better than submission. Garnett says that if it comes to the worst, he can turn bushwhacker, and we all came to the conclusion that if this kind of peace continues, bushwhacking will be the most respectable occupation in which a man can engage.

After his capture on May 10, Jefferson Davis was taken by General Wilson's troopers back to Macon. On the 13th he was put on the train heading for Washington, D.C. En route, passing through Augusta, Davis and his guards proceeded through downtown, where people crowded to see the downcast president. Sister Cora had gotten a letter from one of the bystanders, "giving a very pathetic account of the passage of the prisoners through Augusta. She says that Telfair St. was thronged with ladies, all weeping bitterly, as the mournful procession passed on, and that even the President's Yankee guard seemed touched by the exhibition of grief." "The more sensitive may have shut themselves up," Frances recorded, "but I am glad some were there to testify that the feeling of the South is still with our fallen President and to shame with their tears the insulting cries of his persecutors." Jefferson Davis would eventually be taken to Fort Monroe, Virginia, where he would spend the next two years, waiting for a treason trial that would never come. He was at last released on May 13, 1867; the government eventually dropped its charges.[36]

A similar fate befell Vice President Stephens. On May 11, Federal soldiers overtook him at his Crawfordville home and arrested him.[37] Mrs. Alfred Cumming, a family friend, was with Stephens and related to Fanny what had happened. "The Yankee guard suffered him to stop an hour at Crawfordville," she wrote on the 15th, referring to Stephens's hometown, "in order to collect some of his clothing" for the long trip northward.

> As soon as his arrival became known, the people flocked to see him, weeping and wringing their hands. All his negroes went to see him off, and many others from the surrounding plantations. Mrs. Cumming says that as the train moved off, all along the platform, honest black hands of every shape and size were thrust in at the window, with cries of "Good-by, Mr. Stephens;" "Far'well, Marse Aleck." All the spectators were moved to tears; the vice-president himself gave way to an outburst of affectionate—not cowardly grief, and even his Yankee guard looked serious while this affecting scene passed before their eyes.

Frances Andrews's journal entry for Wednesday, May 17 touches on three subjects: commendation of the considerate, civil conduct of

---

[36] Edward K. Eckert, *"Fiction Distorting Fact": The Prison Life, Annotated by Jefferson Davis* (Macon: Mercer University Press, 1987), xl.

[37] The former Confederate vice president was confined at Fort Warren, near Boston, until his release on October 13, 1865 (Thomas E. Schott, *Alexander H. Stephens of Georgia: A Biography* [Baton Rouge: Louisiana State University Press, 1988], 451–52).

Confederates; denunciation of the outrageous misconduct of Yankees to Georgia civilians; and admiration for a young Southern soldier.

Johnston's army has nearly all gone. The last large body of troops has passed through, and in a few weeks even the stragglers and hangers-on will have disappeared. There have been no camp fires in our grove since Sunday, but five of the dear old Rebs are sleeping in our corn-crib tonight. They said they were too dirty to come into the house, and they are so considerate that they would not even sleep in an out-house without asking permission. Hundreds, if not thousands of them have camped in our grove, and the only damage they ever did—if that can be called damage,—was to burn a few fence rails. In the whole history of war I don't believe another instance can be found of so little mischief being committed as has been done by these disbanded, disorganized, poverty-stricken, starving men of Lee's and Johnston's armies. Against the thousands and tens of thousands that have passed through Washington, the worst that can be charged is the plundering of the treasury and the government stores, and as they would have gone to the Yankees anyway, our men can hardly be blamed for taking whatever they could get, rather than let it go to the enemy. They were on their way to far-distant homes, without a cent of money in their pockets or a mouthful of food in their haversacks, and the Confederate stores had been collected for the use of our army, and were theirs by right, anyway. They have hardly ever troubled private property, except horses and provender, and when we think of the desperate situation in which they were left after the surrender, the only wonder is that greater depredations were not committed. And at the worst, what is the theft of a few bundles of fodder, or even of a horse, compared with hanging men up on a slack rope and poking them with bayonets to make them tell where their valuables were hid;[38] or to pulling the

---

[38] Miss Andrews is referring to an incident she relates in her journal entry of July 28, 1865, how Federal soldiers tied up an old gentleman, Dionysius "Nish" Chenault by the thumbs, trying to get him to divulge the location of valuables.

cover off a sick woman as the Yankees did that one at Barnesville, and exposing her person to make sure she had no jewelry or money concealed in the bed with her? The Northern papers are full of wild stories about Southern lawlessness, though everybody in this country can testify that the two or three thousand sleek, well-fed Yankee troops who have come here to take "peaceable possession" of the country have committed ten times more depredations than the whole Confederate army during its march into Pennsylvania.[39] Some of them broke into Col. Tom Willis's cellar the other day, and when they had drunk as much of his peach brandy as they could hold, they spit into the rest to keep the "d—d rebels" from having it. They strut about the streets of Washington with negro women in their arms and sneak around into people's kitchens, tampering with the servants and setting them against the white people. Sometimes the more respectable negroes themselves are disgusted at their conduct. Mrs. Irvin says her old cook collared one the other day and pushed him out of the kitchen.

I was greatly touched the other day by the history of a little boy, not much bigger than Marshall,[40] whom I found in the back yard with a party of soldiers that had come in to get their rations cooked. Metta first noticed him and asked how such a little fellow came to be in the army. The soldiers told us that his father had gone to the war with the first volunteers from their county, and had never been heard of again, after one of the great battles he was in. Then the mother died, and the little boy followed a party of recruits who took him along with them for a "powder monkey," and he had been following them around, a sort of child of the regiment, ever since.

---

[39] As Lee's army marched into Pennsylvania in June 1863, the commanding general issued strict orders against his troops seizing or damaging civilian property, with the exception of fence rails and horses (Edwin B. Coddington, *The Gettysburg Campaign: A Study in Command* [Dayton, OH: Press of Morningside Bookshop, 1979 (1968)], 153–54).

[40] Daniel Marshall ("Marsh") was Frances's younger brother, born October 24, 1853. He was thus the only one of Judge Garnett's sons not to have served in the Confederate army.

I asked him what he was going to do now, and he answered: "I am going to Alabama with these soldiers, to try to make a living for myself." Poor little fellow! making a living for himself at an age when most children are carefully tucked in their beds at night by their mothers, and are playing with toys or sent to school in the daytime. Metta gave him a piece of sorghum cake, and left him with his friends.

"We had just finished eating and got into our wrappers," recorded our diarist on May 18,

when two rebel horsemen came galloping up the avenue with news that a large body of Yankee cavalry was advancing down the Greensborough road, plundering the country as they passed. We hastily threw on our clothes and were busy concealing valuables for father, when the tramping of horses and shouting of men reached our ears. Then they began to pass by our street gate, with two of their detestable old flags flaunting in the breeze. I ran for Garnett's field-glass and watched them through it. Nearly all of them had bags of plunder tied to their saddles, and many rode horses which were afterwards recognized as belonging to different planters in the county. I saw one rascal with a ruffled pillowcase full of stolen goods, tied to his saddle, and some of them had women's drawers tied up at the bottom ends, filled with plunder and slung astride their horses. There was a regiment of negroes with them, and they halted right in front of our gate. Think of it! Bringing armed negroes here to threaten and insult us! We were so furious that we shook our fists and spit at them from behind the window where we were sitting. It may have been childish, but it relieved our feelings. None of them came within the enclosure, but the officers pranced about the gate until I felt as if I would like to take a shot at them myself, if I had had a gun, and known how to use it. They are camped for the night on the outskirts of the town, and everybody expects to be robbed before morning. Father loaded his two guns, and after the servants had been dismissed, we hid the silver in the hollow by the chimney up in the big garret, and father says it shall not be brought out again until the country becomes more settled. A furious storm came up just at sunset, and I hope it will confine the mongrel crew to their tents.

As it turned out, Judge Andrews, his family and their property were not victimized by "the mongrel crew." For this Fanny gave considerate credit to "Marse Lot," the post commandant.

It is some advantage to live at a military post when the commandant is a man like Capt. Abraham, who, from all accounts, seems to try to do the best for us that he knows how. Our men say that he not only listens, but attends to the complaints that are carried to him by white people as carefully as to those brought by negroes. The other day a Yankee soldier fired into our back porch and came near killing one of the servants. I saw a batch of them in the back garden, where the shot came from, and sent Henry to speak to them, but they swore they had not been shooting. Henry knew it was a lie, so he went and complained to "Marse Lot," who said that such molestation of private families should be stopped at once, and we have not heard a gun fired on our premises since. It is a pretty pass, though, when a gentleman can't defend his own grounds, but has to cringe and ask protection from a Yankee master.

Miss Andrews never tired, it seems, of drawing distinction between good Rebels and bad Yankees, and of bemoaning the current state of Southern society. Here, from May 19:

I have witnessed the breaking up of three Confederate armies; Lee's and Johnston's have already passed through Washington, and Gen. Dick Taylor's is now in transit, but all these thousands upon thousands of disbanded, disorganized, disinherited Southerners have not committed one-twentieth part of the damage to private property that was committed by the first small squad of Yankee cavalry that passed through our county. We are beginning to hear from all quarters of the depredations committed by the regiments, with their negro followers, that came through town yesterday. Their conduct so exasperated the people that they were bushwhacked near Greensborough, and several of their men wounded. They then forced the planters to furnish horses and vehicles for their transportation. Henry says that one of their own officers was heard to remark on the square, that after the way in which they had behaved he could not blame the people for attacking them. When they bring negro troops among us it is enough to make every man in the Confederacy turn bushwhacker.

During and after the Civil War the "Negro ball" was an ugly political and societal trope both in the South and the North. During the U.S. presidential election of 1864, Democratic propagandists manufactured a leering lithograph of such a mixed-race event, and circulated it as inflammatory propaganda against Republican "miscegenators."[41] In Atlanta, after Sherman's capture of the city, there was allegedly held a Negro ball so debauched that when the *Macon Intelligencer* published an account of it, the paper was threatened with lawsuit by a civil leader who was said to have been there—and had allegedly behaved very badly.[42]

When Frances Andrews refers to two such interracial events held in Washington during May 1865, involving freedwomen and Federal soldiers, her allegation deserves notice even if it cannot be corroborated—it's what White residents were evidently talking about.

May 24, Wednesday.—Capt. Abraham—the righteous Lot—and his garrison left town this morning, and no others have come as yet to take their place. They were much disgusted at their reception here, I am told, and some of them were heard to declare that there was not a pretty woman in the place. No wonder, when the only ones that associated with them were negroes. They had two negro balls while they were here, the white men dancing with the

---

[41] Harold Holzer, *The Civil War in 50 Objects* (New York: Viking, 2013), 277–85.

[42] *Atlanta Daily Intelligencer*, September 10, 1864.

negro women. One night they held their orgy in Bolton's Range, and kept everybody on the square awake with their disgraceful noise. They strutted about the streets on Sunday with negro wenches on their arms, and yet their officers complain because they are not invited to sit at the tables of Southern gentlemen!

All about were the signs of a society in distress, if not crisis: absence of governmental authority, economic uncertainty among Whites and Blacks alike, absolutely no vision of how the two races would get along together in the post-slavery South. "The whole country is in disorder," Frances recorded on May 25,

and filled with lawless bands that call themselves rebels or Yankees, as happens to suit their convenience. They say it is not safe for a person to go six miles from town except in company and fully armed, and I am not sure that we shall be safe in the village, the negroes are crowding in so. "Marse" Abraham did protect us against them, in a way, and if his men hadn't tampered with them so, I shouldn't be sorry to see him back till things settle down a little. At present nobody dares to make any plans for the future. We can only wait each day for what the morrow may bring forth. Oh, we are utterly and thoroughly wretched!

Two days later, she added, quite on the same note:

We are a poverty-stricken nation, and most of them are too poor to buy new clothes. I suppose we are just now at the very worst stage of our financial embarrassments, and if we can manage to struggle through the next five or six months, some sort of currency will begin to circulate again. I have clothes enough to bridge over the crisis, I think, but mother's house linen is hopelessly short, and our family larder brought down to the last gasp. Father has a little specie, saved from the sale of the cotton he shipped to Liverpool before the war, but the country has been so drained of provisions that even gold cannot buy them.

Then there were the Yankees' insults to prized and honored Confederates. Even the uniforms that Fanny Andrews still loved to see—"I
think I will hang a Confederate uniform on a pole and keep it to look
at," she had written on May 14—were under assault. "One of the latest
proposals of the conquerors is to make our Confederate uniform the
dress of convicts," she painfully wrote on the 25th. "The wretches! As
if it was in the power of man to disgrace the uniform worn by Robert
E. Lee and Stonewall Jackson! They couldn't disgrace it, even if they
were to put their own army into it."

Two days later came the final insult.

> After sitting awhile with Nora I went to see Mrs. Elzey and found
> her cutting off the buttons from the general's coat. The tyrants
> have prohibited the wearing of Confederate uniforms. Those
> who have no other clothes can still wear the gray, but must rip
> off the buttons and decorations. The beautiful Hungarian knot,
> the stars, and bars, the cords, the sashes, and gold lace, are all
> disappearing. People everywhere are ransacking old chests, and
> the men are handing out the old clothes they used to wear before
> the war, and they do look so funny and old-fashioned, after the
> beautiful uniforms we had all gotten used to! But the raggedest
> soldier of the Confederacy in his shabby old clothes is a more he-
> roic figure in my eyes than any upstart Yankee officer in the finest
> uniform he can get into. Yet, it is pitiful, as well as comical, to see
> the poor fellows looking so dowdy. I feel like crying whenever I
> think of the change and all that it means.

Mrs. Elzey, and others, were performing the mandated stitchery, as the
journalist recorded on May 30:

> Gen. Elzey stayed to tea, and Gardiner Foster dropped in. The
> general wore a gray coat from which all the decorations had been
> ripped off and the buttons covered with plain gray cloth, but he
> would look like a soldier and a gentleman even in a Boston stove-
> pipe hat, or a suit of Yankee blue. Some of our boys put their dis-
> carded buttons in tobacco bags and jingle then whenever a Yank

comes within earshot. Some will not replace them at all, but leave their coats flying open to tell the tale of spoliation. Others put ridiculous tin and horn buttons on their military coats. The majority, however, especially the older ones, submit in dignified silence to the humiliating decree. Old-fashioned citizen's suits that were thrown aside four years ago are now brought out of their hiding-places, and the dear old gray is rapidly disappearing from the streets.

"Making do" under the new regime took on many forms: in dress, with livelihood and in such pastimes as writing and reading ("the mails are broken up so that we can send letters only as chance offers, by private hand, and the few papers we get are published under Yankee censorship, and reveal only what the tyrants choose that we shall know"). Even preparing meals became a challenge. Because the larder at Haywood had been "brought down to the last gasp," much scrambling and improvisation in the kitchen were necessary.

We have so much company that it is necessary to keep up appearances and set a respectable table, which Mett and I do, after a fashion, by hard struggling behind the scenes. The table looks generally well enough when we first sit down, but when we get up it is as bare as Jack Sprat's. We have some good laughs at the makeshifts we resort to for making things hold out. We eat as little as we can do with ourselves, but we don't want father's guests to suspect that we are stinted, so Metta pretends to a loss of appetite, while I profess a great fondness for whatever happens to be most abundant, which is always sure to be cornfield peas, or some other coarse, rank thing that I detest. It would all be very funny, if it were not so mortifying, with all these charming people in the house that deserve to be entertained like princes, and are used to having everything nice. Metta's delicate appetite and my affection for cornfield peas are a standing joke between us. She has the best of it, though, for she simply starves, while I "nawsierate," as Charity says. I make a face at the bag of peas whenever I go near it in the pantry. I don't know what we should do if it was not for Emily and Charity. They join in our consultations, moan over our difficulties, and carry out our plans with as much eagerness as old Caleb Balderstone,[43] in keeping up the credit of the family. Who would ever have believed that we could come to this? I can hardly believe it is I, plotting with the servants in the pantry to get up a dinner out of nothing, like the poor people I read about in books. It requires a great deal of management to find time for both parlor and kitchen, and to keep my manners and dress unruffled. However, Mett and I find so much to laugh at in the comedies mixed up with our country's tragedy that it keeps us in a good humor.... The servants, however, are treasures. With the exception of those who went to the Yankees, they all behave better and work harder than they did before. I really love them for the way they have stood by us.

Among "all these charming people in the house that deserve to be entertained like princes" were Cousin Bolling from Cuthbert and a Captain Hudson, who visited the family at Haywood on Sunday, May 28, "and chatted with us a long time."

They taught us some thunderous German words to say when we feel like swearing at the Yankees, because Cora said she felt like doing it a dozen times a day, but couldn't because she was a woman. I remember this much: "Potts-tousand-schock-schwer an oat—" and my brain could carry no more. I don't know how my spelling would look in German; I would prefer a good, round, English *"damn"* anyway, if I dared to use it.

The next evening, a Monday, the Elzeys joined Dr. Bolling Pope and Captain Hudson for dinner, despite Haywood's scanty larder. "We had a pleasant little party," Fanny recorded later that night.

---

[43] Caleb Balderstone was a character in Sir Walter Scott's novel *The Bride of Lammermoor* (1819). He was an aged servant at Ravenswood who cloaked his master's impecuniosity with artful graciousness.

I have not seen people enjoy themselves so much since our country fell under the tyrant's heel. Gen. Elzey was really merry, and I was delighted to see him recovering his spirits, for he has been the picture of desolation ever since the crash came. I love him and Mrs. Elzey better than almost anybody else outside my own family. Father, too, is so fond of Mrs. Elzey that he laughs at her fiery rebel talk, no matter how hot she grows, and lets her say what he wouldn't tolerate in the rest of us. Our household is divided into factions—we out-and-out rebels being most numerous, but the Unionists (father and mother) most powerful; the "Trimmers" neither numerous nor powerful, but best adapted to scud between opposing elements and escape unhurt by either. I think mother is inclined to waver sometimes and join the rebels through sympathy with the boys, but she always sticks to father in the long run. However, we did not quarrel at all to-day; we Rebs had such strong re-enforcements that the others had no showing at all.

Adding to Frances's delight was that for the first time in a long while, on the evening of the 29th, the family's dining table teemed with good things; "mock turtle soup, barbecued lamb, and for dessert, sponge pudding with cream sauce, and boiled custard sweetened with sugar—no sorghum in anything." A few days before, a family friend had given young Marsh a pet lamb named Mary Lizzie. Everyone knew her fate, though; "Marsh was persuaded to consent to the slaughter," and Mary Lizzie served as centerpiece for the dinner table. (Besides, Mary Lizzie "was mischievous, eating things in the garden.") The parents did their part as well.

The pudding and boiled custard were due to an order father has sent to Augusta for groceries, and mother felt so triumphant over the prospect of having something in the pantry again, that she grew reckless and celebrated the event by using up all the sugar she had in the house. There was plenty of everything, so Mett recovered her appetite and I suddenly lost my fondness for corn-field peas.

Captain Lot Abraham, post commandant, had left Washington with his troops on May 24. A few days later, on the 28th, a new group of occupiers arrived under a Captain Shaeffer. "I have not seen any of them, but I know they are frights in their horrid cavalry uniform of blue and yellow. It is the ugliest thing I ever saw; looks like the back of a snake." About them our journalist expressed doubts that they would behave any better than those of "Marse Lot," especially concerning the Black folk. "The newcomers under Capt. Schaeffer seem to be as fond of our grove as were Capt. Abraham's men. Some of them are always strolling about there, and this morning two of them came to the house and asked to borrow 'Ginny Dick's fiddle!'" (She was referring to a servant who had been purchased in Virginia.)

I suppose they are going to imitate their predecessors in giving negro balls. Abraham's men danced all night with the odorous belles, and it is said that the "righteous Lot" himself was not above bestowing his attentions on them. I hope Dick will have more self-respect than to play for any such rabble. He always was a good negro, except that he can't let whisky alone whenever there is a chance to get it.

Of the freed people as a whole, Miss Andrews feared for their future.

Poor darkeys, they are the real victims of the war, after all. The Yankees have turned their poor ignorant heads and driven them wild with false notions of freedom. I have heard several well-authenticated instances of women throwing away their babies in their mad haste to run away from their homes and follow the Northern deliverers. One such case, Capt. Abraham himself told father he saw in Mississippi. Another occurred not a mile from this town, where a runaway, hotly pursued by her master, threw an infant down in the road and sped on to join the "saviors of her race," with a bundle of finery clasped tightly in her arms. Our new ruler is as little disposed to encourage them in running away as was "Marse Lot," but their heads have been so turned by the idea of living without work that their owners are sometimes obliged to turn them off, and when they run away of their own accord, they are not permitted to come back and corrupt the rest. In this way they are thrown upon the Yankees in such numbers that they don't know what to do with them, and turn the helpless ones loose to shift for themselves.

Worse still, the new conquerors expressed impatience with the Blacks. "They are very capricious in their treatment of negroes," Frances had earlier observed, "as is usually the case with upstarts who are not used to having servants of their own." She generalized as to Yankees and Black folk:

they are so bothered with them, that they will do almost anything to get rid of them. In South-West Georgia, where there are so many, they keep great straps to beat them with. Mrs. Stowe need not come South for the Legree of her next novel. Yankees always did make notoriously hard masters; I remember how negroes used to dread being hired to them, before the war, because they worked them so hard.

June–July 1865

Eliza Frances Andrews titled this portion of her *War-Time Journal* "Foreshadowings of the Race Problem." Her title alone suggests again that her wartime diary of December 1864–April 1865, as valuable as it is, is coupled with personal and frank observations of events during May–August, which serve as a looking-glass on how White Southerners in the several months after Appomattox dealt with the tumult and turmoil of "Reconstruction"—that fear-laden amalgam of the disappearance of Confederate political and military authority; the gradual, halting implementation of the freed people's emancipation; the trembling anticipation of how the new post-Lincoln administration would propose and attempt to enact some form of reinstitution of its political authority; and what uncertain terrors an occupying Federal military presence would wreak in the conquered South.

In an "Explanatory Note" at the start of this Chapter Six, she begins by discussing her father's "devotion to the Union," meaning "his judgment…that secession must inevitably be a failure," and that a Confederacy based on secession would eventually implode. Most importantly, "his common sense told him that slavery was bound to go, sooner or later, and if emancipation must come, it would be better that it should take place peacefully and by carefully prearranged steps than with the violence and unreason which he foresaw were sure to follow in case of war."

> He was a large slave-holder himself, and honestly believed, like most of his class, that a condition of mild servitude secured by strict regulations against abuses, was the best solution of the "negro problem" bequeathed us by our ancestors. We were in the position of the man who had the bull by the horns and couldn't let loose if he wanted to, for fear of being gored. Yet, in spite of the dangers and difficulties that beset this course, his pride and faith in the future of the great republic his father had fought for, were so great, that if forced to choose, he would have

preferred emancipation, under proper safeguards, rather than disruption of the Union.

Already, however—and recall that Frances was writing in summer 1865, well before the U.S. Congress enacted the Fifteenth Amendment to the Constitution—there was fearsome talk of the South's vast, newly freed Black population, at least the adult male portion of it, receiving from the federal government the political right to cast ballots in public elections. Miss Andrews describes her father's feelings on the subject: "But while he believed that peaceable and gradual emancipation would have been a lesser evil than disunion, he was bitterly and unalterably opposed to negro suffrage, and regarded it as the greatest of all evils brought upon us by the war."

Fanny wrote her "Explanatory Note" as she was editing her wartime journal for publication three or four decades after the war. Looking back through those years, she sighs—almost audibly to our ears: "the passion and fury of the time were not favorable to moderation, and the fatal mistake was made, that has petrified the fifteenth amendment in our national constitution, and inject a race problem into our national life. There it stands to-day, a solid wedge of alien material cleaving the heart wood of our nation's tree of life."

The very title of Frances Andrews's chapter—"Foreshadowings of the Race Problem"—at once invites us to venture into the intellectual realm of a cultured, educated, twenty-five-year-old Georgia woman of respectability and manners, and at the same time cautions us against the temptation to view her opinions on the subject in the context of our own today.

President Johnson was but a month in office when he proclaimed that across the nation—including the former Confederate states, even though they had not formally been readmitted back into the Union—June 1 would be a day of fasting and prayer in honor of the memory of the slain Lincoln.[1] It is not to be unexpected that on that day our feisty Fanny, instead of observing solemnity and supplication, would plan to spend it in gay socializing:

> *June 1, Thursday.*—I dressed up in my best, intending to celebrate the Yankee fast by going out to pay some calls, but I had so many visitors at home that I did not get out till late in the afternoon. I am sorry enough that Lincoln was assassinated, Heaven knows, but this public fast is a political scheme gotten up to throw reproach upon the South, and I wouldn't keep it if I were ten times as sorry as I am.

The rest of our journalist's entry for this Thursday addressed three pressing subjects: the occupation of Little Washington by Federal soldiers; the freed people wandering about; and the difference between Northern officers who were seeing things in the South as they were versus the Northern officials in Washington who were enacting policies out of supposition and ideology.

> The "righteous Lot" has come back to town. It is uncertain whether he or Capt. Schaeffer is to reign over us; we hope the latter. He is said to be a very gentlemanly-looking person, and above associating with negroes. His men look cleaner than the other garrison, but Garnett saw one of them with a lady's gold bracelet on his arm, which shows what they are capable of. I never look at them, but always turn away my head, or pull down my veil when I meet any of them. The streets are so full of negroes that I don't like to go out when I can help it, though they seem to be behaving better about Washington than in most other places. Capt. Schaeffer does not encourage them in leaving their masters, still, many of them try to play at freedom, and give themselves airs that are exasperating. The last time I went on the

---

[1] E. B. Long, *The Civil War Day by Day: An Almanac 1861–1865* (Garden City, NY: Doubleday & Company, 1971), 692 (June 1 as "a day of humiliation and prayer in honor of Abraham Lincoln").

street, two great, strapping wenches forced me off the sidewalk. I could have raised a row by calling for protection from the first Confederate I met, or making complaint at Yankee headquarters, but would not stoop to quarrel with negroes. If the question had to be settled by these Yankees who are in the South, and see the working of things, I do not believe emancipation would be forced on us in such a hurry; but unfortunately, the government is in the hands of a set of crazy abolitionists, who will make a pretty mess, meddling with things they know nothing about. Some of the Yankee generals have already been converted from their abolition sentiments, and it is said that Wilson is deviled about out of his life by the negroes in South-West Georgia.

Then comes something to give one pause.

June 4, Sunday.—Still another batch of Yankees, and one of them proceeded to distinguish himself at once, by "capturing" a negro's watch. They carry out their principle of robbing impartially, without regard to "race, color, or previous condition."

Alas, we see here an apparent instance of Frances Andrews's tinkering with her war-contemporaneous text some years later. The troublesome evidence is the phrase, "race, color, or previous condition"— one which only worked its way into the national discourse after it had been drafted in the Fifteenth Amendment in early 1869 (bestowing the right to vote regardless of "race, color, or previous condition of servitude"[2]). This was more than three years after our journalist recorded her entry of June 4, 1865; the phrase almost certainly would not have been commonplace at the time of her writing. The infraction, if we infer correctly, is, in truth, slight. But having announced in her prologue a "desire to avoid as far as possible any unnecessary tampering with the original manuscript," we must take note of it, if only to watch

---

[2] Alfred H. Kelly and Winfred A. Harbison, *The American Constitution; Its Origins and Development* (New York: W. W. Norton & Company, 1963 [1948]), 470.

for any further anachronism in her delicate discussion of "the race problem."

Let's not let this, however, distract us from one of the journalist's most tangential points: the hypocritical Yankees, here in Georgia ostensibly to ensure the safe and fair treatment of the newly freed Blacks, were stealing from them. "Ginny Dick," the slave brought from Virginia, had hidden his watch and chain from the snooping occupiers. "Maum Betsy," on George Palmer's plantation, told someone that she "knowed white folks all her life, an' some mighty mean ones, but Yankees is de fust ever she seed mean enough to steel fum niggers." Not only from them, but from Whites, too. Fanny mentioned this day that Federal soldiers entered the bank downtown and proceeded to empty it of $100,000 that had been deposited there in the name of Virginia banks.

> One of the men came to our house after supper, while we were sitting out on the piazza, and just beginning to cool off from a furious political quarrel we had had at the table. Father could not see very well without his glasses, and mistook him for a negro and ordered him off—an error which I took care not to correct. He then made his errand known, and produced an order from Capt. Abraham for father's carriage horses. Garnett and Capt. Hudson quickly moved towards him, ready to resist any insolence. He was mighty civil, however, and tried to enter into conversation by remarking upon the pleasantness of the weather, but people about to be robbed of their carriage horses are not in a mood for seeing the pleasant side of things and nobody took any notice of him, except old Toby, who is too sensible a dog and too good a Confederate to tolerate the enemies of his country. I don't know how father and Garnett managed it, but the fellow finally went off without the horses, followed by a parting growl from Toby.

Hovering over all, both races alike, were the twin prospects of eking out a living and coping with the vagaries of this uncharted, episodic emancipation. When two Confederate officers, invited by Garnett, arrived at Haywood for dinner, Fanny was relieved that she had enough to feed them. "We are all poor together," she observed frankly, "and nobody is ashamed of it." "We live from hand to mouth like beggars," she confided in her diary on June 5. Judge Andrews had sent to Augusta for groceries, but until they arrived, the only coffee and sugar at Haywood came from the labors of one of the servants, Uncle Osborne. "He is such a good carpenter that he is always in demand," Fanny commented, "and the Yankees themselves sometimes hire him." In a footnote, she told of Uncle Osborne's sad fate after he left the Andrews family.

> For some years he prospered and became owner of a comfortable home of his own. When sickness and old age overtook him, my father invited him to come and eat from his kitchen as long as he lived. It was not advisable to send him food at his home, because he had become weak-minded, and there could be no assurance that the charity intended for him would not be appropriated by idlers and hangers-on. He came to us regularly for a year or two, only missing a day now and then, on account of sickness or bad weather. At last he failed to appear for a longer time than usual, and on inquiring at his home, it was found that he had not been seen there since he started out, several days before, for his accustomed visit to "old marster's kitchen." Search was then made and his dead body found in a wood on the outskirts of the village. He had probably been seized with a sudden attack of some sort, and had wandered off and lost his way looking for the old home. It was a source of bitter regret to my father, and to us all, that his faithfulness and devotion should have met with no better reward.

To Miss Andrews, the tale of this faithful Negro "is a pathetic example of the unavoidable tragedies that have so often followed the severing of the old ties between master and servant throughout the South."

Adding to the anxiety of the Andrews family—indeed, of all White residents of Wilkes County and beyond—was the mixed

messaging given out by the occupiers. On June 5, a Yankee expropri-
ated a mule by order of "'Marse' Abraham," which Fanny was sure
they'd never see again. (The animal was returned the next day; Fanny
dismissed the return of the mule, which "Garnett says is pretty good
evidence that it wasn't worth stealing.") As for Blacks in Wilkes
County, Captain Abraham earned gratitude from the Whites when he
strived "to restrain their insolence on the streets." But he earned disgust
as well amidst talk that "he went to their balls and danced with the
black wenches!" Captain Schaeffer, the other garrison officer, when
faced with runaways come to town, either "has them thrashed and sent
back home, or put to work on the streets and made to earn their rations." While Abraham was rumored to partake of the balls, Schaeffer
would have nothing to do with them; hence to Fanny he "seems to be
a more respectable sort of a person."

> People are so outraged at the indecent behavior going on in our
> midst that many good Christians have absented themselves from
> the Communion Table because they say they don't feel fit to go
> there while such bitter hatred as they feel towards the Yankees
> has a place in their hearts.... It is dreadful to hate anybody so, and
> I do try sometimes to get these wicked feelings out of my heart,
> but as soon as I begin to feel a little like a Christian, I hear of some
> new piece of rascality the Yankees have done that rouses me up
> to white heat again.

"There must surely be something in the wind, they are gathering
here in such numbers," Miss Andrews wrote of Washington's garrison
on June 6.

> Still another batch of Yankees, on this afternoon's train, and our
> men say their commander promises better than even Schaeffer.
> They say he looks like a born gentleman, while Schaeffer was
> nothing but a tailor when he went into the army. A precious lot
> of plebeians they are sending among us! It is thought this last
> comer will rule over us permanently, but they make so many

changes that no one can tell who is to be the next lord para-mount.

Though in the Yankees' clutches, Frances consoled herself with thoughts that History would render a kind judgement for her country and its cause.

They have everything their own way now, and can tell what tales they please on us, but justice will come yet. Time brings its re-venges, though it may move but slowly. Some future Motley or Macauley will tell the truth about our cause, and some unborn Walter Scott will spread the halo of romance around it. In all the poems and romances that shall be written about this war, I prophesy that the heroes will all be rebels, or if Yankees, from some loyal Southern State. The bare idea of a full-blown Yankee hero or heroine is preposterous. They made no sacrifices, they suffered no loss, and there is nothing on their side to call up scenes of pathos or heroism.

Life with Yankees!

June 7, Wednesday.—I started out soon after breakfast and got rid of several duty visits to old ladies and invalids. There is cer-tainly something in the air. The town is fuller of bluecoats than I have seen it in a long time. I crossed the street to avoid meeting a squad of them, but as I heard some of them make remarks upon my action, and didn't wish to do anything that would attract their notice, I bulged right through the midst of the next crowd I met, keeping my veil down and my parasol raised, and it wouldn't have broken my heart if the point had punched some of their eyes out. While we were at dinner Gardiner Foster and Sallie May Ford came in from Augusta, and left immediately after for Elberton. They say that when the prayer for the President of the United States was read for the first time in St. Paul's Church, not a single response was heard, but when Mr. Clarke read the "Prayer for Prisoners and Captives," there was a perfect storm of "Amens."

The complexities of parting with the family servants are suggested by Frances's writing, again on June 7.

I am afraid we shall have to part with Emily and her family. Mother never liked her, and has been wanting to get rid of her ever since "freedom struck the earth." She says she would enjoy emancipation from the negroes more than they will from their masters. Emily has a savage temper, and yesterday she gave mother some impudence, and mother said she couldn't stand her any longer, and she would have to pack up and go. Then Emily came crying to Mett and me and said that Mistis had turned her off, and we all cried over it together, and Mett went and shut herself up in the library and spent the whole afternoon there crying over Emily's troubles. Mother hasn't said anything more about it to-day, but the poor darkey is very miserable, and I don't know what would become of her with her five children, for Dick can't let whisky alone, and would never make a support for them. Besides, he is not fit for anything but a coachman, and people are not going to be able to keep carriages now. I felt so sorry for the poor little children that I went out and gave them all a big piece of cake, in commiseration for the emptiness their poor little stomachs will sooner or later be doomed to, and then I went and had a talk with father about them. He laughed and told me I needn't be troubled; he would never let any of his negroes suffer as long as he had anything to share with them, and if mother couldn't stand Emily, he would find somebody else to hire her, or see that the family were cared for till they could do something for themselves. Of course, now that they are no longer his property, he can't afford to spend money bringing up families of little negro children like he used to, but humanity, and the natural affection that every right-minded man feels for his own people, will make him do all that he can to keep them from suffering.

On Thursday, June 8, our journalist got a bit of cheering respite. Out on an afternoon buggy ride with her friend Mary Day, she encountered four Confederate soldiers, recently released from hospital, walking toward their encampment. The ladies' offer to take them aboard was politely declined; they had only a short distance yet to go. "Two of them had very bright, intelligent faces, and one smiled so pleasantly that Mary and I agreed it was worth driving five miles just to see him," she explained. "I told them that just the sight of their gray coats did my heart good, and was a relief to my eyes, so long accustomed to the ugly Federal blue."

Then, the next evening, more jollity was to be had when brothers Henry and Garnett, with Captain Hudson (whose first name has yet to be offered by our diarist), returned from a barbecue at Captain Steve Pettus's plantation, having "indulged too freely in the captain's favorite form of hospitality" ("Henry clean done up, Capt. Hudson just far enough gone to be stupid, and Garnett not quite half-seas over"). With their friend Mary Wynn, Fanny and Mett danced with the gentlemen a bit after supper; then "we went out on the lawn and sang Confederate songs." The war was over, and lost, but there was still patriotic music and its attendant memories. "I love all the dear old Confederate songs," Frances recorded, "no matter what sort of doggerel they are—and some of them are dreadful. They remind me of the departed days of liberty and happiness."

Then, a couple of weeks later, there arrived still another new Northern officer as post commandant in Washington, "a New York counter-jumper named Cooley." To Frances Andrews, the refined lady of patrician bearing, having a mere store clerk "who now reigns over the land" was yet another instance of insulting Yankee effrontery. But after a while, she had to admit that "his whole conduct, while in command of our town, was characterized by a desire to make his unpopular office as little offensive as possible." As example, she told a little story under date of June 21. Charley Irvin had administered a thrashing to one of his family's servants, "old Uncle Spenser" for having displayed impudence toward his mother. When Captain Cooley learned of it, he fined Charley fifteen dollars. Irvin was offended, as he made manifest on the town square when he presented the captain with his payment.

Sensing a confrontation, people gathered to hear about the indignant fine.

"Here is fifteen dollars you made out of me," proclaimed Charley. Giving the crowd what it wanted, he added a taunt, implying that Cooley's fine had been less about meting out justice than about personal pocket-lining. "Put it in your pocket; it will pay your board bill for a month, and get you two or three drinks besides."

The counter-jumper immediately sensed the insult, as he turned to a bystander, Barnett, and asked, "What is the law in this country? Is a man allowed to defend himself when he is insulted?"

Mr. Barnett answered that it depended on the nature of the insult.

Cooley countered, "Do you think this one sufficient to warrant me in knocking that man down?"

Barnett: "I do think so."

The crowd was sensing a fight.

"Yes," cried Charley, "if you have any spirit in you, you *ought* to knock me down. Just come and try it, if you want a fight; I am ready to accommodate you."

But it seems he wasn't "spoiling for a fight" after all, and concluded that it was beneath the dignity of a United States officer to engage in a street broil.

The next day, Miss Andrews added,

Charley says that Capt. Cooley went to him this morning and told him that he would have punished old Spenser for his insolence to Mrs. Irvin if Charley had complained to him, instead of taking the law into his own hands. Charley told him that the protection of his mother was a duty that he would delegate to no man living while he had the strength to perform it. "I'll knock down any man that dares to insult her," he said, "whether he is a runaway nigger or a Yankee major-general, without asking your permission or anybody else's. My life isn't worth much now, anyway, and I couldn't lose it in a better cause than defending my blind mother." Bravo, Charley!

For every temperate, even gentlemanly Northern officer (Captain Cooley), however, it seems that there were ninety-nine of the baser, crueler sort (thieving Yankees). This Fanny makes abundantly clear in her journal.

> Miss Kate Tupper is at her brother's, completely broken in health, spirit, and fortune. She was in Anderson (S.C.) during the horrors committed there, and Mr. Tupper thinks she will never recover from the shock. All her jewelry was taken except a gold thimble which happened to be overlooked by the robbers, and her youngest brother was beaten by the villains about the head and breast so severely that the poor boy has been spitting blood ever since. Old Mrs. Tupper, one of the handsomest and best-preserved old ladies of my acquaintance, turned perfectly gray in five days, on account of the anxieties and sufferings she underwent. The two daughters of the old gentleman with whom Cousin Liza boarded that summer she spent in Carolina before the war, were treated so brutally that Mr. Tupper would not repeat the circumstances even to his wife. Oh, how I do hate the wretches! No language can express it. Mr. Alexander tells me about a friend of his in Savannah who has taught her children never to use the word "Yankee" without putting some opprobrious epithet before it, as "a hateful Yankee," "an upstart of a Yankee," "a thieving Yankee," and the like; but even this is too mild for me. I feel sometimes as if I would just like to come out with a good round "Damn!"

On June 22, brother Henry, the physician, came home with a gratifying story. "Henry came home to supper with his first greenback, which he exhibited with great glee," Frances wrote on June 22; "it is both a pleasure and a profit." *Profit*, because anything bringing money into the family was indeed welcome; *pleasure* as Henry expressed, brandishing his greenback : "I earned it by pulling a Yankee's tooth, and I don't know which I enjoyed more, hurting the Yankee or getting the money."

Still there were indignities, especially when Yankees consorted with Negroes—a recurring scandal in the words of our journalist.

Capt. Cooley has established a camp in Cousin Will Pope's grove, and the white tents would look very picturesque there under the trees, if we didn't know they belonged to the Yankees. Our house is between their camp and the square, so that they are passing our street gate at all hours. We cannot walk in any direction without meeting them. They have established a negro brothel, or rather a colony of them, on the green right in front of our street gate and between Cousin Mary Cooper's and Mrs. Margaret Jones's homes. Whenever Mett and I walk out in company with any of our rebel soldier boys, we are liable to have our eyes greeted with the sight of our conquerors escorting their negro mistresses. They even have the insolence to walk arm in arm with negro women in our grove, and at night, when we are sitting on the piazza, we can hear them singing and laughing at their detestable orgies. This establishment is the greatest insult to public decency I ever heard of. It is situated right under our noses, in the most respectable part of the village, on the fashionable promenade where our citizens have always been accustomed to walk and ride in the evenings. I took a little stroll with Capt. Hudson a few evenings ago, and my cheeks were made to tingle at the sight of two Yankee soldiers sporting on the lawn with their negro "companions." There is no way of avoiding these disgusting sights except by remaining close prisoners at home, and Cousin Mary and Mrs. Jones can't even look out of their windows without the risk of having indecent exhibitions thrust upon them.... I hope the Yankees will get their fill of the blessed nigger before they are done with him. They have placed our people in the most humiliating position it is possible to devise, where we are obliged either to submit to the insolence of our own servants or appeal to our Northern masters for protection, as if we were slaves ourselves—and that is just what they are trying to make of us. Oh, it is abominable!

Perhaps during the re-reading and editing process of her war-time journal decades later, Miss Andrews felt obliged to explain the sentiment she expressed here, for she adds, as a footnote:

It is possible that these associations may not have been, in all cases, open to the worst interpretation, since Northern sentiment is, theoretically, at least, so different from ours in regard to social intercourse between whites and negroes; but, from our point of view, any other interpretation was simply inconceivable.

Throughout her war diary, Eliza Frances Andrews had written of her father's Unionist sympathies: "the Union men in the South—the honest ones, I mean, like my father" (prologue); "he did what he thought was right" (April 21, 1865). In her entry of May 4, she addressed herself more squarely to her mixed feelings:

I was not ashamed of father's being a Union man when his was the down-trodden, persecuted party; but now, when our country is down-trodden, the Union means something very different from what it did four years ago. It is a great grief and mortification to me that he sticks to that wicked old tyranny still, but he is a Southerner and a gentleman, in spite of his politics, and at any rate nobody can accuse him of self-interest, for he has sacrificed as much in the war as any other private citizen I know, except those whose children have been killed. His sons, all but little Marshall, have been in the army since the very first gun—in fact, Garnett was the first man to volunteer from the county, and it is through the mercy of God and not of his beloved Union that they have come back alive.

Judge Andrews's Unionism was so well-known that, in summer 1865, he was being talked about as a potential provisional governor of Georgia, now that Joe Brown no longer held authority.[3] On June 21,

---

[3] Judge Andrews had previously run for Georgia governor, in 1855 as candidate for the Americanist Know-Nothing Party (Robert M. Willingham Jr., "Garnett Andrews" in Kenneth Coleman and Charles Stephen Gurr, eds., *Dictionary of Georgia Biography*, 2 vols. (Athens: University of Georgia Press, 1983), 1:31.

though, Fanny was relieved to enter into her journal the news that her father would not be appointed, after all:

> Father, I am glad to say, has not been appointed provisional governor, so I can say what I please about our new rulers without any disrespect to him. I know he would have done everything in his power to protect our people had he been appointed, but at the same time it would have been his duty to do many hard things, from the obloquy of which he is now spared, and his name will not be stained by being signed to any of their wicked orders. My dear old father, in spite of his love for the Union, is too honorable a man, and too true a gentleman to be mixed up in the dirty work that is to be done…. Poor, dear old father, he can't help loving the old Union any more than I can help loving the Confederacy. But even if he is a Union man, he is an honest and conscientious one, and was just as stanch and outspoken in the hottest days of secession—even more so than he is now. I will never forget the night when the bells were ringing and the town illuminated for the secession of Georgia, how he darkened his windows and shut up the house, and while Mett and I were pouting in a corner because we were not allowed to take part in the jubilee, he walked up and down the room, and kept saying, as the sound of the bells reached us: "Poor fools, they may ring their bells now, but they will wring their hands—yes, and their hearts, too, before they are done with it!" It has all come out very much as he said, but somehow, I can't help wishing he was on the same side with the rest of us, so there wouldn't be all this quarreling and fretting.

"We are all stirred up now about that public meeting yesterday," Frances recorded on Friday, June 23.[4]

> The whole town is in a ferment about some resolutions that were passed. I can't learn much about them, but it seems father was

---

[4] Willingham dates the meeting Washington's citizens as occurring on June 24 (*History of Wilkes County*, 190).

active in pushing them through. One of them, thanking the Yankee officers for their "courteous and considerate conduct," was particularly odious. There was a hot discussion of them in the courthouse and Garnett was so angry that he left the room and wouldn't go back any more. The returned soldiers held an opposition meeting after dinner before the courthouse door, and declared that instead of repenting for what they had done, they were ready to fight again, if they had the chance, and they say that if these objectionable resolutions are published, they will pass a counter set. Henry came home furious that father should have been mixed up in any such business, but he didn't know much more about what happened than I do. He wouldn't go to either meeting because he said he didn't approve the first one, and he didn't want to show disrespect to father by taking part in the second, or letting anybody talk to him about it. Henry is like me; he can't talk politics without losing his temper, and sometimes he gets so stirred up that he goes off to his room and won't come to the table for fear he might forget himself and say something to father that he would be sorry for. Serious as it all is, I can't help wanting to laugh a little sometimes, in spite of myself, when I begin to see him swell up and hurry out of the way, as if he had a bomb in his pocket and was afraid it would go off before he could get out of the house.

"But it is dreadful," she sighed; "I wonder what we are all coming to." Our journalist may be forgiven for applying Southerners' plight to the old adage, "sink or swim," but her maritime allusions allow her to launch upon an extended commentary on just how she felt, two months after Joe Johnston's surrender in North Carolina.

There may have been some use in talking and wrangling about what to do, in the beginning, when the choice was open to us, but now, as Garnett says, right or wrong, we are all in the same boat, and the whole South has got to sink or swim together. We are like people that have left a great strong ship and put out to sea in a leaky little raft—some of us because we didn't trust the pilot, some, like father, because they had to choose between their

156

friends on the raft, and comfort and safety aboard the big ship. Now, our poor little raft has gone to the bottom, run down by the big ship, that in the meantime, has become a pirate craft. But father can't see the change. He grew old on the big fine ship and longs to get back aboard on the best terms he can. And this seems to be about all the choice that is left us; to make such terms as we can with the pirate crew and go into voluntary slavery, or resist and be thrown into chains. I don't suppose it will make much difference in the end which course we take, but it has always been my doctrine that if you have got to go to the devil anyway, it is better to go fighting, and so keep your self-respect.

"The latest act of tyranny," Miss Andrews recorded on Sunday, June 25, "is that handbills have been posted all over town forbidding the wearing of Confederate uniforms. We have seen the last of the beloved old gray, I fear." Then, writing for her eyes only ("I believe I would burst sometimes, if I didn't have this safety-valve," she had confided six weeks earlier), Fanny added, "I can better endure the gloomy weather because it gives us gray skies instead of blue."[5]

As is usual for a people under military occupation, there were many more insults yet to come. On June 27, walking with Jim Bryan, Fanny heard the "complete history of the old striped rag that the Yankees have raised on the courthouse steeple, where my lone star once proudly floated." Mention of the old courthouse flagpole and its current occupant brought back memories of five and a half years before.

I consider that flag a personal insult to Cora and me, who made the first rebel one ever raised in Washington. And such a time as we had making it, too, for we had to work on it in secret and smuggle it out of sight every time we heard any one coming, for fear father might find out what we were at and put a stop to our work. But we got it done, and there it floated, while the bells were singing for

---

[5] After the war, it was said of former general Jubal Early, quite unreconstructed, that he preferred gray skies to blue.

secession, just as that horrid old Yankee banner floats there now, the signal of our humiliation and defeat.

Our diarist was not alone in her detestation of that "old striped rag." She entered into her entry for the 28th that during a morning visit by Tom Cleveland and Jim Bryan she had hear that "the young men of the village are trying to contrive some way of getting to the top of the court-house steeple at night and tearing down the Yankee flag." The problem was, though, that Federal garrison troops were quartered in the court-house, "and they keep such close watch that there is no chance to carry out the design."

Such ruminations led to Fanny's reflections not only on what her father's Unionist sympathies had meant in 1861, but also what it meant now, in the conquered Confederacy still to be a *Reb*.

Poor, dear, old father, my conscience hurts me to think how I have disobeyed him and gone against his wishes ever since the war began. We are all such determined Rebs that I sometimes wonder how he can put up with us as well as he does—though we do have awful family rows sometimes. We barely missed one this evening, when I came in and commenced to tell the news, but luckily the supper bell rang just in the nick of time, though father was so upset he wouldn't say grace. That old flag started it all. We children were so incensed we couldn't hold in, and father reproved us for talking so imprudently before the servants. I said I hated prudence—it was a self-seeking, Puritanical sort of virtue,[6] and the Southerners would never have made the gallant fight we did, if we had stopped to think of prudence. Mother turned this argument against me in a way that made me think of the scene in our house on the night when that first rebel flag was raised. We try to avoid politics at home, because it always brings on strife, but a subject of such vital

---

[6] In an article for *Scott's Monthly Magazine*, printed in September 1869, Miss Andrews has a character exclaim, "O, I hate prudence; it is a mean, selfish, Yankee sort of virtue" (Elzey Hay, "Mercenary Matches," *Scott's Monthly Magazine* 8/3 [September 1869]: 674).

and general interest *will* come up, in spite of all we do.... I don't want to be disrespectful of him, but Henry and I are born hotheads, and never can hold our unruly tongues.

In truth, Frances recalled that before Georgia seceded, she actually sympathized with her father's politics: "I loved the old Union, too—the Union of Washington and Jefferson—as much as I hate the new Union of compulsion and oppression, and I used to quarrel with Henry and Cora for being such red-hot secessionists." But then came war and its ravages.

I would have done justice to Yankee virtues, if they had had any, but since that infamous march of Sherman's, and their insolence in bringing negro soldiers among us, my feelings are so changed that the most rabid secession talkers, who used to disgust me, are the only ones that satisfy me now. And I am not the only moderate person they have driven to the other extreme. Not two hours ago I heard Garnett say that if they had shown one spark of magnanimity towards us since we gave up the fight, he would be ready to enter their service the first time they got into a foreign war. "But now," he say, "I would fight in the ranks of any army against them."

Here our journalist adds a footnote: "Were it not for the bitter wrongs of Reconstruction and the fatal legacy it has left us, the animosities engendered by the war would long ago have become...a mere fossil curiosity."

Chief among the victims of those bitter wrongs were the very people whom the federal government desired to assist and protect. "The negroes," she wrote, "are already becoming discontented with freedom, so differed from what they were taught to expect."

Instead of wealth and idleness it has brought them idleness, indeed, but starvation and misery with it. There is no employment for the thousands that are flocking from the plantations to the towns, and no support for those who cannot or will not work. The disappointed ones are as much incensed against their "deliverers" as against us, and when they rise, it will not be against either Yankee or Southerner, but against the white race. Unfortunately, many of them have been drilled and made into soldiers. They have arms in their hands, and when the time comes, will be prepared to act the part of the Sepoys in India, thanks to Northern teaching. At the beginning of the war I was frightened out of my senses, when I read the frightful story of Lucknow and Cawnpore,[7] for fear something of the kind would happen here, but the negroes had not been corrupted by false teachings then, and we soon found that we had nothing to fear from them. Now, when I know that I am standing on a volcano that may burst forth any day,[8] I somehow, do not feel frightened. It seems as if nothing worse could happen than the South has already been through, and I am ready for anything, no matter what comes. The strange part of the situation is that there was no danger when all our men were in the army and only women left to manage the plantations. Sister never even locked her doors at night, though there was often not a white man within three miles of her; but as soon as the Yankees came and began to "elevate the negro" by putting into his ignorant, savage head notions it was impossible to gratify, then the trouble began, and Heaven only knows where it will end.

Interracial tensions were so high that Frances recorded her private prediction, "the next war they get into, I think, will be against the negroes." Her prophesying was no less dire than her sociological soothsaying.

A race war is sure to come, sooner or later, and we shall have only the Yankees to thank for it. They are sowing the wind, but

---

[7] During the Sepoy mutiny, 1857, in India, British garrisons, including women and children, suffered terribly when the rebels besieged Cawnpore and Lucknow (D. S. Richards, *Cawnpore & Lucknow: A Tale of Two Cities—Indian Mutiny* [Barnsley England: Pen and Sword Books, 2007]).

[8] The Goodriches title their chapter 22 "Standing on a Volcano" and quote Miss Andrews (*The Day Dixie Died*, 225, 237).

they will leave us to reap the whirlwind. No power on earth can raise an inferior, savage race above their civilized masters and keep them there. No matter what laws they make in his favor, nor how high a prop they build under him, the negro is obliged, sooner or later, to find his level, but we shall be ruined in the process. Eventually the negro race will be either exterminated or reduced to some system of apprenticeship embodying the best features of slavery, but this generation will not live to see it. Nothing but experience, that "dear teacher" of fools, will ever bring the North to its senses on this point, and the fanatics who have caused the trouble will be slow to admit the falsity of their cherished theories and confessed themselves in the wrong. The higher above his natural capacity they force the negro in their rash experiments to justify themselves for his emancipation, the greater must be his fall in the end, and the more bitter our sufferings in the meantime. If insurrections take place, the United States government is powerful enough to prevent them from extending very far, but terrible damage might be done before they could or would send succor. Our conquerors can protect themselves, but would they protect us, "rebels and outlaws"? Think of calling on the destroyers of Columbia for protection![9] They have disarmed our men, so that we are at their mercy.

Then she caught her breath: "but I am going to stop writing, or even thinking about politics and everything connected with them if I can." Before she closed her ledger book though, she could not help but write a bit more on that seemingly favorite subject of hers: *Yankees*.

There is an atmosphere of greed and vulgar shopkeeper prosperity about the whole Yankee nation that makes the very poverty

---

[9] Federal forces marched into Columbia, South Carolina, on the morning of February 17, 1865. Fires soon broke out, and after they died down, a third of the city lay in ashes. Confederates blamed the Yankees for the fires, but Federals argued that the Rebels had set cotton ablaze during their evacuation (Marion Brunson Lucas, *Sherman and the Burning of Columbia* [College Station: Texas A & M University Press, 1976], 128).

and desolation of the South seem dignified in comparison. All the best people in the Border States—Kentucky, Missouri, Maryland, and poor little Delaware—were on our side, while the other kind sided with the Yankees. This is why all the soldiers and refugees from these States are so nice; the other sort staid at home to make money, which people with vulgar souls seem to think will make them ladies and gentlemen.

Meanwhile, in the absence of any widespread "system" enacted and enforced by the Federal occupiers, in a touch-and-go process Whites and Blacks tried out tentative answers to common questions: what will the freed people do? where will they live? how will they earn money, or who will give them food? Frances Andrews's entry of June 28 hints at how Judge Andrews was working through these issues with his own slaves. (Her mention of "the old terms" meant the quiet option of maintaining the master-servant relationship till everyone could figure out what to do.)

Father called up all his servants the other day and told the men that if they would go back the plantation in Mississippi and work the rest of the year, he would give them seven dollars a month, besides their food and clothing; but if they chose to remain with him here, he would not be able to pay them wages till after Christmas. They were at liberty, he told them, either to stay with him for the present, on the old terms, or to take their freedom and hire out to somebody else if they preferred; he would give them a home and feed them till they could do better for themselves. In the altered state of his fortunes it will be impossible for him to keep up an establishment of twenty or thirty house servants and children, who are no longer his property. The poor ignorant creatures have such extravagant ideas as to the value of their services that they are sadly discontented with the wages they are able to get. There is going to be great suffering among them, for Southerners will not employ the faithless ones if they can help it, and the Yankees cannot take care of all the idle ones, though they may force us to do it in the end. I feel sorry for the poor negroes. They are not to blame for taking freedom when it is brought to their very doors and almost forced upon them. Anybody would do the same, still when they go I can't help feeling as if they are deserting us for the enemy, and it seems humiliating to be compelled to bargain and haggle with our own servants about wages.

"I don't know what is to become of the free negroes," Fanny confided in her journal.

Every vacant house in town is packed full of them, and in the country they are living in brush arbors in the woods, stealing corn from the fields and killing the planters' stock to feed on....They are growing more discontented every day, as freedom fails to bring them all the great things they expected, and are getting all manner of insolent notions into their heads.

Thus far with her journal entries, by the end of June 1865, Frances Andrews had captured the gist of the first several months of Reconstruction in Georgia.

- Even though some of Georgia's half-million slaves had been freed before the end of the war, in the months after Appomattox Whites and Blacks alike tried to figure out how society and the economy would work with emancipation.
- Suddenly freed, Blacks wandered toward towns, not seeking work so much as lapsing into vagrancy and theft. As Mildred Thompson has written in her early history, *Reconstruction in Georgia*, "To the negro, freedom meant all that slavery had not been. Slavery signified work, generally in the field, labor under constant supervision, restriction in habitat, and subjection to patrol. Therefore, if freedom meant anything at all it must be idleness, roving from place to place, flocking into towns, and doing generally as pleasure dictated. Vagrancy and loafing, natural reactions when the restraint of slavery was removed, were fostered among negroes by the belief, as

tenacious as their certainty of judgment day, that at Christmas time the white folks' lands would be divided and every negro would have his share, commonly estimated at forty acres and a mule....in the summer and fall of 1865, vagabondage was the general condition of the freedmen."[10]

- As at Washington, Federal officers in such cities as Augusta and Milledgeville sought to control the prevailing vagrancy by ordering compulsory work.

- White Southerners hoped to redefine race relations without Northerners' influence. "To be left alone to work out the negro problem without interference from the North was the intense desire of the South," as Thompson puts it.[11]

- Just as Little Washington was occupied by Federal troops on May 5, so too were other Georgia cities about the same time. From their concentrations at Macon and Savannah, U.S. soldiers fanned out to Augusta (May 3), Athens (May 4), Atlanta (May 16) and Milledgeville (May 21). Other towns along the coast and throughout the interior followed. These occupying forces at times became embroiled with the local citizenry, particularly if they included Black soldiers.

- The Yankees, as Miss Andrews attests, more than once helped themselves to the inhabitants' goods and possessions. One middle Georgia citizen, N. G. Foster of Madison, felt so disgusted that he wrote directly to President Johnson on May 10: "True, there is no war upon us, but then it is not peace. Armed men still cover our whole land, and though they do not claim the right to take whatever they wish, they manage in one way or another to procure all they desire. Almost daily houses are entered and pilfered."[12]

- As for the social commingling—on June 28, Fanny complained that in an encampment of Blacks near Haywood, "they are very noisy, especially at night, when they disturb the whole

---

[10] Thompson, *Reconstruction in Georgia*, 43, 45.
[11] Ibid., 66.
[12] Ibid., 138.

neighborhood with their orgies"—this same presidential correspondent complained, "the negro girls for miles and miles are gathered to the camps and debauched."[13]

- Foster warned that heavy-handed policies of the occupiers would rile ex-Confederates like Garnett Andrews: "I have not conversed with a soldier who had returned, that does not express a perfect willingness to abide the issue. They say they made the fight and were overpowered, and they submit. Nothing will again disturb the people but a sense of injustice."[14]

The feeling of injustice that Mr. Foster had warned the president about provoked a troubling incident in Washington. Another of Captain Pettus's bibulous barbecues (see June 9) had on the first of July led Garnett, Henry, and a few other men to stagger home. ("I never did believe in these entertainments for men only," Fanny opined; "they are so apt to forget themselves when there are no ladies about to keep them straight.") Garnett straggled in, tipsy enough so as not to utter a word to anybody lest he betray his condition.

But the serious part of the business is Henry's exploit. The whole affair might have passed off as a joke, but for that. He came home too far gone for anything except to be put to bed, but before making that proper disposition of himself, he went round to the hotel, where Capt. Cooley and the other officers of the garrison were boarding, and "cussed out" the whole lot. Garnett, and Anderson Reese, who had taken charge of him, did their best to hold him back, and apologized to the commandant, explaining that Henry was in liquor, and they hoped no notice would be taken of his irresponsible utterances. But the Yankee saw that they were pretty far gone on the same road themselves, and I suppose did not regard the apology any more than he ought to have regarded the insult, under the circumstances. To make matters worse, when they had at last gotten Henry quiet and were carrying him

---

[13] Ibid., 138.
[14] Ibid., 139.

off home, as they were passing through the square, he happened to spy a party of Yankee soldiers on a corner, and stopped to pay his respects to them in language which made them furious. Garnett tried to appease them by explaining his brother's condition, which was sufficiently apparent of itself to anybody not looking for an excuse to annoy a "d—d" rebel.

Things for Henry got worse before they got better. The next morning the family learned that Captain Cooley intended to have Henry arrested. Judge Garnett intervened and had service of the warrant delayed a bit till Henry could find a friend to post bail. This at least kept him out of jail, but Fanny was not pleased at all. "Any Southerner would have dropped the matter at once after finding that Henry was in his cups and not responsible...but this Yankee shopkeeper prefers to defend his honor with the long arm of the law." She suspected that Cooley, fuming because "our returned soldier boys have bedeviled him in a thousand ways that he can't take up," had determined "to make an example of somebody," and that somebody just happened to be Henry Andrews.

It all ended well, though. Captain Cooley merely fined Henry $25, maybe $30, explaining that he would have dropped the whole business except that Henry's intemperate language had so angered his men that Cooley had to do something.

The Fourth of July had once been a "national" holiday, but for Frances Andrews—who still spoke of her "country" as meaning the Southern states, not the United ones—it was a meaningless occasion. Just a few days before she had written that "the negroes and Yankees are going to celebrate" the Fourth, but that some men in Washington were thinking of holding a counter-event on July 6: a barbecue "for the purpose of showing their contempt for the 4th." She, Garnett, the Elzeys, as well as other family friends agreed that participating in the July 6 barbecue would show disrespect for Judge Andrews, the venerated Unionist. Fanny resolved that "simply to ignore the Yankees is more dignified than any positive action."

This she did when Tuesday, July 4 arrived.

I was awakened at daybreak by the noisy salutes fired by the Yankees in honor of the day. They had a nigger barbecue out at our old picnic ground, the Cool Spring, where they no doubt found themselves in congenial society, with their black Dulcineas. They have strung up one of their flags across the sidewalk, where we have to pass on our way to the bank, so I shall be forced to walk all around the square, in future, to keep from going under it.

The decent people of the town celebrated this anniversary of our forefathers' folly by keeping themselves shut up at home…. The Yankees gained it no favor, waking people up before day with their vexatious salutes. Every good rebel, as he turned over in bed, gave them and their day a silent execration for disturbing his slumbers. I never heard such hideous noises as they made—but I suppose it was only proper that the reign of pandemonium should be celebrated with diabolical sounds.

"Our negroes all went to the mongrel barbecue," she added, leaving she and Mett to do all the household chores.

As for the protest barbecue planned for July 6, the post commandant threatened to take action, as Miss Andrews noted. "Capt. Cooley is reported to have said that if the barbecue projected for the purpose of throwing contempt on the Fourth does take place," she wrote on the 1st, "he will leave his post and send a garrison of negro troops here." That prospect was chilling, as she confided in her journal: "If he carries out the threat I hope our citizens will resist, be the consequences what they may. I would rather die than submit to such an indignity." As it turned out, despite Cooley's threat, "the rebel 'cue'" (as she termed it) was held on July 6. And as she had resolved, Fanny did not go; afterward she was glad she hadn't: "Capt. Semmes tells me it was hot enough to roast a salamander, and nobody enjoyed it very much."

On June 22, Fanny had observed "a negro brothel, or rather a colony of them, on the green right in front of our street gate." A week later she complained that "the mongrel population on the green in front of our street gate has increased until all the tents and hovels are teeming like a pile of maggots." Finally, though, there came some form of resolution to what our journalist clearly felt was an insulting consequence of Blacks' emancipation. On July 7, she recorded, "The Yankees have pulled down the shanties in front of our street gate at last, and turned the negroes out of doors." What Frances Andrews called "a negro brothel," was in fact a makeshift tent-camp populated by freed people who, having left their masters, really had no place to go. Fanny seemed to sense this in her continued writing:

> They are living as they can, under trees and hedges, and some of them have no shelter but an old blanket stretched over a pole, or a few boards propped against a fence. It is distressing to see the poor wretches in such a plight, but what is to be done? The Yankees have taken them out of our hands, and we Southerners are not to blame for what happens to them now. I hate to go into the street, because in doing so I have to pass that scene of wretchedness and vice. They live by stealing—and worse. Everybody in the neighborhood suffers from their depredations. The common soldiers associate with them, but the officers do not, under the present administration. They seem to have no scruples about beating and ill-using them if they trouble their sacred majesties. One of their favorite punishments is to hang offenders up by the thumbs, which I think is a horrible piece of barbarism. It would be much more merciful, and the negroes would understand it better, if they would give them a good whipping and let them go. I am almost as sorry for these poor, deluded negroes as for their masters, but there is indignation mingled with my pity. There are sad changes in store for both races, who were once so happy together. I wonder the Yankees do not shudder to behold their work. My heart sickens when I see our once fat, lazy, well-fed servants reduced to a condition as miserable as the most wretched of their brethren in Africa.

The "sad changes in store for both races" were evident as well among the Whites. "The grand old planters, who used to live like lords," she wrote, were now "toiling for their daily bread." "Maj. Dunwody," she wrote, "is trying to raise a little money by driving an express wagon between Washington and Abbeville, and Fred writes from

Yazoo City that he found one of his neighbors, the owner of a big plantation in the Delta, working as a deck-hand on a dirty little river steamer, hardly fit to ship cotton on."

All around came evidence of the passing of Fanny's beloved Confederacy. A friend of Garnett's, Col. Coulter Cabel, stopped in on July 14 as he made his way home from Richmond. Now prohibited from wearing his uniform coat, and straitened by "the exigencies of a Confederate pocketbook," he was now attired "in the suit of seedy black resurrected from heaven knows where." Two days later, the Elzeys set out from Washington on their long journey back home to Baltimore. Saying goodbye, Fanny remarked, "General, I feel if I am shaking hands with the Confederacy; you are the last relic of it that is left us."

Having Captain Cooley and his garrison occupying the courthouse beneath their detestable striped rag was bad enough, but in came the self-righteous abolitionist missionaries sent by the Freedmen's Bureau. On June 27, Frances recorded in her journal of the Northerners in Washington:

> They have a miserable, crack-brained fanatic here, now, named French, who has been sent out from somewhere in New England to "elevate" the negroes and stuff their poor woolly heads full of all sorts of impossible nonsense. Cousin Liza was telling us the other day what she had heard about him, how he lives among the negroes and eats at the same table with them, and she got so angry before she finished that she had to stop short because she said she didn't know any words bad enough to describe him. Mett told her that if she would go out and listen the next time Emily got into a quarrel with some of the other negroes, she wouldn't have to consult the dictionary, and Cora said if we would wait till Henry came home, she would call him up and let him say "damn" for us, and then we had to laugh in spite of our indignation.

Fanny, Mett and Cora detested the "crack-brained fanatic," but many of the Blacks idolized him. One July day, the Andrews sisters were visiting with General Toombs's daughters "when the rest of the company rushed to the windows to see the negroes pass on their way to hear the New England apostle Dr. French, give his lecture.... The negroes looked very funny in their holiday attire, going to hear 'the Frenchman,' as they call this missionary from the Freedman's Bureau, expound to them the gospel according to Phillips, Garrison & Co."

Here Frances Andrews touches upon one of the Reconstruction era's signal events: the establishment of a Freedmen's Bureau to address the problems created by the sudden emancipation of four million slaves. The organization was created by Congress in early March 1865, with the primary task of overseeing the lease of abandoned or confiscated land to Southern freedmen. Another purpose of the Freedmen's Bureau was to provide Blacks with at least a rudimentary education. Northern teachers had begun moving South even during the war. Most of them were women, but some, as in the case of this Dr. French in Little Washington, were male ministers or missionaries. Of course, they were abolitionists, too, as Fanny alludes in her mention of "Phillips, Garrison & Co." Wendell Phillips and William Lloyd Garrison were among the most famous denouncers of slavery in the decades before the war. Both men were Bostonians: Phillips, a moving orator; Garrison, an impassioned newspaperman, having established the *Liberator* in January 1831.[15]

Needless to say, Fanny Andrews was no fan of "the Frenchman," who attracted crowds of Blacks in frequent outdoor meetings. One of these, as she wrote in her journal entry of July 21, was spoiled by a sudden thunderstorm. "I was sorry for the poor darkeys to get their Sunday clothes spoilt," she remarked, "but I hope 'the Frenchman' will catch a cough that will stop that pestiferous windpipe of his."

French had come with Brig. Gen. Edward A. Wild, who took over command of Washington's military garrison sometime in July.[16] Miss Andrews had written on May 5 of the arrival of the first Federal troops in Washington ("about sixty-five white men, and fifteen negroes"), but she doesn't say whether or when the latter left town or were ordered

---

[15] McPherson, *Ordeal by Fire*, 44–45, 399, 403.
[16] Willingham, *History of Wilkes County*, 178.

away. Instead, as in late July, she writes, "we have great fears of a negro garrison being sent here, and then, Heaven have mercy on us!" Evidently French brought with him an "escort of negro troops"; Fanny noticed how "they flirt around with the negro women." Their Caucasian comrades were bad enough: "the white Yankees are getting so rude that ladies are afraid to walk on the streets alone." Particularly galling to Fanny was the sight of blue-uniformed men sashaying along downtown with dark-skinned women. Frances recorded having heard two friends complain that Yankee soldiers had ordered them from the sidewalk "to make way for their negro companions."

Still, our journalist entered into her private book honest expressions of sympathy for the newly freed slaves. "My feeling for them is one of unmixed pity," she wrote on July 21.

> The apostles of freedom are doing their best to make them insolent and discontented, and after a while, I suppose, they will succeed in making them thoroughly unmanageable, but come what will, I don't think I can ever cherish any very hard feelings towards the poor, ignorant blacks. They are like grown up children turned adrift in the world.... The streets of Washington are crowded all the time with idle men and women who have no means of support.... The poor negroes don't do us any harm except when they are put up to it.... Such things happen only in places where they have been corrupted by the teachings of such wretches as this French and Wild.

"This state of things is about the best we can expect under the new *regime*," she continued, "but there is no telling how long the Yankees will let well enough alone." Fanny worried that the inculcations of General Wild and Dr. French would make her family's remaining servants "insolent," which was Southerners' customary term for surly, indolent, or disrespectful Blacks. Even worse: "Mammy says that Dr. French told them in one of his speeches that some of them would be called upon to rule over the land hereafter—a pretty strong hint at negro suffrage"—a specter thoroughly haunting to Frances Andrews and others of her class and society. Even Captain Cooley was becoming annoyed. "Damn French," Fanny had heard him reportedly declare; "I had trouble enough with the Negroes before he came, and now they are as mad as he is." This caused our journalist to comment, "Bravo! Little Yank; I really begin to respect you."

Of "the Frenchman" we know little. At Washington he created quite a stir by announcing that he would officiate at the weddings of all Black couples not already betrothed under the old regime. Hundreds attended the mass marriage ceremony; on July 31, Miss Andrews noted "it has become a fashion among them to be married by him, though he takes the last cent they have, as a fee"; "Dr. French has been cheating and imposing upon them all the time, but the poor, ignorant creatures can see nothing wrong in him whom they call their 'white Jesus.'"

We have more about General Wild. Massachusetts-born, a physician, he enlisted in his state's very first infantry regiment. He rose in rank to become colonel of the 35th Massachusetts, serving in the Army of the Potomac. He lost his left arm in the battle of South Mountain, Maryland; after recovery, he was promoted to brigadier general. An ardent abolitionist, he spent the rest of the war recruiting and commanding "Wild's African Brigade."[17]

As post commandant in Washington, Wild exercised an authority both broad and brutal. "He tied up Mr. Chenault by the thumbs and kept him hanging for an hour, trying to exert from him treasure that he did not possess," Miss Andrews recorded on July 28; Nish (short for Dionysius) was a corpulent man, so this treatment was excruciating.[18] The Federals also tied up Chenault's son till he fainted from the pain. Wild had a Washington citizen fined, as Fanny put it, "merely for

---

[17] Ezra J. Warner, *Generals in Blue: Lives of the Union Commanders* (Baton Rouge: Louisiana State University Press, 1964), 557–58.

[18] Miss Andrews mentions the Federals' torture of Dionysius ("Nish") Chenault in her article "Romance of Robbery," published in the *New York World*, August 21, 1865 (Charlotte A. Ford, "Eliza Frances Andrews: A Fruitful Life of Toil," *Georgia Historical Quarterly* 89/1 [Spring 2005]: 29).

saying that he wished the bullet that hit Wild's arm had taken off his confounded head." "And the Yankees pretend to be a civilized people!" she exclaimed, adding mournfully, "It is sad to think how things are changing. In another generation or two, this beautiful country of ours will have lost its distinctive civilization and become no better than a nation of Yankee shopkeepers."

All of this was preparatory to Frances's journal entry of July 30. At the time, General Toombs was away, slipping through northeast Georgia in order to avoid capture and arrest.[19] Mrs. Toombs—Julia—remained at her fine home on Main Street, until that Sunday, when Wild strode in and commandeered the place. "He only allowed her to take her clothing and a few other personal effects, peering into the trunks after they had been packed" in search for valuables. (Fortunately, Julia had already stored much of her silver and other precious belongings at Haywood.) Fanny's sister Cora was at Julia's home that day and said that Wild's demeanor was "as hard and unfeeling as a rock" and that "his negro sergeant actually seemed ashamed of him."

Then, the very next day, came word that General Wild had been arrested!

After having received complaints from Washington's prominent citizens, such as the Chenault and Toombs families, the Union commander in Georgia, Maj. Gen. James Steadman, recalled to Augusta not only General Wild but Dr. French as well. The afternoon train of July 31 brought in a squad of Federals, whose commander brought Steadman's order. Upon hearing the news, as Fanny wrote, "we clapped our hands and shouted for joy." Sister Cora spun into a pirouette; brother Marsh (the eleven-year-old) did somersaults across the piazza; brother Henry threw his hat to the ceiling three times; even father, usually so reserved, burst into laughter.

The Andrews family was not alone; some youths loaded and fired the old cannon on the public square. And they got away with it!

---

[19] Ulrich Bonnell Phillips, *The Life of Robert Toombs* (New York: Burt Franklin, 1968 [1913]), 254.

August 1865

"Wild and French have gone their way; the Reign of Terror in our town is over for the present," Fanny wrote on August 2. She might be considered a bit hyperbolic ("Reign of Terror") but for her pained recounting of Wild's outrages. He made his way to the Chenaults' looking for treasure; Nish and two other men were hung up by their thumbs as the Federals tried to get them to talk—Fanny noted that Nish "fainted three times." Mrs. Chenault and her daughter Sallie were sent to a room and there, under inspection by a Black woman, were strip-searched ("they stopped and objected to undressing any further, but were compelled to drop it to the waist"). Then, evicting its occupants, Wild's men ransacked the house and came up with watches, family jewels, and $150 in gold. "Miss Chenault says she doesn't suppose there was much left in the house worth having, when the Yankees and negroes had gone through it," Fanny recorded. Then, adding further insult, Nish's wife was arrested for slapping one of her female servants, who, emboldened by the Federals' presence, "was insolent to her." All of this led our journalist to remark, "if the Yankees cashier Wild, it will give me more respect for them than I ever thought it possible to feel."

"I sincerely pray that no more negro troops may be sent here," she wrote on August 1. That was the day that "Gen. Wild's negro bodyguard" left Washington. At the depot there gathered a considerable crowd; Whites began taunting the departing soldiers, who "cursed the white citizens who happened to be there, threatened to shoot them, and were with difficulty restrained by their Yankee officers themselves from making good their threat." "Our white men were compelled to submit to this insolence," Frances wrote, "while hundreds of idle negroes stood around, laughing and applauding it."

Wild's escort left, but in Washington Black civilians remained, very noticeably: "the town is becoming more crowded with the 'freedmen' every day, and their insolence increases with their numbers." The mere act of walking about town was vexing:

> I went to walk with Mary Semmes in the afternoon, and every lady we met on the street had some unpleasant adventure. A negro called to Cora, in the most insulting manner, from an upper window on the square, and two drunken Yankees ran across the street at Mary and me and almost knocked us down, whooping and yelling with all their might. Things are coming to such a pass that it is unsafe for ladies to walk on the street.... Every available house is running over with them, and there are some quarters of the village where white people can hardly pass without being insulted.

Just as troubling were Miss Andrews's concerns for the Blacks' physical condition.

> The negroes are nearly all idle, and most of them live by stealing. I don't know what is to become of them in winter, when fruits and vegetables are gone. Sometimes my sympathies are very much excited by the poor creatures, notwithstanding their outrageous conduct—for which the Yankees are more to blame, after all, than they. The other day I met a half-grown boy with all his worldly goods in a little wallet slung over his shoulder. He was a poor, ignorant, country darkey, and seemed utterly lost in the big world of little Washington. He stopped at our street gate as I passed out, and asked in a timid voice, almost breaking into sobs: "Does you know anybody what wants to hire a boy, mistis?" I was so sorry for him that I felt like crying myself, but I could do nothing. The Yankees have taken all that out of our hands, and deprived us of the means of caring for even our own negroes. There is nothing for it but to harden our hearts against sufferings we never caused and have no power to prevent. Our enemies have done it all; let them glory in their work.

Then, too, were Frances Andrews's intermittent expressions of sadness over what was happening to her and her people. Gone were the days of busy entertaining, with "our house a sort of headquarters for the officers of two Confederate armies." All of those wartime wayfarers had gone their separate ways, "and Washington is becoming nothing but a small, dull country village again." Much worse, "the bitter realities of a hard, sordid world" were undeniable: "a sense of grinding oppression, a deep humiliation, bitter disappointment for the past, and hopelessness for the future," as she grieved in her writing of August 7. It made her long for the exciting war days, "for war, with all its cruelty and destruction, is better than such a degrading peace as this."

Yet our enterprising journalist could snap herself out of melancholy when social occasions offered accompaniment and entertainment. On Thursday and Friday, August 17 and 18, she and a handful of others rode to visit Ella Daniel at her elegant home in Woodstock, eighteen miles away. They danced, talked, dined, played cards, and simply enjoyed each other's company. On their way back, "we laughed and sang rebel songs, and the whole party were as jolly and as noisy as if we had been half-tight."

Then, at home, brought in by the mail, was a bunch of Yankee newspapers. "I hate the Yankees more and more, every time I look at one of their horrid newspapers and read the lies they tell about us." Just as bad—maybe worse—than the articles were the woodcut illustrations in the New York-based *Harper's Weekly* and *Frank Leslie's* that caricatured or ridiculed prominent Southerners. "I get in such a rage when I look at them that I sometimes take off my slipper and beat the senseless paper with it," she exclaimed. "No words can express the wrath of a Southerner on beholding pictures of President Davis in a woman's dress; and Lee, that star of light before which Washington's glory pales, crouching on his knees before a beetle-browed image of 'Columbia,' suing for pardon!"

In *Frank Leslie's Illustrated Newspaper* of June 3, 1865, a wood engraving shows Jefferson Davis being captured in South Georgia on May 10; with four Federals grabbing at him, Davis is shown wearing a woman's dress. In his memoir, Davis wrote that when he and Varina were surprised by the Yankees' approach, he grabbed his raglan, or light overcoat, which later turned out to be his wife's. Mrs. Davis also threw a shawl over his head and shoulders. Eager to humiliate the Rebel leader, the Northern press hallooed that Davis had tried to escape in his wife's clothing. *Leslie's* described its woodcut as showing Davis, "in petticoats, morning dress and a woolen cloak." In other similar cartoons, the shawl became a bonnet, the raglan turned into a dress, even a hoopskirt.[1]

Robert E. Lee, as Miss Andrews complains, was similarly belittled in a woodcut that appeared the *Harper's Weekly* on August 5, 1865. The illustration shows a number of penitent Southerners bowing before a female Columbia, seeking pardon. Most abject, and in the foreground, is Lee, bent on one knee, head cast downward as he seeks forgiveness.[2]

No wonder Fanny Andrews was disgusted! This got our journalist going about what we would today call "bias in the news media."

---

[1] Mark E. Neely, Harold Holzer, and Gabor S. Boritt, *The Confederate Image: Prints of the Lost Cause* (Chapel Hill: University of North Carolina Press, 1987), 84; Stephen Davis, "How Yankees Turned a Raglan and Shawl into a Dress and Petticoats," *Civil War News* 43/12 (December 2017): 39.

[2] As a high-ranking Confederate, General Lee was excepted from Andrew Johnson's amnesty proclamation of May 29, 1865. As stipulated by the president, though, Lee applied for pardon by writing directly to the president under date of June 13. He followed it up a few months later by taking the loyalty oath as required by Johnson. The government, however, took no action, and at the time of his death Lee had not been bestowed his full rights of citizenship. Finally, at the urging of Virginia senator Harry F. Byrd, Congress passed a resolution restoring those rights in July 1975. President Ford signed the measure at Arlington House (Steve Davis, "Citizenship for General Lee," *Lincoln Herald* 81/2 [Summer 1979]: 94–102). I thank Salvatore Cilella of Atlanta for helping me locate the Lee/Columbia drawing in *Harper's*.

The world is filled with tales of the horrors of Andersonville, but never does it hear about Elmira and Fort Delaware.[3] The "Augusta Transcript" was suppressed, and its editor imprisoned merely for publishing the obituary of a Southern soldier, in which it was stated that he died of disease "contracted in the icy prisons of the North." Splendid monuments are being reared to the Yankee dead, and the whole world resounds with paeans because they overwhelmed us with their big, plundering armies, while our Southern dead lie unheeded on the fields where they fought so bravely, and our real heroes, our noblest and best, the glory of human nature, the grandest of God's works, are defamed, vilified, spit upon. Oh! you brave unfortunates! history will yet do you justice. Your monuments are raised in the hearts of a people whose love is stronger than fate, and they will see that your memory does not perish. Let the enemy triumph; they will only disgrace themselves in the eyes of all decent people. They are so blind that they boast of their own shame. They make pictures of the ruin of our cities and exult in their work. They picture the destitution of Southern homes and gloat over the desolation they have made. "Harper's" goes so far as to publish a picture of Kilpatrick's "foragers" in South-West Georgia, displaying the plate and jewels they have stolen from our homes! "Out of their own mouths they are condemned," and they are so base they do not even know that they are publishing their own shame.

Domestic matters, then as now, obtruded, such as life at Haywood without servants.

Our circumstances are so reduced that it is necessary to reduce our establishment and retrench our expensive manner of living....

---

[3] At Elmira, New York, and Fort Delaware, on Pea Patch Island in the Delaware River, were two notorious Northern Civil War prisons, but they were not the deadliest (2,933 recorded POW deaths at the former, 2,460 the latter); 4,454 Confederate prisoners died at Camp Douglas in Chicago (Lonnie Speer, *Portals to Hell: Military Prisons of the Civil War* [Mechanicsburg, PA: Stackpole Books, 1997], 324–25).

Sister and I do most of the housework.... Sister attended to the bedrooms this morning, while Mett and I cleaned up downstairs and mother washed the dishes. It is very different from having a servant always at hand to attend to your smallest need, but I can't say that I altogether regret the change; in fact, I had a very merry time over my work. Jim Bryan came in while I was sweeping the parlor, to invite Garnett, Mett, and me to a party at his house. Then came John Ficklen with Ella Daniel, now on a visit to Minnie Evans, and Anna Robertson and Dr. Calhoun dropped in later. I had my head tied up in a veil to keep the dust off, and a linen apron round my waist. They called me "Bridget" and laughed a great deal at my blunders and ignorance, such as dusting the top shelves first and flirting the trash behind me as I swept. However, I will soon learn better, and the rooms really did look very nice when I got through with them. I never saw the parlor and library so tidy. I was in high good humor at the result of my labors, and the gentlemen complimented me on them. I don't think I shall mind working at all when I get used to it.... But it does seem to me a waste of time for people who are capable of doing something better to spend their time sweeping and dusting while scores of lazy negroes that are fit for nothing else are lying about idle.... I think it is an advantage to clean up the house ourselves, sometimes, for we do it so much better than the negroes.

From plantation mistress to house sweeper, Eliza Frances Andrews had changed her lifestyle dramatically in the course of time, December 1864 to August 1865, in which she composed her journal. Under date of August 25, she philosophized on how all of this made her feel.

Aug. 25, Friday.—The Ficklens sent us some books of fashion by Mr. Boyce from New York. The styles are very pretty, but too expensive for us broken-down Southerners. I intend always to dress as well as my means will allow, but shall attempt nothing in the way of finery so long as I have to sweep floors and make up beds. It is more graceful and more sensible to accept poverty as it comes than to try to hide it under a flimsy covering of false appearances. Nothing is more contemptible than broken-down gentility trying to ape rich vulgarity—not even rich vulgarity trying to ape its betters. For my part, I am prouder of my poverty than I ever was of my former prosperity, when I remember in what a noble cause all was lost. We Southerners are the Faubourg St. Germain[4] of American society, and I feel, with perfect sincerity, that my faded calico dress has a right to look with scorn at the rich toilettes of our plunderers. Notwithstanding all our trouble and wretchedness, I thank Heaven that I was born a Southerner,—that I belong to the noblest race on earth—for this is a heritage that nothing can ever take from me. The greatness of Southern character is showing itself beyond the mere accidents of time and fortune; though reduced to the lowest state of poverty and subjection, we can still feel that we are superior to those whom brute force has placed above us in worldly state.

---

[4] Faubourg Saint-Germain was the historic district of Paris where French nobility and aristocracy preferred to reside.

Epilogue

Writing probably forty years later—in her journal entry of August 27, 1865, she posted a footnote stating that she was writing "at present (1907)"—Eliza Frances Andrews composed an epilogue as a reflection on all she had experienced and written about during the last year of the war and its immediate aftermath.

We feel it meet and right to let our journalist end her narrative by speaking in her own words.

> HERE the record ends, amid the gloom and desolation of defeat—a gloom that was to be followed ere long by the still blacker darkness of Reconstruction. Yet, I would not have the reader draw from its pages a message of despair, but of hope and courage under difficulties; for disaster cheerfully borne and honorably overcome, is not a tragedy, but a triumph. And this, the most glorious of all conquests, belongs to the South. Never in all history, has any people recovered itself so completely from calamity so overwhelming. By the abolition of slavery alone four thousand millions of property were wiped out of existence. As many millions more went up in smoke and ruin of war; while to count in money the cost of the precious lives that were sacrificed, would be, I will not say an impossibility, but a desecration.
>
> I do not recall these things in a spirit of bitterness or repining, but with a feeling of just pride that I belong to a race which has shown itself capable of rising superior to such conditions. We, on this side of the line, have long since forgiven the war and its inevitable hardships. We challenged the fight, and if we got more of it in the end than we liked, there was nothing for it but to stand up like men and take our medicine without whimpering. It was the hand that struck us after we were down that bore hardest; yet even its iron weight was not enough to break the spirit of a people in whom the Anglo-Saxon blood of our fathers still flows uncontaminated; and when the insatiable crew of the carpet-baggers fell upon us to devour the last meager remnants left us

by the spoliation of war, they were met by the ghostly bands of "The Invisible Empire," who through secret vigilance and masterful strategy saved the civilization they were forbidden to defend by open force.

To conquer fate is a greater victory than to conquer in battle, and to conquer under such handicaps as were imposed on the South is more than a victory; it is a triumph. Forced against our will, and against the simplest biological and ethnological laws, into an unnatural political marriage that has brought forth as its monstrous offspring a race problem in comparison with which the Cretan Minotaur was a suckling calf; robbed of the last pitiful resource the destitution of war had left us, by a prohibitory tax on cotton, our sole commercial product; discriminated against for half a century by a predatory tariff that mulcts us at every turn, from the cradle to the grave; giving millions out of our poverty to educate the negro, and contributing millions more to reward the patriotism of our conquerors, whose imperishable multitudes as revealed by the pension rolls, make the four-year resistance of our thin gray bands one of the miracles of history; yet, in spite of all this, and in spite of the fact that the path of our progress has been a thorny one, marked by many an unwritten tragedy of those who went down in the struggle, too old, or too deeply rooted in the past to adapt themselves to new conditions, we have, as a people, come up out of the depths stronger and wiser for our battle with adversity, and the land we love has lifted herself from the Valley of Humiliation to a pinnacle of prosperity that is the wonder of more favored sections.

And so, after all, our tale of disaster is but the prelude to a triumph in which one may justly glory without being accused of vainglory. It is good to feel that you belong to a people that you have a right to be proud of; it is good to feel coursing in your veins the blood of a race that has left its impress on the civilization of the world wherever the Anglo-Saxon has set his foot. And to us, who bore the storm and stress and the tragedy of those dark days, it is good to remember that if the sun which set in blood and ashes over the hills of Appomattox has risen again in splendor on the smiling prospect of a New South, it is because the

foundations of its success were laid in the courage and steadfast-
ness and hopefulness of a generation who in the darkest days of
disaster, did not despair of their country.

THE END

Interlude

Elzey Hay's Articles in *Scott's Monthly Magazine*

EDITOR'S INTRODUCTION

After the war, along with countless other Southerners rebuilding their lives, Miss Andrews scraped together a means of living. In February 1865 Frances had written about "the career I have marked out for myself" without mentioning what sort of career that might be. Doubtless one of its tenets involved writing, and the income (if even slight) it might bring her.

It is likely that the composition of her journal had shown her that she possessed a flair for writing. Besides, in the shattered ex-Confederacy, any potential source of personal income was to be pursued, so Eliza tried her hand at newspaper writing. Following the sisters' return to Washington in April 1865, there had occurred a local robbery. Fanny wrote an account of the incident that, as she entered in her journal on August 5, "I intend trying to sell to one of the New York papers."[1] She did indeed send "Romance of Robbery" to the *New York World*. The editor must have liked it at first glance, for the piece appeared in the paper on August 21, 1865, with a byline that read merely, "From our own Correspondent," without mentioning her name.[2] Thus encouraged, Miss Andrews submitted more articles to the *World*. One, "Georgia: The Elections, a Peep behind the Scenes," shows the daring of a young woman offering published thoughts about politics in her state. Possibly with the help of her older cousin Eliza, she also began editorial writing in the local *Washington Gazette*. In one piece, appearing in

---

[1] *War-Time Journal*, 366 (entry of August 5, 1865).

[2] "Romance of Robbery" in S. Kittrell Rushing, ed., *Journal of a Georgia Woman*, 61.

1869, she expressed her opposition to women's suffrage, believing that women's proper sphere in society was moral and cultural, rather than political. "It would be a gross injustice if the men were to combine with a few fanatical women, and force female suffrage upon the whole sex, the great majority of whom do not want it any more than a majority of the Southern people wanted negro suffrage," she wrote; "a people that have swallowed the camel of negro suffrage will not strain long at the gnat of woman's rights." (Congress had passed the Fifteenth Amendment in February 1869 and required the Georgia legislature's ratification of it as a condition of readmission to the Union.)[3]

Another early Andrews article appeared in July 1866 in *Godey's Lady's Book*, the popular women's magazine published in Philadelphia. In the style of the day, nineteenth-century female authors usually wrote under pseudonyms (often masculine ones). Miss Andrews's was "Elzey Hay"; Arnold *Elzey*—eventually to become a Confederate major general—was a family friend, and *Hay* was taken from the name of the family home. Titled "Dress under Difficulties," the essay describes ladies' fashions in the wartime South—a signal that the observant Miss Andrews was quite comfortable writing about civilian life in the Confederacy, echoing one of the salient strengths of *The War-Time Journal.*[4]

Selling articles to New York newspapers and Philadelphia magazines was well and good, but there were closer publications in which Miss Andrews's articles (and poetry) appeared: her hometown *Washington Gazette*, the *Augusta Chronicle, Macon Telegraph, XIX Century* (Charleston) and *Banner of the South* (Augusta).[5]

---

[3] Rushing, ed., *Journal of a Georgia Woman*, xxvii, xxxi, 68–74 ("Georgia: The Elections, a Peep Behind the Scenes"); Kenneth Coleman, ed., *A History of Georgia* (Athens: University of Georgia Press, 1991 [1972]), 214.

[4] "Dress under Difficulties; or, Passages from the Blockade Experience of Rebel Women. By Elzey Hay, of Georgia," *Godey's Lady's Book* 72 (July 1866): 32–37. Also in Rushing, ed., *Journal of a Georgia Woman*, 74–84.

[5] S. Kittrell Rushing, "Editor's Introduction" in Eliza Frances Andrews, *A Family Secret: A Novel* (Knoxville: University of Tennessee Press, 2005), xi.

After the war a cluster of literary magazines popped up in the South though most of them proved short-lived: *The Land We Love* (Charlotte, 1866–1869), *Richmond Eclectic / New Eclectic / Southern Magazine* (1866–1875), *Southern Opinion* (Richmond, 1867–1869), and *Southern Review* (Baltimore, 1867–1879), as well as a few others in the postbellum decades.[6]

Then there was *Scott's Monthly Magazine.*

Georgia-born William J. Scott (1826–1899) practiced law a few years and wrote for newspapers in LaGrange and Rome before entering the Methodist ministry. When the war broke out, Scott was preaching at Wesley Chapel in downtown Atlanta.[7] After Appomattox, as Scott later wrote, the South lay defeated, impoverished, and ruined. "I saw then that she needed industrial reorganization quite as much as political reconstruction," he explained, "and I saw, also, that she required, beyond all else, literary elevation and enfranchisement. To aid in the accomplishment of these desired results, I established the magazine."[8] The first issue was dated December 1865. Annual subscription rates ran $4 to $5 during its four-year run, and paid advertising helped. At its peak, *Scott's* had a circulation of perhaps up to 5,000 before it succumbed to hard times in December 1869.

The Reverend Scott published prominent Southern authors such as Paul Hamilton Hayne, Sidney Lanier, and Henry Timrod; he later claimed that he was able to pay Timrod $25 for "Our Willie," which turned out to be the Carolinian's last poem. But his magazine was also

---

[6] Jay B. Hubbell, *The South in American Literature 1607–1900* (Durham: Duke University Press, 1954), 716–19.

[7] James C. Bonner, "William J. Scott," in Kenneth Coleman and Charles Stephen Gurr, eds., *Dictionary of Georgia Biography*, 2 vols. (Athens: University of Georgia Press, 1983), 2:874–75.

[8] Ray M. Atchison, "*Scott's Monthly Magazine*: A Georgia Post-Bellum Periodical of Literature and Military History," *Georgia Historical Quarterly* 49/3 (September 1965): 294.

"a proving ground for many amateur authors," as one historian has put it.[9]

Among these latter was Elzey Hay/Frances Andrews. Historians have accepted that it was Mary T. Tardy, in *The Living Female Writers of the South*, who identified "Elzey Hay" as Eliza Frances Andrews in 1872.[10] In her book, Tardy quotes Elzey Hay as believing "the great beauty of anonymous writing is to protect one against the bores and the other annoyances of a small reputation, till one can claim the advantages of a great one." Tardy also states that "her [Andrews's] identity was published to the world without her knowledge," but does not elaborate.[11] One publisher who let the cat out of the bag—and may be the one Tardy refers to—was the Reverend Scott. When his magazine published one of Elzey's articles in 1868, the volume's index listed the piece as "In Fashion and Out of Fashion. By Miss Fannie Andrews."

Between spring 1866 and autumn 1869, *Scott's Monthly Magazine* carried at least eight articles by Elzey Hay. The titles convey both the intellect and imagination of their author: "Names and Their Uses," "Women as Judges of Character," "In Fashion and Out of Fashion," "Modern Essayists and Periodical Literature," "Professions and Employments Open to Women," "The Art of Lying," "Origin of Good Manners," and "Mercenary Matches." The former demonstrates a kind of anthropological curiosity, not to mention an erudition remarkable for a woman in her mid-twenties; the latter reinforces our understanding of Frances Andrews as something of a mid-nineteenth-century protofeminist. Here we publish all eight of them in their entirety, rescuing them from seclusion and oblivion.

---

[9] Atchison, "Scott's Monthly Magazine," 294–96, 302; *Scott's Monthly Magazine*, Business File, Kenan Research Center at the Atlanta History Center.

[10] King, "Introduction," xiv.

[11] [Mary T. Tardy], *The Living Female Writers of the South* (Philadelphia: Claxton, Remsen & Haffelfinger, 1872), 216.

Names and Their Uses[1]

What's in a name? that which we call a rose,
By any other name would smell as sweet.
So Romeo would, were he not Romeo called,
Retain that dear perfection which he owes,
Without that title.

There are, perhaps, few lines of the oft-quoted Shakespeare more
frequently or more erroneously used than the foregoing. They are in
everybody's mouth, familiar as a common proverb, but no one, I believe, has ever presumed openly to question the poet's philosophy,
though every heart bears unconscious testimony to its falsity. Say what
you will, there is something in a name, and no small thing, either. If a
rose were called *stinkweed* nobody would smell it; the very name would
make people hold their noses in the presence of such a flower; so that
even granting "a rose by any other name to smell as sweet," mankind
would not reap the benefit of that sweetness, and thus we might lose
something by a name, even if the rose did not.

The very fact that a rose is not called stinkweed, or some other
ugly name, proves that the framers of our language instinctively fitted
things with appropriate appellations, roses, violets, daisies, stinkweeds,
"old maids," dog-fennel—all have names that suit them, and no one
would consider it a matter of indifference, whether daisies were called
dog-fennel, or *vice versa*.

That there is something in a name, Shakespeare tacitly acknowledges in the one he has chosen for the play from which were selected
the verses that suggested this essay. Suppose Romeo were Thomas
Smoote, and Juliet, Betsy Gobbins, would not this far-famed tragedy

---

[1] *Scott's Monthly Magazine* 2/1 (June 1866): 439–46.

be converted into a ridiculous farce? Imagine Thomas Smoote apostrophizing Betsy Gobbins thus:

> "But soft; what light from yonder window breaks?
> It is the east, and Betsy is the sun."

If "Romeo and Juliet" were Thomas Smoote and Betsy Gobbins, there would be a comic meaning in the lines:

> "Oh Thomas, Thomas, wherefore art thou Smoote?
> Deny thy father and refuse thy name,
> Or, if thou wilt not, be but sworn my love,
> And I'll no longer be a Gobbins."

But the great English poet was far too wise for any such tampering with names; he understood human nature too well not to appreciate their importance to a writer of fiction. In real life, where we are brought into actual contact with people, where their appearance, character and manners stand out in much bolder relief than their names, the latter are of comparatively little importance, and we may have very agreeable associations connected with very ugly names, and may actually learn to love one for the sake of its owner. But in novels and plays the case is very different; the person himself is never actually brought under our observation, while his name is constantly before our eyes, and thus assumes such importance that I have sometimes heard people object to a novel because they did not like the name of the hero or heroine. Weak, silly, or foolish people, they may have been, but such are often the best exponents of human nature. The best of us, almost involuntarily, form some impression of a person or character from the name. This is so well known to writers, that they almost invariably fit their personages with appropriate and characteristic names, which are worth pages of description. Shakspeare's comic characters only are Gobbins and Falstaffs, while his heroes are Othellos, Hamlets and Romeos. Even the fairies have significant appellatives. That mischievous little sprite, Puck, has a mischievous little name, and slips into it as easily as he drops into an old gossip's bowl "in very likeness of a roasted crab," or cuts his antics in the legs of a "three foot stool." Puck is as well established a mythological character as Cupid or Apollo, but if he were named fairy John or fairy James, I verily believe none but the most devout readers of Shakspeare would ever have heard of him.

Ariel, the "airy spirit" who came to the good Prospero, is as different from Puck in name as in nature. There is something light and ethereal in the very sound of the word, which, without further description, would give us an idea of the spirit's joyous flitting to and fro on errands of love and mercy.

In few things does our great modern novelist, Dickens exhibit higher excellence than in the art of naming. You know, the moment a character is mentioned, what it is going to be. The names of Nicholas Nickleby, Martin Chuzzlewit, etc., are, I suspect, intended to burlesque the high-sounding and often snobbish titles which some authors of fiction bestow upon their heroes, and it shows the power and genius of the man, that he can stir up a romantic interest about people with such unmusical, plebeian names. To the pretentious and vulgar, he gives pretentious and vulgar names, as Morleena Kenwigs and George Washington Jefferson Brick, while Straightforward Miss Betsy Trotwood bears one as plain and simple as her face. Mr. Pecksniff's bears his character in every syllable of it, and so does Tom Pinch's and Mr. Pickwick's, Sam Weller's and Uriah Heep's. What name but *Uriah* is mean and sneaking enough for such a villain? They are not far-fetched inventions, these names. Every one can point out, within the range of his own personal knowledge, people whose names exactly suit their characters, stations and occupations—people who seem as it were, made to order, to fit their names, and such congruity is always striking and amusing. I know a tailor named Mr. Patch, a market gardener, Mr. Bubbage, a quack doctor of medicine, ycleped Clinkscales, and twenty others equally appropriate, but cannot mention them for obvious reasons.

A very striking coincidence, relating to this subject, I met with a little village in Georgia, where two Federals, an officer and a private soldier, who chiefly distinguished themselves by ill conduct towards the inhabitants, were Captain Saint and Mr. Angel. Notwithstanding their distress and indignation, the poor villagers could not suppress a few witticisms, upon the names of those who had proved anything but "ministering spirits" to the little town of ____.[2]

There seems to be a class of names set apart and especially appropriated to old maids. When not Miss Sallys and Miss Bettys, they are Miss Sophronias, Miss Aramintas, or Miss Amandas, and so the story writers make them.

There is a class, *descriptive* names, I may call them, which are used by the author of "Ten Thousand a Year" with much effect. Oily Gammon, a scheming lawyer; Mr. Dismal Horror, a ranting preacher, who wrote a book called Groans from the Bottomless Pit; Hon. Swindle O'Gibbet and Hon. Empty Belly, penniless politicians; Mr. Woodlouse, a scurvy editor; and Sir Harkaway Rotgut Wildfire, a drunken, hot-headed, fox-hunting old baronet, are all masterpieces of their kind and highly amusing; but names of the other class, which are equally descriptive, without appearing to be made up for the occasion, are generally, I think, more pleasing in a novel, because more natural.

I suppose the custom of giving or having names to be the very oldest in existence. The first thing bestowed upon Adam, after his creation, was a name, and the first gift of Adam to Eve was a name. Surnames, or family names, as we have them, were unknown until a comparatively recent period on the world's history. The ancients frequently had some honorable appellation bestowed upon them for feats of courage and daring, almost the only praiseworthy exploits known to them, but these were mere personal distinctions, and not handed down from father to son, as our surnames are. People were also distinguished by qualities of mind and body, or from the circumstances of their lives. This was especially the case where different persons of the same name were brought prominently before the public, and it was necessary to have each well identified. The Ptolemies, for instance, were known as Ptolemy Philadelphus (loving his brother), Ptolemy Philopater (loving

---

[2] "The little town" in Georgia is, of course, Washington.

his father), Ptolemy Physcon (ton-bellied). The Antiochi, as Antiochus Epiphanes (the illustrious), Antiochus Grypus (the long nosed), etc. The nick name often became so prominent that the other was dropped altogether.

We have some appearances of family names in the foundation of ancient tribes, but these were soon extended to whole tribes or nations; so that Israelite or Ishmaelite was no more of a personal distinction than is Frenchman, Spaniard or John Smith in modern times. The name of Caesar was extended to the office made illustrious by the nephew of that great man, before the word Emperor was adopted, so that Augustus Caesar, Tiberius Caesar, merely meant Augustus the Caesar, or Emperor, Tiberius the Emperor. Two emperors of the same family rarely succeeded each other, yet the name Caesar was retained as a title of office, and not as a family distinction, and was afterward preserved in the kaiser of Eastern Europe.

Surnames seem to have taken their rise with the feudal system. When lands were distributed by a conqueror among his followers, they added to their own names those of the domains over which they ruled, and he who was simply Robert or William before, now became Robert or William of ____, some place. Hence the aristocratic meaning of that little particle *de*. It is the French for *of* or *from*, and he who could put *de* before his name showed, beyond a doubt, that he was lord of some place, or at least that some of his ancestors had been chief personages of or from some territory—no matter how small—which is just as good for the purposes of heraldic nomenclature. When William the Conqueror introduced the Feudal system and French language into England, the rough old Saxon names gave way to the de Veres, the de Lanays, and others who took possession of their lands, and to this day an English noblemen will wrangle about his right to a *de*, as if it were the dearest part of himself. Hence the plebeian names, while the nobility being chiefly of Saxon origin, are rough and uncouth, while the nobility bear traces of Norman descent in the softness and elegance of theirs.

Of course no one will understand me to assert that all aristocratic names, where the French language has ever prevailed, have *de* before them. Generally speaking, those names which come from land or places are the most aristocratic, while those which rise from occupations are the most plebeian. But many of the most noble names were gained by noble deeds in chivalric times, and some, again, rose from very trifling circumstances. The proud Plantagenets took their name from a bunch of straw or sedge that an ancestor wore in his helmet during one of the crusades. Those names are quite as aristocratic, and even more honorable, than those which spring from lordly domains. Names, too, like wine and pedigrees, improve with age. In our days there is an element in the nobility of names hardly recognized by our ancestors. Genius and learning have raised our Bunyans, Goldsmiths and Johnsons far above all that land and lineage can do.

Fortune, too, is constantly abusing some and exalting others; so that it is not uncommon to find the most plebeian names in the most exalted stations, and *vice versa.* This is not so much the case in Europe, where an almost impassable gulf separates their exclusive aristocracy from that inferior class of beings which constitutes the mass of mankind, as in our own country, especially the Northern States, where a monied aristocracy exists. Here our ladies of fashion are frequently Browns, Greens, Wigginses, Taylors, while we find Hamiltons and Howards in the most ignoble stations. This is all very right and proper; though there is something in a name, it should not be of sufficient importance to uphold a rascal to the prejudice of an honest man. If Tom Scroggins be a good, sensible fellow, and Ernest d'Aubeyon a lout, then let Tom rise and Ernest fall, each to his true level.

Of plebeian names we cannot tell so much, for history treats of the noble and great, and their names alone are found in its pages, while the humble walks of every-day life are ignored alike by history and tradition. We know, however, that the common people often took their names from their occupations. Many of the trades and mechanical arts have given names to a long line of descendants, and no patronymic in the books of heraldry can boast so numerous a progeny as the Taylors, Drapers, Coopers, Millers and Smiths. It would hardly be orthodox for a writer on names to let the Smiths pass unmolested, but it may comfort John Smith to know that there are, in other languages, some names as much laughed at as his own. I have heard Galli called the Italian Smith, and Duval might as well be called the French.

After what has been said about names taking their rise from occupations, it must strike every one that there was once a prodigious number of Smiths in the world, compared with the followers of other avocations—and such was really the case. The middle ages, when men first began to adopt surnames, were warlike times, and swords, spears, shields, armor, horse-shoes, and all the implements of war were in great demand. Smiths were the men to supply their wants, and consequently large numbers of them sprang into existence. While one half of the world were breaking lances, the other half were making them.

Great use was also made, by the common people, of the prefixes Mac and Fitz, signifying son. Thus two Johns were distinguished as John McLeod and John McLean; John the son of Leod and John the son of Lean. He who was the son of somebody had more of a pedigree, and was more aristocratic than he who was merely a cooper or tailor. Indeed, some of the Macs and Fitzes are among the most aristocratic names in Great Britain. Half the noble old Highland families are Macs, while there are few prouder names in England than Fitzgerald and Fitzroy—though the latter originated in dishonor. More common among the people than Mac and Fitz was the use of the word son, whence we have the Jackson, Johnson and Hobson families. Names ending in *son* will generally be found to have a plebeian sound, though some of them have been ennobled, like many others, by the bearers.

It is curious to study the changes which a name undergoes in passing from one language to another. Thus, our James in France becomes Jacques, while in Spain, whose liberality of language extends to proper names, he may be either Jacobo, Diego or Santiago, as best suits his fancy. John is Jean or Jehan in France, Juan (pronounced Hooan) in Spain, while in Italy he is dignified with four syllables—Giovanni. Jane, female name corresponding with John, is Jeannette in France and Juana in Spain. Some names, after traveling in foreign countries, come back to us so changed that they cannot be recognized, and are adopted into the language as new. This is the case with Isabel, who left England as plain Elizabeth, but, after wandering through Spain, came back home as Isabel, and does not now even acknowledge relationship to her former self.

We laugh at the Germans for their jaw-breaking names, but this is because we have in our country mostly the plebeian names of emigrants, who come generally from the very lowest classes. We hear of the Haslockers, Jogstetters, Fushtwangers, but the noble Falkensteins and Rosenbergs stay in Europe to enjoy their fortunes and their peerage. I really think a good German name the finest in the world, except a noble old English one. There is a sonorous roll in the long syllables that is quite majestic. Great injustice is done the German names in our pronunciation of them. I have heard Wreigelspeigel (bad enough in itself) called *Wrigglespraggle*, Hearnsberger Hanspiker, and many other corruptions equally bad. Americans are very much addicted to chopping off and corrupting names, and the process is seldom improving. It is a subject of complaint in one family of this country, that their ancestral name, de Torksay, has been cut down to Toxey. So du Bois has been changed to Dubose, and Fouché to Fouch. Even where the elegance of the word is not impaired, the change is unfortunate, as it destroys one means of tracing out ancestral connections—a subject of interest, if not of importance to every family. This difficulty might be illustrated in the case of a family near Richmond, Virginia, who spell their name Euroughty, but by some strange chance it has come to be pronounced Darby. From them we get Darbytown and the Darbytown road, now historical as being the scene of important operations during the late siege of Richmond.

Many foreign names have been engrafted with our own, and have become so familiar that they scarcely seem foreign, while the hearers of them are as staunch Americans as if they were Browns or Joneses. It is amusing to translate some of these names, and instructive also, if the families that bear them are of any importance. One of the most aristocratic of them, a female name, signifies, when rendered into English, Swineherd, or hog drover. The meaning of the other is "Drunken-fellow." Almost any surname is passable, if not tacked to an unsuitable christian name, as incongruous in sound as calico dress and diamonds in appearance. A certain class of silly people have a great fancy for giving their children romantic and heroic names, which contrast sadly with the appearance, manners and surnames of the urchins.

I like an aristocratic surname with a plain, modest given one, as Archibald Campbell, John de Treville, etc., because of the utter absence of pretension in them. On the other hand, the vulgarest kind of plebeian names are those which reverse the former order, and tack an Arabella, a Volumnia or an Adolphus behind a Noodles, a Dowdle or a Boozer.

Bible and classical names have always been great favorites with the people, and the former are very suitable, for they are all sufficiently plain and unpretending to do for anybody. A pretty woman may be called Ruth; so may an ugly one, or a stupid one, an intelligent one, a grave one, or a gay one, without anything in the name to stand in disagreeable contrast with her manners or appearance. So any man may be Mark or Peter—indeed, some Bible names have been appropriated so long by plain people that they seem to belong to them. Not so with the classics. I always thought it dangerous to give children classical or historical names, because so few people can stand the associations which they call up. I have seen the veriest dunces called Cicero and Aristides, and I know a snubbed looking Camilla whose awkward, ungainly motions make a poor comparison with that "swift Camilla," who

> "Scoured the plain
> Flew o'er the unbending corn,
> And skimmed along the main."

I suppose everybody knows George Washingtons and Julius Caesars, who resemble their great namesakes as much as my little dog Plato does the philosopher.

These remarks do not apply to the naming of negroes. The very names that it is dangerous to give white children suit the blacks to perfection, because there is something ludicrous in the contrast which always fills the mind with a pleasant feeling of amusement—at least such was the case before slavery was abolished in the Southern States. There was no better name of a sleek, shining, old black "mauma" than Psyche or Minerva, while "uncle Pompeys" and "daddy Cyruses" were such favorites that there was one on every plantation. The negro was regarded as such an indisputably inferior being, that we no more expected him to emulate Cyrus or Pompey than we expected our dog Diogenes to emulate that philosopher. Indeed, mythological and classical names have been so long appropriated, in the South to negroes and pets, that they have fallen into common contempt among the Southerners, being much more intimately associated in their minds with dogs, horses and slaves, than with their original illustrious bearers.

But the day of aunt Daphnes and uncle Israels has forever passed away. They belong to the dead and buried glories of our old plantation life. Since their emancipation, the more intelligent negroes have adopted surnames by which they will henceforth be distinguished among themselves and strangers, though the present generation of Southerners will never recognize the change. It might be supposed that the surnames they adopt would hereafter afford some clue as to who were the owners of certain families, but such is by no means the case. Not a solitary instance have I known of a freedman's adopting the name of the master who owned him at the time of emancipation. I was at the house of a planter one day when the quondam slaves came home from the lecture of an Abolition preacher. One of the women ran to her young mistress, with every demonstration of pleasure, exclaiming: "Oh, Miss ____, I have got two names now, like white folks. I ain't no long just Polly—I'm Mrs. Hamp Tatom."

"Ah," said the lady, seeming highly amused, "that is a very nice name; how did you come by it?"

"Well, you see Hamp's grandfather used to belong to a Mr. Tatom; so Hamp took that name, and Dr. French married us right this evening; so I'm Mrs. Tatom"[3]

---

[3] Miss Andrews relates this in her *War-Time Journal*, entry of July 21, 1865.

The negro has one element of an aristocratic nature strongly developed; he always adopts the name of the owner of the remotest ancestor with which he is acquainted—if it be a short one. He has a great aversion to long or uncommon names, and it is creditable to his instincts of congruity that he always chooses plebeian ones. All the freedmen whose names I have heard, are Finches, Tatoms, Longs, etc. There are no Hamptons, Gordons, Mortimers among them, though some of these names are among those of the largest slaveholders in the South, and it might reasonably be expected that some of the freedmen would bear them, having been called by the names of their owners through long ages of servitude. I believe it gives general satisfaction to the planters, that their names are not used by their former slaves, a thing which they would consider as degrading and desecrating to their honorable patronymics.

Of all fortunate names, those that afford a play upon words are the worst. Every miserable punster thinks he must exercise his wit upon such an one, until the bearer of it almost wishes he had been born with no name at all. The same old puns are repeated with an air of originality by different people in different places, and the poor victim must be highly amused each time, as if he were regaled with a new and striking witticism. I doubt whether a person named Pope ever visited a new place without being tortured with stale old puns about himself and the Roman Pontiff. Miss Pope meets a sentimental young man who immediately professes himself ready to turn Roman Catholic. Miss Pope knows what is coming now, for she has heard it a hundred times, but being a good natured girl, and seeing the poor fellow's stereotyped wit struggling to escape, she gives it an opportunity, by expressing her disapproval of his new religion. Then it bursts forth: he electrifies Miss Pope with the startling pun, combining both flattery and wit: "Oh, I cannot help worshiping the Pope." More vulgar minds amuse themselves with ideas of kissing the Pope's toe, prostrating themselves in his presence, etc., etc., all with equal originality and brilliancy.

But it is at their marriages that people feel the full inconvenience of names that can be punned up. Weddings are great occasions for the revival of obsolete old jokes, more respectable for age than cleverness, and puns are never omitted, if one can be screwed out of the name of either bride or bridegroom. Miss Rose Hall marries Mr. Charles Thorne, and every individual soul that comes to the wedding has to crack his joke about "every rose having its thorn"—what a pity that a rose should turn to a thorn, etc. etc., till poor Rose wishes herself an old shoe, or anything else that will not admit of a pun. Some puns are so far-fetched that nobody can see the point without explanation, or rather there is no point to see—like one that went round the newspapers some years ago, the pith of which consisted in an incomprehensible play upon the words Canaan and Canandagua.

If very good and original, a pun upon a person's name may be tolerated occasionally, but there are very, *very* few of this sort. The best I ever heard was made by a gentleman who called, one hot summer afternoon, to see a young lady named Kate, and sinking into an easy chair, exclaimed:

"Give me a fan, or I'll suffo-*cate!*"

However, I would advise all people, under all circumstances, to beware of punning on the names of their acquaintances. The books of rhetoric define a pun as the lowest form of wit, and I think those upon people's names may be defined as the lowest of the lowest order of wit.

But there is more in a name than has yet been told. I have often heard an eminent politician say that he doubted whether the secessionists would ever have carried their point had they not branded the opposite party with the name of submissionists. Nothing is more revolting to the mind of spirited people than the idea of tameness and pusillanimity; so many men voted for secession merely because they could not stand being called by such ugly names. If this be true there was the fate of a nation involved in a name. The importance of a name may be seen in the fact that political parties always try to dub their opponents with some opprobrious epithet. Thus the Union men attempted to throw ridicule upon secession by calling its advocates Fire Eaters, but as the Southerners happen to be a very fiery race, this nickname had the contrary effect. So with the name Rebel, which the

Northern people thought to fasten upon us as a term of reproach, but which the Southerners adopted as their favorite name. Even now, when the very name of *Confederate* is dead and buried, the Southern women teach their children to call themselves "Little Rebels," and the soldiers always loved to be addressed as *Reb* or Rebel. The Northern people made a great mistake in the selection of this name, which had been glorified by our ancestors in the old Revolution. One stanza of a favorite rebel song ran thus:

> "Rebels before,
> Our fathers of yore;
> Rebel the righteous name
> Washington bore.
> Why, then, be ours the same,
> Name that he snatched from shame,
> Making it first in fame
> Foremost in war."[4]

If they had called us *traitors* it would have done harm—but Rebels, since '76, have been held in honor among the descendants of old Revolutionary heroes.

The rebels were more fortunate in the name bestowed upon their enemies. When a Southern turns up his nose and says *Yankee*, he imagines that he has expressed all the hatred and contempt which language can convey. This is not mere national prejudice, either, for long before the rebellion, Yankee was a name which nobody would own. Europeans called all Americans Yankees, but Southerners resented such appellation as a mortal affront, while the other Yankees staved it off upon

---

[4] The lines are from "God Save the South!" (lyrics by George Henry Miles, AKA Ernest Halphin, and music by Charles W. A. Ellerbock). When published in Richmond, the song was hailed as "our national Confederate anthem" although it never gained that distinction (James A. Davis, *Maryland, My Maryland: Music and Patriotism during the American Civil War* [Lincoln: University of Nebraska Press, 2019], 15–17; E. Lawrence Abel, *Confederate Sheet Music* [Jefferson, NC: McFarland & Company, 2004], 93–96).

New England, and New England made Connecticut the scape goat. Here the odious epithet rested, because it could be pushed no further, and not, I opine, because the people of Connecticut were desirous of appropriating it to themselves. The late war, however, has settled the boundary of that nickname; there will never again be confusion as to who are Yankees. The line of separation is drawn deep and dark by a stream of blood that flows between Yankees and Rebels.

There are few instances of political parties naming themselves, or if they do so, the name they take is soon set aside for another which their enemies fasten upon them, or which they adopt, as the Southern-ers did *Rebel.* Nations at war, like children in a quarrel, always call each other bad names, which are used as a means of stirring up the people at home. History is full of instances in which the populace has been roused to frenzy by a name. What excitements have been caused in Paris by the single name of Bourbon! What enthusiasm has been raised in the imperial army by the magic word Napoleon! It would fill a book to tell the mischief that has been caused in England by the one word Popery. For ages it was an instrument in the hands of unscrupulous politicians, by which they put the nation in ferment, and shed innocent blood. Say "wooden shoes" to a burly English yeoman, and he will begin to puff and swell as in the days when *Bonaparte* was the bugbear with which mothers frightened their naughty children.

It is true that undue importance is often attached to a name. In-deed, it is but too common for people to mistake names for things. I venture to say that nine people out of ten imagine copper to be the chief ingredient in copperas, merely because the names are similar— whereas, the two things have no more to do with each other than tin and tinder. I knew an old man who prided himself upon having been a Democrat in politics for thirty-five years, and considered that fact a striking proof of his unchanging integrity and consistency. Now, the most superficial knowledge of political history is enough to teach one that having always borne the same political name is no great argument of a man's consistency. The two great parties of England, Whig and Tory, have sometimes so completely reversed their situations that the

Tories of one day hold precisely the opinions of the Whigs a few years back, and *vice versa*. What then, become of the principles of a man who measures his fidelity by a name?

Such an one falls into a worse error than simple little Juliet, whose mistake, at least, was not pernicious.

The confession may seem out of place, but I know at least one young writer who spent almost as much time and thought in selecting a title for his first essay, and a *nom de plume* for himself, as in writing the whole piece from beginning to end.

Women as Judges of Character[1]

The word character, as used in the following pages, is intended to denote those qualities which mark the social rather than the intellectual man; or, in other words, it refers rather to the heart and disposition, than to the understanding. A man's intellect is no part of his character, though the two may modify and influence each other in various degrees. Appreciation of talent is mainly an act of the understanding, while nothing more than a little observation, coupled with a moderate share of common sense, is necessary to form a correct judgment of character. Knowledge of character seems to be rather an intuition, than the result of any process of reasoning, for we often find it largely developed among those who are little capable of making or comprehending a syllogism. Children, so far as their experience goes, are generally keen and accurate judges: they seem to know by instinct whom to love and whom to fear, whom to caress and whom to avoid, and they can tell at a glance who are lovers of children and who are not. I have always had great respect for the intuitions of children: their instinctive perceptions of the motives and dispositions of men, are often of greater worth than the most painful and elaborate deductions of grown people.

On the same principle, it seems to me, that women are, perhaps, as a class, better judges of character than men, though less capable of forming a correct estimate of talents. It is woman's province to deal with the heart, rather than the head, and as talent belongs to the latter, while character is chiefly dependent upon the former, the reason is plain why women should judge better of the one than of the other. Female judgment is by no means so reliable in its estimate of mental as of moral and social qualifications. This is sometimes absurdly manifest in the behavior of ordinary women, who have become the wives of talented men. They look up to their husbands with a sort of dread,

---

[1] *Scott's Monthly Magazine* 4/4 (October 1867): 769–72. [Interestingly, her name on this on is "Elsey" Hay.]

wondering awe, admiring them because other people do, and not because they understand themselves what they admire. Unable to distinguish one kind of talent from another, these undiscriminating creatures coolly take it for granted that their lords are endowed with all. One imagines, that because her spouse has made a fine speech, he must be a poet and musician, also; another, whose lord has published some clever verses in the north-west corner of the Hopkinsville Gazette, would be mightily offended if one should hint a suspicion that he is not quite the equal of Cousin in metaphysics, or of Agassiz in natural science. I have heard the wife of an eminent surgeon, whose professional duties left him no time for general cultivation, quote the opinions of her husband as infallible in politics and literature; I have heard Mrs. Doctors of Divinity gravely promulgate the bulls of their reverend partners with regard to military operations, and Mrs. Politicians demolish whole systems of theology with the disapprobation of M. C.'s, who hardly knew the Psalms of David from the songs of Beranger—if, indeed, they had ever heard of either. The coolness with which these undiscriminating females sometimes set aside the opinions of other people, with an "Oh, but Mr. _____ says so-and-so," as if there were no appeal from that decision, is positively exasperating to intelligent beings who happen to hold opinions of their own, which they respect quite as much as Mr. _____'s, out of his own especial province.

All this, however, is no argument against the skill of even very ordinary women, in judging of character. Let a wife be never so blinded as to the mental endowments of her husband, she will not fail to note the minutest obliquities and eccentricities of his character, and to shape her conduct accordingly. Women, as a general thing, are much closer observers than men, and hence their judgment is more to be relied on in cases where observation, rather than reflection, is necessary to the formation of a correct opinion. Men, being of a more reflective turn, observe less minutely—though, as de Quincey says, when reflective people do give their attention to a subject, they are the keenest observers in the world with regard to that particular thing, so when a man becomes interested in the study of a particular character, his judgment is perhaps more reliable than that of a woman, not equally interested.

Men of sense, with right principles, always have great respect for the judgment of women, in matters which do not fall beyond their sphere or capacity; but silly men and boys never have—especially boys of eighteen or nineteen, just beginning to enjoy the inestimable privilege of going out at night. Boys at this stage of existence imagine that wisdom is only to be gained by strutting about the streets after dark, and because women are shut out from this and similar sources of information which are open to "us men," they look upon the sex as mere babes in knowledge and experience, and entertain a thorough contempt for their judgment in all affairs beyond the simplest details of housewifery. Only the other day, I heard Master Arthur, a young friend of mine just out of round jackets, wishing for something to read. His sister Kate recommended an article in the Saturday Review, whereupon the young gentlemen exclaimed disdainfully, "Do you reckon *I* would care to read anything that *women* like?" This same young gentleman's father, one of the most cultivated men in Georgia, always makes Kate look over the papers first, to tell him what is worth reading, not having time to examine for himself, on account of professional engagements. It is true, there are some women whose recommendation of a book or paper ought to keep any sensible person from reading it, but men of understanding can always distinguish between these and women whose taste and judgment can be relied on. I am sure no man would, though some grown-up boys might, declare themselves against any book "that *women* like."

Although I regard knowledge of character as in a certain sense intuitive, yet I have no faith in the pretensions of those who profess to read everybody at a glance—who pass judgment upon character on the evidence of countenance alone. Our Creator seems to have printed some index of every man's character on his face, but he has not given us power always to interpret the writing at a glance. There is no one who can read every face he sees, though there are some faces which every one can read. I am somewhat inclined to distrust the judgment of a person who boasts that he can read every man's countenance like a book, for it is mere charlatanry to profess to judge of anything without sufficient evidence. Our very strong instincts about faces are nearly always correct, though it would not be correct always to have such strong instincts, because physiognomy seldom reports so strongly. When it does, however, its report is pretty sure to be correct. Every one can remember instances in which his own settled prejudices either for or against a countenance have been verified on more intimate acquaintance with the character of the person to whom it belonged. When we know a person's character, we always find that his physiognomy corresponds to some part of it, though the expression may not have been sufficiently distinct for us to have detected the trait without other means of knowledge. The generality of countenances bear no very marked expression, because the generality of people have no very strongly marked character. Ruskin, one of the most acute and critical observers of the age, says that the majority of faces are indicative of either vanity or sensuality, and when we consider what common failings these are, the remark will excite no surprise. I have noticed that the traits which are capable of being most strikingly portrayed on the features, are obstinacy and cunning—the one depending for its expression mainly on the mouth, the other on the eye. With regard to the latter, it is a little singular that the vice which most courts secrecy should be the one most obviously betrayed.

It seems to me that physiognomy is a better test of talent than of character. Wicked hearts are not always so surely betrayed by bad countenances, as are empty heads by vacant faces. A knave may sometimes put on a benevolent look designedly, but a fool can never put on a wise one, even supposing it were possible for him to discover that he is a fool, and form the design of looking wise. One sees this fact exemplified to some extent in the physiognomy of the lowest class of our rustic population, better known, in our Georgia phraseology, as "crackers." Some of them wear such vacant, idiotic expressions of countenance, that one would scarcely take them to be of the same race with the corresponding class in towns and villages. Wherever a large number of people are collected together, the general spread of intelligence is greatly facilitated, and hence the lower classes in cities are, as a general thing, less ignorant than the "cracker" population of remote rural districts. The difference of expression may be merely that the city "rough" has more vices depicted on his visage than the country bumpkin—but expression, of whatever kind it be, saves his face from the look of staring vacancy worn by the man "who never had a dozen thoughts in all his life." The larger experience of the city rowdy puts more ideas into his head and more expression into his face than the limited knowledge of the lowest class of rustics can accord to them. Whether the ignorance of the latter is not preferable to the kind of knowledge often acquired by the former, and whether a look of harmless stupidity is not more agreeable than one of knowing iniquity, are questions which do not belong to the subject at present under discussion.

The nose probably has more to do with the expression of a face, than any other feature; there are some feelings, as contempt and aversion, which could not be visibly portrayed without it. I am aware that this opinion runs the risk of shocking my sentimental readers, for the nose is usually regarded as a most unpoetical feature. There is a popular prejudice in favor of the eye as a medium of expression, and, indeed, every feature is treated with more consideration than the nose. Poets sing of lustrous eyes and ruby lips, but never a note is tuned to the praise of a Grecian nose which really is a rarer beauty than either. A pain or a sore, in any other part of the face, meets with sympathy and respect, but a boil or a bruise on the nose only excites laughter. People seem to associate something ludicrous with the very idea of a nose. I was at a dinner party once, when it was announced that a young officer, known to most present, had got his nose shot off at the battle of ___, and everybody began to laugh, though I think the poor fellow was really more to be pitied than if he had lost an arm or a leg. Now, I must protest against this injustice to the nose. It reminds one of the old fable about the stomach and the members, and people who treat noses with so little respect, would, if they were to lose their own, find themselves in as sad a light as that of the refractory members, when the stomach ceased to perform its functions. The loss of no other feature disfigures the appearance so much, yet, in describing a face, people will enter into the most minute details concerning the eyes, mouth, hair, complexion, etc., but not a word do they think it worth while to utter regarding the nose, the most conspicuous, and so far as looks are concerned, the most important of them all. The substitution of black eyes for grey, or blue for brown, would not change the expression of a face half so much as the substitution of a *petit nez retrousse* for a Grecian or Roman profile. Let any one gifted with an aquiline beak, just give it a push upwards with his finger, and hold it so, while he examines his face in a mirror, and he will find that no grimace he can make will so completely change its expression. The result will be equally marked, if one flattens the end of one's nose against a window-pane. It is said that if the entire persons of a number of people with eyes of every shape, size and color, be concealed, and only the eyes exposed, it will be impossible to distinguish one pair from another; but if the same experiment be tried with noses, I will warrant a very different result. Hence, it would seem that the nose is at least a more *marked* feature than the eye.

But it is not on noses, nor eyes, not mouths, nor on all combined, that the best judges rely for their estimate of character. A single sentence, a word, a gesture, often betrays more than the closest study of a placid countenance could reveal. We all like to think ourselves very hard to find out, but the majority of us are not so deep as we imagine. Our Creator has wisely ordered it so that no man's character can be entirely concealed from his fellows. It is necessary that people who are brought into close or frequent contact should know each other: a pretty state of confusion this world would be in, if every creature in it were ignorant of the character of those with whom he has to deal!

The best way to find people out in a short time, is to travel with them. The variety of incident, a scene, and society, is so great on a journey, that the numerous qualities which make up a character are brought into more constant exercise, and consequently more forcibly revealed to others, than they would be in the same length of time during a quiet sojourn in one place.

At their own houses is also an excellent place to study people, because *home* is a place where we all luxuriate in doing as we please, and the most practiced man or woman of the world, however much disposed to act a part, is sure to forget him or herself (oh, for a common pronoun singular!) now and then, and relax into naturalness, just from the unbending influence of home. One may act a part forever before the world, but the deepest of us must sometimes be himself at home.

In Fashion and Out of Fashion[1]

There are some people who make a practice of railing against every new fashion that comes in vogue, for no other reason apparently, than because it is the fashion: "What is the sense of it?—what is the use of it?—where is the reason of it?" they sneeringly ask of every mode that makes its appearance—as if the same queries might not suggest themselves, with equal propriety, concerning the antiquated styles which they make such a merit of keeping up. To people who are always asking, What is the use of being in the fashion? we may very properly retort, What is the use of being out of it? The truth is, it is both unreasonable and impertinent to look for either use, sense, or reason in fashion—a thing whose glory is eccentricity, whose wisdom is folly, whose reason is caprice. Fashion is no more to be regulated by reason than the strains of a musical fantasy, or the vagaries of a midsummer night's dream. Its chief aim is at novelty and variety; its acknowledged object in society is to startle and amuse by endless changes. The soul of its existence is that very fickleness which is so much censured by prudes whose narrow purses allow them to rail against fashion more freely than to follow its endless caprices. Very often, I fear, there are a few sour grapes mixed up with the philosophy of people who so ostentatiously parade their contempt for the follies of fashion. A lady who can afford a new bonnet every few weeks, and whose mantuamaker spares her the trouble of directing how each new gown shall be trimmed, will generally keep on much better terms with the fickle goddess than one who has to get an old bonnet done over every season, or who can only sport a fashionable covering by cutting down last winter's cloak into a poplin jacket. The folly, if there be any, in such cases, is not in fashion, but in those who attempt, without sufficient means, to imitate its extravagances. Fashion was never intended for poor people; it ignores poverty, and hoots at economy; it takes no account of small incomes and large

---

[1] *Scott's Monthly Magazine* 5/5 (May 1868): 263–68.

families of girls. Unfortunately for the purses of poor women, the caprices of fashion are constantly controlled by those who never have to
consider the cost of them, and to whom the most sudden and decided
changes cause not a moment of anxious reflection. They can jump
from short skirts to sweeping trains, from Spanish jackets to Arab man-
tles, from "catalans" to "sky-scrapers," without a thought, while their
more humble imitators are at their wits' ends to keep up in the race
after this fleeting will-o'-the-wisp. If the Empress of France had to rip
and alter old clothes—if she had to turn last winter's silk before appearing at the first *fete* of the present season—if she knew what it was
to let a breadth into last summer's muslin before it would set well over
the new style of hoops—if she had to cut up and gore that green poplin
skirt before it could be made to hang properly, the changes of fashion
might, perhaps, be less rapid and capricious, and if she could once feel
the despair that strikes some breasts when the style changes suddenly
and decidedly, so that a short sacque can, by no stretch of ingenuity,
be converted into a long talma, nor a tight coat sleeve expanded into a
flowing *manche a la juire*, the five Miss Jenkinses would never be so
sadly put to it in trying to follow her arbitrary decrees.

And yet, after all, I question whether the Empress of France, who
sets fashions for all the world, thinks half so much about them as many
a poor little country belle, who spends all the week in planning and
working to make a fine appearance on Sunday. The ladies who dress
most are not always the ones that think most about what they wear.
They have milliners and dress-makers to think for them, while they
have only to enjoy the results of such deliberation. Long familiarity
with well filled wardrobes prevents them from forming that exaggerated estimate of the importance of dress which is natural to one who
works hard for every bit of finery she possesses—just as a man who
enjoys uninterrupted health does not appreciate his immunity from
sickness so highly as one whose sense of the blessing is quickened by
an occasional twinge of the gout, or a passing fit of indigestion. The
grandest duchess of Belgravia feels not half so fine in her point lace and
diamonds as the Devonshire farmer's daughter in her new muslin dress

and pink ribbons. We generally value a thing in proportion to the labor and trouble it costs us to obtain it: hence, the poorer members of fashionable circles are apt to rate the importance of dress much more highly than their wealthier and more dashing associates, and women in little country towns talk more about the fashions than would a convention of professional *modistes*. The belles of Madison Square and Pennsylvania Avenue would be startled could they witness the anxiety with which a country farmer's daughter, who has come two miles to lay out the proceeds of her dairy, inquire of the village milliner, "how is the way to make muslin dresses this year?" and "if pink or blue ribbins is goin' to be the fashion for bonnets this summer?" as if the fate of her soul depended upon pink or blue "ribbins," or the "way how" to make muslin dresses.

"The follies of fashion" is an old song in the ears of most people, if not an old tune in their mouths; but it seems to me that if the philosophers who are so fond of moralizing upon that theme would reflect a little upon the folly of those who persist in worshipping at a shrine that was never set up for their devotions, they might sometimes vary the tone of their meditations. There can be no folly in adopting any mode whatever, not positively indecent or injurious, if one's means will permit; but it is both foolish and out of taste for people to attempt what their means or their situation in life will not warrant them in doing. The main cause of the fickleness of fashion is to baffle such people in their pursuit of her. Nobody cares to dress like her waiting-maid, but we all know that waiting-maids are much given to aping the modes in favor with their mistresses. Now, these presumptuous imitations, whether gotten up by servant-maids or by respectable young ladies in rural districts, who do their own millinery and dress-making, are very apt to be more or less of burlesques upon the prevailing fashions. That potent goddess does not like to have her ways burlesqued any more than we common mortals, so she instantly changes her costume, and appears to the baffled gaze of her impotent pursuers in a shape which they cannot hope to acquire before the capricious divinity again shifts her mantle and leaves them as far from their purpose as ever. If Miss

Dora Hopkins has to lament that long white wrappings go out of vogue, just as she has succeeded in patching up her old delaine shawl into something bearing a faint resemblance, in species, to Miss Brockenborough's flowing Arab of white alpaca, she may partly thank the success of her own efforts for the fact which she so much deplores. Miss Brockenborough might have been content to wear the white Arab a few weeks longer, had she not beheld Miss Dora Hopkins' imitation with the old white delaine shawl. Now, it would be far wiser, and in better taste, for all classes of Hopkinses to let fashion alone, and dress as their fortunes and convenience might dictate. I do not mean that any one should take pains to keep persistently and conspicuously out of fashion, because that would be more foolish and inconvenient than the opposite extreme; neither is it necessary to cry out against every new mode, and declare that you never will be seen in this or in that as long as you live, because the probabilities are, that you will, as soon as its novelty ceases to startle you—and, indeed, you would be very ridiculous not to adopt any style which should become so general, like crinoline, for instance—that you would appear odd or uncouth without it. There is a just mean between all extremes which persons of small incomes would do well to observe, without striving to imitate either fashionable extravagance or unfashionable eccentricities. Those people who live in a chronic state of protest against the fashions frequently give themselves more trouble in their efforts to dress persistently out of the mode, than another class of foolish women take in trying to keep up with it. They have an idea that there is some peculiar merit in dressing differently from the rest of the world, though they have to change their style as often, to keep out of fashion, as other people do to keep in it. As crinoline expands, the circumference of these worthies contracts to the size of a dinner plate, and as others collapse, they expand in proportion. When large bonnets are worn, they wonder how people can disfigure themselves with such monstrosities, and when small ones come in, they are equally busy with the problem as to "how people can," etc. Bonnets have been a pet grievance with these moralists, in all ages, though the style that they make war on in one generation may be the very one adopted by their successors in the next. They look upon stylish dressing, in general, as a sure index of a frivolous mind; and the young lady who is first to adopt a new style of bonnet is too fast ever to come to any good. They entertain a comfortable sense of their own superiority over the idle creatures who are wasting time and thought in the vain pursuit of pomp and fashion, never seeming to consider that more time and thought may be wasted, and even more personal vanity displayed, in dressing flagrantly and conspicuously out of fashion, than in quietly submitting to its decrees. Milliners say that they have more trouble in pleasing old ladies, who, influenced possibly, by the recollection of how pretty their once rosy faces used to look in the fashions of forty years ago, insist upon wearing bonnets of some exploded shape that has not been seen for half a century, than in gratifying the caprices of their most fashionable customers. It is the universal testimony of dress-makers and milliners that the most fashionable women are the least capricious about what they wear. If once that a dress or a bonnet is quite *a la mode,* they think no more about it, while an old-fashioned prude will torment one with orders and counter-orders, and a thousand minute directions which must each be carried out to the letter. Old ladies are the special terror of country milliners. A poor little hard-working *modiste* told me that she once had to rip up a bonnet in order to add a quarter of an inch in breadth to the front, for an old lady who was very much afraid of getting into the fashion. The milliner, by mistake, added a half, instead of a quarter, of an inch; whereupon the bonnet was sent back to be ripped again, and reduced by the width of the wire cord that held it in shape. Anybody who has ever seen an old lady in a milliner's shop, measuring all the bonnets with a little piece of tape to make sure of one exactly the size of that she had fifty years ago, objecting to this one because the straw is too light, to that one because of some innocent little bow of ribbon, to another because there is a suspiciously modern air lurking about it—whoever, I say, has observed all this, will be convinced that the most fashionably dressed people are not always the ones who think most about their clothes.

The immodesty of fashion is a favorite theme with prudes of all ages and sexes. Old ladies, village editors, and nice young men in paper shirt-collars,[2] contrive to find something which shocks their delicacy in every new style that is introduced. When there are just grounds for such objections, I have not a word to say against them; but the unreasonableness and inconsistency of some of these prudish strictures upon dress and manners are so apparent as almost to incline one to err on the opposite extreme. Every generation seems to have its own pet indecencies and pruderies—its gnats to strain at and its camels to swallow. Immodesty and prudery change their shape as often as hats and bonnets. Our grandmothers did not hesitate to expose their persons in short, scant, and what we would consider insufficient clothing. A few years ago, our modern belles displayed what ought to have been hidden by the artful contrivances of "tilting" skirts, while the established indecencies of the present season are extreme low dressing and tightly gored skirts stretched over great protruding *ventres* of gutta-percha. These things are all equally to be condemned, but who shall cast the first stone? A "Saturday Reviewer" declares that modern young ladies are often taunted with the question, "What would your grandmother say to you?" but he significantly adds, "It would be well to look at the other side of the picture and see what these young ladies would say to their grandmothers." Old people are very apt to forget the fashionable indelicacies of their own day in denouncing what they consider the gross monstrosities of ours. I confess I would as soon think of appearing on the streets in my chemise as in the costume of my grandmother's portrait; and yet, that same old grandmother was all but ready to faint with horror the first time she beheld her degenerate offspring in a looped-up muslin skirt, with several inches of embroidered petticoat displayed below. No fashion that has appeared within the last ten years seems to have scandalized the gossips of country towns so deeply as that very petty and convenient style of looping up dress skirts, which

---

[2] This alludes to Elzey Hay's article, "Paper-Collar Gentility," first reprinted by Ida Raymond in *Southland Writers* (1872) and from there republished in Rushing, ed., *Journal of a Georgia Woman*, 104–106.

immediately preceded the introduction of our modern walking dresses. I once saw two old women grow quite hysterical over the very moderate display of white muslin made by a young lady who happened to be walking in front of them—their offended modesty taking no account of the two pair of stout ankles which were visible beneath their own short and narrow gown of modest grey. Why the display of a little strip of embroidered muslin should have been considered more vulgar than an equal breadth of foot and ankle, I am at a loss to conceive. Neither seems open to very serious objections on the score of delicacy; but as to grace and beauty, the petticoats—save in a few exceptional cases— have the best of it. Prudes of all ages seem to be peculiarly sensitive on the subject of petticoats, though these last really are the most harmless and inoffensive of garments, except in dusty streets, where they have a bad habit of getting soiled. As to "tilting" hoops, extreme low dressing false *ventres*, and all other actual indelicacies, I must confess myself wholly on the side of the prudes; nor do I think such modes at all justifiable on the ground that worse things have been approved and practiced before. One excuse, perhaps, and that a very lame one, might be urged in palliation of the fashionable indelicacy of any existing period—namely: that so long as it is generally practicable, custom takes off the edge of it somewhat, and the world looks upon it as a matter of course; so that in following or submitting to its whims, a woman is not so conspicuously or flagrantly indecent as if she were to adopt some peculiar or unsanctioned indelicacy.

If the censors of fashion would confine their strictures to what is essentially immodest or indelicate, no one would have just cause of complaint against them; but most prudes have a way of confounding innocent absurdities with indecencies, for no better reason than because both happen to be in vogue at the same time. When "tilting" hoops and mammoth "waterfalls" were in their prime, the "nice young men" of a little town out West met in solemn conclave and resolved that they would not bestow their valuable attentions upon any young lady who patronized the obnoxious modes. On what grounds the "waterfall" was classed as an indelicacy, even the most impure imagination would be at a loss to conceive. If a lady should choose to wear a cotton bale at the back of her head, there would be no immodesty in the act; and though the huge masses of false hair that some of us used to fasten there might have been almost as burdensome as carrying a cotton bale, they were quite as inoffensive to decency. When men undertake to meddle with the fashions, they are very apt to do something foolish. Dress is as much out of their province as trade and politics are out of ours, and we resent their interference as bitterly as they would resent our meddling with prices current or election returns. Men have nothing to do with our clothes, except to pay for them—and admire them, if they choose; but as to fault-finding, we will have none of that. Half the men in the world don't know silk velvet from thread cambric, nor wine-color from drab; and I am not sure that anybody would respect them the more for it if they did. Men ought to know just enough about the fashions to tell whether a woman is well or ill-dressed, without knowing what makes her so. Less knowledge on their part would destroy the pleasure of dressing for their appreciation—more would betray a contemptible interest in trifles.

With regard to the mere eccentricities, or absurdities, if you will, of fashion, it is unreasonable to carp at them on any account, because, being mere matters of caprice, they are not amenable to the judgment of reason, or even of taste. The most that can be said for any fashion is, that it is *the fashion* and against this decision, judgment, taste, reason, may contend in vain. We of the present day have no more right to sneer at the towering head-gear of our ancestresses than have modern old ladies to make war on our little bonnets, for it is more than probable that, if we live long enough, most of us will wear structures similar to those on the heads of old portraits, and not only wear them, but think them beautiful. Even caprice is not inexhaustible, and fashion must often repeat itself. Every mode is approved and admired in its day, else it would not be the mode, and as fashion is confessedly governed by the most arbitrary caprice, there is no reason for one generation to suppose that it can boast any superiority over another in the aesthetics of dress. It is natural, I suppose, that every woman should feel a partiality for the fashions of her youth, because, as she of course looked her best then, she will readily be led to conclude that the style of dress then worn was more tasteful and becoming than any she may have adopted since. For a like reason, any style that we have been accustomed to see in fine old pictures, will, if revived in the dress of any period, naturally recommend itself to the taste of cultivated people. The magic touch of art can beautify almost anything, and the author of "Georgia Scenes," after declaring that somebody was "as pretty as a lady in a picture," thought farther praises superfluous.[3]

But there is one point, besides immodesty, at which toleration for the eccentricities of fashion ought to cease: I mean when they trespass beyond their legitimate sphere of dress, and undertake to prescribe models of shape or color to the human face and form, in defiance of One who has declared, "Thou canst not make one hair white or black." God has made our bodies as He would have them, and any attempt to alter His work will, sooner, or later, be punished with pain and disease. The manner of coveting them has been left entirely to us, and we are at liberty to exercise our taste, skill, or caprice upon our clothes. Fashion may punish rebels against her legitimate authority by causing them to appear awkward and uncouth, but she has not the same means of establishing the empire which she sometimes attempts to usurp. A woman may appear odd, or even ridiculous, for declining to adopt any very prevalent style of dress, but she will never suffer, even that far, for refusing to distort her body in deference to some passing freak of the day. In the highest triumph of blondes, a well dressed brunette will never seem old or out of fashion simply for having black hair and eyes, nor during the reign of tight corsets will one be disagreeably conspicuous because she has not the figure of a wasp. I do not pretend to say that excessive corpulence is not conspicuously ungraceful, as is a long nose, a big mouth, or any other personal misfortune, but these things

---

[3] Reference is made to Augustus Baldwin Longstreet (1790–1870), attorney, Methodist minister, and writer, whose *Georgia Scenes* (1835) places him among the best humorists of the Old Southwest (Young et al., eds., *Literature of the South*, 362–63).

are beyond the reach of fashion, and she has no remedy for them. It is true, fashion often runs in the direction of the personal peculiarities of its leaders, but if those peculiarities happen to be deformities, they can never become so much the mode that one will look odd for not aping them to the utmost extreme. A leader of fashion will of course introduce styles to set off her own especial graces, or to conceal her defects, and of course such graces immediately become particularly in vogue, and even defects may become fashionable by the means taken to conceal them. Let the Empress of France show a slight tendency towards *embonpoint*, and obsequious Madame la Mode will set all womankind to inflating themselves with bustles, pads, and heaven only knows what, and then plump beauties and low dresses have their day. An imperial tendency in the opposite direction will find Fashion lacing and squeezing her subjects into the smallest possible compass, and then corset-makers, undertakers, and lean women have their day. Queen Victoria's thick ankles put all womankind into long trailing skirts, while an ominous widening of the part in Eugenie's hair made it necessary for her loyal subjects to build towers of puffs, flowers, and false curls on top of their heads, as though they, too, had symptoms of baldness to conceal. The sterner sex are not independent of similar caprices of *physique* and fashion. A bow-legged potentate may keep all mankind in full trousers for half a generation, and the memory of a hump-shouldered king lived long after him in the full curling wigs which adorned the heads of nobles and dandies in the last century. A good story to the same moral occurs in an old fairy book. A certain king had offended a wicked fairy, who, in revenge, declared that his wife should bear a son with a nose as long as his father's foot. The king died before his son was born; so the youngster came into the world a reigning monarch. As soon as the size of his proboscis became known at court, fashionable mothers set to work upon the noses of their offspring, pulling and doctoring, in the hope of enlarging them, until the *Balzeans* and *Rachelles* of those days invented the convenience of gigantic false noses, which could be adjusted as easily as a modern calf or *chignon*.

Long noses became as fashionable throughout the young sovereign's dominions as are deformed feet among Chinese women, and thus was fulfilled the prediction of a friendly fairy, who, unable to break the spell of the malicious enchantress, had counteracted it by declaring that the long-nosed prince should never be conscious of his deformity, nor wish it otherwise.

What kings, queens, and court celebrities do for fashions in general, minor personages accomplish on a smaller scale. Every little town has some local fashion which may be referred to its own special leader of the modes. I remember one instance in which a peculiar, and by no means graceful, hitch, on the part of an affected beauty, set all the young misses within her sphere of influence to wriggling and twisting themselves as if they had St. Vitus' dance; and every country milliner knows that the bonnet of the village belle is the model that she will have to work by for all other young ladies in the community. The whimsical, and sometimes undignified, origin of fashions is frequently brought by critics in charge against them, and it must be granted, by her warmest adherents, that Madame la Mode is something of a toady. Fashion is truly the servant of great people, and the mistress of small ones. She will follow rank and opulence through every turn of human caprice, while obscurity and insignificance are left to follow her best they may. If this difference between the leaders and followers of fashion were always taken into consideration, perhaps there would not be so many satirical remarks directed against the former. Fashion belongs legitimately to the sphere of those who have the power to direct, or at least the means to follow, and if others choose to take her yoke upon themselves, they have no right to complain of her as an arbitrary or tyrannical mistress.

Modern Essayists and Periodical Literature[1]

There is a certain class of sayings which every generation likes to repeat for itself. No matter how often or how well they may have been said before, we must say them over for ourselves in our own fashion. Even what Addison and Steele wrote for their generation was not stated so entirely to the satisfaction of a later period that it could dispense with its Charles Lambs and Sidney Smiths, while the place of these last is supplied in one day by the Saturday Review and its contemporaries. The class of sayings to which I refer comprises those light reflections upon the morals, manners and events of the day which express the sentiments of the existing generation, but fail to comprehend the changing views of a new era. There was a time when not to have read the "Spectator" through and through, page by page, was considered as unpardonable a piece of ignorance as it would be in our day to have a volume of Dickens unexplored, but now the sayings of Sir Roger de Coverley and his companions are familiar only to the comparative few who delight in the classics of English literature. The inimitable Elia, whose essays such an immaculate judge as Dickens has pronounced the very best ever written, is hardly so generally read at present as our living contemporary, the humorous "country parson," or that more sparkling essayist, whose writings charm all England, in the Saturday Review. There is a fashion in literature as well as in dress, and the style of novelists and essayists undergoes as many changes as the cut of our coats, or the shape of our boots. A Homer or Milton may be produced but once or twice in a nation's lifetime, but each generation must make its own essayists, just as it makes its own fashions, its own manners, its own history.

There is scarcely any class of literary compositions in which great originality of thought is less to be expected than in light essays. It is impossible that subjects which each generation has discussed in its own

[1] *Scott's Monthly Magazine* 6/4 (October 1868): 674–79.

way should be very new or striking in themselves, and hence an author's manner of treating them must be both, in order to justify him in repeating what has been said, or nearly said, before. It is often argued, by a certain class of critics, that there has been nothing really new or original in literature for several generations, because, they maintain, the fund of human thought has been pretty well exhausted, so that modern writers of all classes merely repeat, in different language, what has already been said by their predecessors. While I am by no means disposed to admit this assertion, with regard to the great mass of literary productions, it can hardly be denied, altogether, of the class of writings now under consideration. Essayists are so numerous that it is almost impossible for an author to hit upon a subject which has not been treated, in some way or other, by his predecessors, or even by his contemporaries. Not long ago, in looking over several different periodicals, I found in one an article on "Women's Heroines"; in another a piece headed "Novel Writing as a Modern Accomplishment;" a third discoursed on "Murderous Novels," and a fourth on "The Ending of Novels." From the similarity of titles, one might have expected a tedious repetition of the same ideas, but such was not the case at all. Each writer seemed to have observed his subject from a different point of view, and each had, if not something new to say, at least some new way of saying it, which made as pleasing a variety for the reader as if the most diverse subjects had been chosen. Light essays, dealing as they do with the little everyday occurrences of life, and never wandering into the untrodden paths of speculative reflection, are made up, for the most part, of things which all of us have thought, or opinions that we have entertained, but which we have never been able to express for ourselves half so well as the essayist has said them for us. We have not, all of us, the happy faculty of giving expression to all of our thoughts, so as to make them enter into and appreciate them as we do, and we are much obliged to anybody else who will take the trouble for us. Nothing is more pleasing than to find a cherished opinion of our own pithily expressed for us in print. It gives a sense of sympathy and appreciation, added to the pleasure of an agreeable surprise. Hence, perhaps, the less original an essay may be as to matter the better, provided this deficiency be supplied by the greater originality and vivacity of style. Style is the dress in which other writings are clothed, but it is the life and soul of a light essay. "Elia" would be positively unreadable in the style of "Rasselas," and the "Autocrat of the Breakfast Table" would have perished with his first utterance had it been clothed in the language of "Edward's Sermons."

The style most in vogue with essayists and readers of the present day is a very easy, familiar one, not unlike the tone of conversation among fast young men in club rooms, and entirely different from the stately diction which was formerly thought necessary to sustain the dignity of written productions. The general tendency of our age is to throw off everything like useless restraint and formality in social relations, and a corresponding relaxation has naturally taken place in the light literature of the day. This class of writings, we know, always takes a tinge from the prevailing tone of social converse, which happens at present to be a remarkably free and easy one. A certain kind of genteel slang flourishes in the very best drawing rooms, and modern young ladies of fashion will speak of a faded belle as "played out," or advise the author of an awkward remark to "dry up" with a boldness that would have made the very hairs of their grandmothers stand on end. But there is hardly a greater difference between the careless *badinage* of a modern flirt and the stately dignity of her great-grandmother than one finds between the chaste purity of the Spectator and the brilliant flippancy of a recent essay. There is not a periodical of the day, from Blackwood's Magazine and the Saturday Review down to the lowest penny newspaper, in which this tendency towards the unrestrained freedom of colloquial language is not apparent. It may be objected by some that the periodical literature of the day is the very last standard to which we should refer for models of modern English composition. With regard to the great mass of inferior publications this is undoubtedly true, but it is not to these that I allude. There is a class of periodicals in England, such as Blackwood's Magazine and the great Reviews, which are just models of English style, as well as faithful exponents of English opinion. Papers which have numbered among their contributors the greatest names in literature, and which are now adorned by the genius of the greatest living writers, may reasonably be consulted as standards of the literary taste and culture of our generation. The best of our light literature generally appears first in Magazines and Reviews, and essayists, especially, seem to prefer this mode of laying their productions before the public. It would be hard to name a single production of essays worthy of notice that have not graced the pages of some Magazine before enriching the shelves of our libraries in book form. Some of the finest specimens of colloquial English ever put upon paper are now appearing weekly in the Saturday Review, while the humorous "A. R. H. B." charms all readers through the pages of Frazer's Magazine. It is, therefore, to the first-class periodicals of our day, and to the books recently collected from them that we are to look for characteristics of the prevailing style of essay writing.

A student of contemporary literature cannot fail to have noticed the unreserved colloquial style which marks the popular essays, and even the more ambitious productions of the last ten years. The more nearly writing can be made to resemble talk—and very free and easy talk at that—the better it is liked. In reading an essay from the Saturday Review, the Cornhill, or Blackwood's Magazine, you can almost fancy your author reclining luxuriously on the damask sofa of some fashionable club room, carelessly throwing out his brilliant observations on matters and things in general, while twisting the corners of a black moustache, between puffings of a fragrant Havana. There is something a little *fast*, so to speak, about the style of a modern essay, which brings to the mind other visions than moldy garrets in Grub street. If you think of your author at all, it is rather as a careless lounger in coffee houses, than as a poor wearied hack, stealing time from night to buy his daily bread. He is *au fait* in all the fashionable slang of the day, and sometimes makes very free use of his knowledge, as any one may observe who will take the trouble to read ten pages in the first Magazine that falls into his hands. He talks about the ways of the world with the air of a man who knows, and his allusions to the customs and manners of fashionable life are never at fault. This is partly owing to the improved condition of authors, whose liberal pay, together with the high estimation in which literary pursuits are held by the modern public, not only opens the door of good society to them, but gives them a commanding position there, and partly to the general tendency of the age, as already noticed, in which the style of popular composition keeps pace with the tone of manners and conversation. Authors, mingling more in fashionable society than formerly, their writings are naturally more affected by the influences at work there. In this connection we must not overlook the influence of the daily press, which affects the style of our higher periodical literature even more extensively than the general tone of society. Newspaper articles are generally dashed off in a hurry by men who have no time to study their words, and are filled with popular slang, to suit the popular taste, which they are intended to gratify. Now, though newspaper slang is by no means to be commended, and the style of our daily press is a model more to be avoided than imitated, yet they exert an indirect influence upon the higher literature of the day, by familiarizing us with the sight of all sorts of dubious expressions in print, thus leading authors unconsciously to be less fastidious in their choice of words.

Essays, being a very humble, unpretending kind of literary composition, have always admitted of a more familiar and conversational style than any other class of writings, but it is only the most recent essayists who have succeeded in actually talking to you on paper. The humorous pathos of Sterne, the brilliant satire of Swift, and even the beautiful simplicity of Goldsmith, never make you forget that your author is writing—not talking to you. Our immediate predecessors, in the earlier half of the present century, which may be styled the golden age of essay writing, show very obvious signs of a tendency towards the present fashion of admitting into their literary compositions what a martinet in criticism would perhaps consider very questionable colloquialisms. Charles Lamb speaks of a man's taking down his enthusiasm "a *peg* or two," while Macauley did not think it beneath the dignity of history to talk about getting things into a *jangle.* Fortunately, such expressions were used with great caution, and always italicized, or surrounded with quotation marks, to show that they were not exactly the thing! But now the Saturday Review, without note of apology, or hesitation, coolly makes use of such phrases as "not a bad thing to take," "those *confounded* tunes," "making a *row*," &c., while the St. James Magazine descends to more local slang, and tells that on a certain occasion "even the ladies were prevailed upon *to take a smile*." Critically speaking, such expressions cannot be considered very elegant or refined, but whatever they may detract from the chasteness of a composition is gained in force and sprightliness, when they are judiciously used. The best writers know how to acquire this vivacity of expression without the sacrifice of other excellences; as, for example, in the passage already noticed from the Saturday Review, where there is no outward and visible sign to that effect, you are really made to feel that the somewhat dubious colloquialisms are nothing more than quotations from the lips of those about whom the author is writing. The expression *making a row* is used by a writer on "Old-fashioned Sins," who, after alluding to the feudal practice of shutting up offenders to starve in dungeons, tells us that in our day one country gentleman will not shut up another in his coal cellars, "because the papers would make *a row* about it." Our essayist knew that country gentleman who should feel any inclination to shut his neighbor up in a coal cellar would be very apt to characterize any notice the newspapers might take of such proceeding as a *row*, and by a happy use of the same expression he describes, in a single word, the class of men to whom he refers, and thus, by the judicious adoption of a popular phrase, acquires a vivacity of expression for which he might have ransacked Roget and Worcester in vain. In another article, after noticing the various annoyances to which one may be subjected by a tiresome or uncongenial traveling companion, our author supposes, for example, a turn for whistling in one's comrade, and tells us that "whistling, we soon perceive, is only the first item in a chapter of atrocities which we might never, perhaps, have thought of observing if it had not been for those *confounded* tunes which have wearied our patient souls." Now, we all know that *confounded* is not exactly the most refined and delicate expletive that could be put upon paper, yet it is precisely the one which an impatient young tourist, exasperated by the incessant whistling of a troublesome companion, would apply to his tunes. Men who have means and leisure to make the tour of Europe are apt to be petted favorites of fortune, impatient of the least annoyance, and our author, imagining himself for the moment to be one of this class, works himself into a fume against whistlers, and vents himself in the language of an imaginary tourist against an imaginary bore. An essayist, as well as a novelist, must make his characters talk in their own language, and his composition loses nothing in polish or refinement by what may fall from the lips of a testy country 'squire, or an irascible young man of fashion. There is a vein of waggery about some of these expressions, which renders them highly effective in humorous compositions, and a writer has often more to gain by wandering from the beaten path of established usage than by a rigid adherence to what are called the best models. A clever young author in my own State, whose talents are far too little known or appreciated, even by his own people, trespasses, with fine effect, against a certain rule in Murray's Grammar by building up a climax somewhat after this fashion: "No home, no friend, no money, no credit, *no nothing.*" Take away that ungrammatical little *no* and the whole climax falls flat as a sand bank, and all force of expression is lost.

The best writers always adapt their style to their subject, and the figures, comparisons and allusions commonly used in light essays are of a plain, familiar nature, whose homeliness a snobbish critic would be apt to mistake for, and a coarse one to confound with, vulgarity. And yet it really requires greater refinement of mind to write or talk in the free and easy style of modern essayists, without overstepping the delicate line between homeliness and vulgarity, than to employ always that prim stateliness of diction in use among the female writers of the last century. It would be more feasible for a low-minded person to write in the style of Miss Augusta Evans's novels than in that of the Saturday Review essays, because the distinction is more strongly marked between stiffness and vulgarity than between ease and vulgarity. There are some people who seem to think that the language of composition must be as distinct as possible from that of conversation, and they always write in a stilted, inflated manner. I have known some who stood in such awe of ink and paper that they could not even read aloud in a natural tone of voice, and many who talk delightfully become stiff and constrained in writing, from their exaggerated ideas of the dignity of the pen. Some of the very best talkers I have ever known wrote the poorest letters. As a case in point, I remember once hearing a clever woman give a very spirited account of a discussion she had overheard between a distinguished judge and a pert young political aspirant, in which she spoke of the former as having "put an extinguisher" on his antagonist. Not long after a common friend read me part of a letter, in which the same lady had undertaken to describe the same occurrence, and the judge's extinguisher on the pert young man dwindled away into his having "very effectually silenced Mr. _____ in his animadversions upon the President's policy."

It is not in the society of the learned that the best specimens of conversational English are always to be found; but perhaps the purest and most idiomatic—certainly the most forcible—language is that spoken by plain people, who are more intent upon expressing their thoughts than upon making sonorous periods. The figurative and colloquial expressions that we see in modern essays are often picked up from the social converse of coffee houses, street corners, and other places of public resort, where, in the unrestrained freedom of common conversation, men are apt to use whatever language best conveys their meaning, without stopping to clothe it in fine-sounding words. The love of big words is a very bad symptom in any literary production, and one which men who have big ideas are not apt to exhibit. I once knew a sensible woman, who, in writing to a gentleman with whom she was but slightly acquainted, let slip the phrase, "I could not get rid of the idea." Immediately it occurred to her that "could not divest myself of," &c., was a more elegant expression than the other, but then she said: "I remembered that I was writing to a man of sense, and so concluded not to alter the sentence. If I had been writing to a fool I would have substituted 'divest myself of' for 'get rid of.'" As a general rule, whenever a little word will express your meaning as well as a big one, give it the preference. The main object of every writer is, or should be, to express his ideas in the most vivid, forcible and telling manner, and this can best be done in the everyday language of conversation, to which people are accustomed. The popular slang of conversation is, of course, as much to be avoided as the stiffness of pedantry, and a writer must have the nice discrimination of a Saturday Reviewer to adopt only such expressions as are forcible or witty, and leave every taint of vulgarity behind him.

In deciding when a dubious expression may be admissible in print one must be sure that it really expresses one's meaning better than any well established phrase, and that there are no good reasons why it should not finally be adopted into the language as good English. There is one vulgar Americanism—*skedaddle*, for instance—which really has no meaning, and will never be seen in print, outside the columns of a daily newspaper, nor heard, except ironically, in good society. It is not only vulgar, but useless and impertinent, because there are a dozen other expressions, established by good usage, which declare more forcibly the meaning it is intended to convey. All such expressions are properly termed slang. They are born and die on a day, and however popular they may be in bar rooms and at street corners, are always impertinent and out of place in print. It would be unpardonable in a writer to talk about *skedaddling* when there are such expressions at his command as "decamp," "make tracks," "to be sent packing," "to be sent about one's business," &c. Each of these phrases contain, besides a certain amount of waggery of expression, a sort of figurative allusion, which renders them highly effective when properly used. A suggestive figure, or a covert allusion always adds greatly to the vivacity of a sentence, and hence their popularity in the current literature, as well as the current talk of the day. Many expressions which pass for *slang* among prudish critics are really nothing more than homely figures of speech. In using any of these popular figures a writer's only care need be to avoid such as are based on coarse and vulgar allusions. There is a great diversity in this respect among the various words and phrases that we see going the rounds of the newspapers. Let us take, for example, that very expressive phrase "played out," which nine critics out of ten would condemn as slang, but which is really nothing more nor less than a figurative employment of a term which is constantly heard at card tables, even in the most respectable homes. There is surely nothing low or vulgar in the idea of a quartette of respectable old people enjoying a quiet game of whist, and the parson of the parish might, with perfect propriety, say to the 'squire that clubs, spades, hearts, or diamonds were "played out." There being nothing essentially coarse in the allusion, "played out" cannot properly be called a *vulgar* expression, however *popular* it may be. As further illustration of the difference between popularity and vulgarity, we may take the phrase "up to the scratch," often seen in public prints and heard in public places. Now, scratching, however necessary it may sometimes be to bodily comfort, is an operation which most of us like to perform in private, and one which is under no circumstances, very much in vogue among people who pay proper attention to personal cleanliness. Hence, I think, we must consider "up to the scratch" an essentially vulgar phrase, and, like most vulgar phrases, it is also an impertinent one, for "up to the mark," or "pass muster" express more happily the meaning it is intended to convey. We shall always find that any low, slang phrase may be dispensed with advantageously for some unobjectionable word or expression.

A striking characteristic of our contemporary essayists—indeed, of modern writers in general—is the highly figurative style which they employ, though their figures are usually of so homely and figurative a nature as to cheat one with the belief that he is reading a most literal, matter-of-fact composition. The Saturday Review begins an essay which has been republished by half the periodicals in America, with the remark that "as long as literature was more or less a man's vocation,....a successful novelist would as soon have thought of flying as of *driving a team of ugly heroines through three volumes*," and the same article is closed with the expression of a hope (in which all good people devoutly concur) that "injured wives and glorified governesses will, in the long run, *take the wind out of the sails* of the glorified adulteresses and murderesses which at present seem the latest and most successful efforts of feminine art." Carlyle, the most original writer of the day, both as to matter and manner, must be considered the father of this style of writing. His works are as figurative as an Easter poem, and hence they are not appreciated by unimaginative people. For the same reason, an imitator of Carlyle is apt to make a failure. In order to employ this style with success a writer must be able to choose his own figures, and see the force of them for himself—a power which implies a greater degree of originality than is often possessed by mere imitators. Writers on trivial or familiar topics should always be modest, often homely, in their use of figurative expressions. Our practical age and race have little patience with empty flourishes of rhetoric, and to please their sober taste a figure must be so expressive as to justify its use—so appropriate and suggestive as scarcely to seem a figure. English readers are more intolerant of bombast than of almost any other affectation of which a writer can be guilty, and a caterer to their fastidious taste must be equally careful to avoid burlesquing his subject by grandiose figures, or debasing it by low ones. When Carlyle finds it necessary to speak of a petty national quarrel, he satisfies his imagination with a homely allusion to the guttering noise of a dirty candle, and tells us that at such a time "there was a little *sputter* of war between Spain and Austria." It is only where he would describe some mighty convulsion like the French Revolution, or the wars of Frederick the Great, that he seeks for his figures in the roaring of tempests and heaving of earthquakes.

Professions and Employments Open to Women[1]

The world acknowledges but one vocation for women. Taste, talent or necessity may often lead them into other pursuits, but they are felt to be out of their natural sphere when engaged in other business than the rearing of children and fulfillment of household duties. I do not, of course, mean to assert that the world actually discountenances the efforts of a woman to live by her own exertions in any honest calling which she may find it necessary to pursue; yet, there is an instinctive feeling that she is out of her natural element the moment she steps—whether by choice or necessity—beyond the sacred circle of home duties. She is felt to be a sort of outsider, placed beyond the pale of that tender, protecting care which shields her more favored sisters from rude collision with the world, and society feels that it has an equal right to pity her and condemn her husband. It is to be observed that the world usually takes it for granted that some man is to blame for every necessity which compels a woman to take up a profession and go to work on her own responsibility, and her husband or nearest male relations are sure to be made the scapegoat. Why don't Mr. A. take care of her? Isn't Mr. B. rich enough to help his cousin? I should think Mr. C. might give her a home. How can Mr. D. let his own niece go knocking about the world in that fashion, and he living in a great big house with only a wife and six children to support? Such are the comments of society upon every accession from its ranks to the band of professional women, and the fear of its idle criticism, no doubt, influences many a worthy man to forego the assistance he might receive from his wife and daughters, and makes many a timid woman hesitate to engage in an honest profession, lest her husband's character and reputation should suffer more than his finances would be benefited by her exertions. Many a poor wife will wear her life away in all kinds of domestic drudgery, when she might, by the lighter labor of giving music lessons, or

---

[1] *Scott's Monthly Magazine* 7/1 (January 1869): 52–60.

coloring photographs, find means to relieve herself of harder work, and add greatly to the comfort of her household besides. Public opinion is always hard upon men who receive pecuniary assistance through the efforts of their wives or daughters, and the entrance of a woman upon any field of labor, outside of home duties, is usually the signal for a general assault upon her nearest male relative.

"My husband would work his fingers to the bone before he'd see *me* teaching school," says Mrs. Jenkins, complacently, as she sits over her work-basket and watches a troop of children pouring through the gate of her neighbor, Mrs. Jones, who has exchanged needle and thread, patches and buttons, for the more remunerative labors of the school room. Between the destructive knees and elbows of the little Jenkinses and the refractory buttons of their papa Mrs. Jenkins probably has a much harder time of it than Mrs. Jones; yet she feels, somehow, that she occupies a position of advantage over the latter, and feels herself entitled to speak of her as "poor Mrs. Jones," with a half-pitying, half-patronizing air, as who should say "she has to work for a living. I don't; Mr. Jenkins takes better care of me than that;" and straightway all the Jenkins circle begin to think disparagingly of Jones a poor village doctor, perhaps, who has never been able to collect a cent on the numberless prescriptions made out for colic-stricken young Jenkinses.

But, after all, the prejudices of Mrs. Jenkins and her little world, however false and distorted in themselves, are the natural offshoot of a social system in which women are regarded as a sort of pet and plaything for the other sex. It is a principle of our modern civilization that women were not made for hand to hand conflict with the world, but to be cherished and cared for by those who were, and when one is forced by necessity, or led by inclination, to step beyond the place reserved for her sex, it is, perhaps, not unnatural that she should be regarded as an object of pity, or a target of criticism by those who remain within its sheltered precincts.

To return to our illustration. Mrs. Jenkins does possess this advantage over Mrs. Jones, that she is accountable to nobody but her husband if the buttons are not sewed on, or the elbows are not patched, while Mrs. Jones is amenable to the public for what transpires in her school-room. Mrs. Jenkins is sheltered by her husband from open contact with the world. Mrs. Jones has to face it in person. It cannot be denied that, in direct contact with the world, women are apt to lose something of that exquisite delicacy, that soft, shrinking dependence upon others which all civilized people, but especially we of the chivalrous South, consider so essential to the perfection of female character, or if they retain it, they are always liable to be imposed upon by the selfish and wounded by the vulgar. In either case there is much to regret, for while nothing can atone for the loss of feminine graces of character and feeling, yet timidity, ignorance of the world, even their tender-heartedness, and the charming incapacity of taking care of themselves which men find so attractive in young girls—that soft, confiding truthfulness which is one of the chief graces of women, all lay them open to be swindled and preyed upon. "But," I think I hear some chivalrous reader exclaim, "these very qualities are women's best protection—her weakness is her strength." And so it would be if the world at large were a knight-errant, going about to redress the wrongs of unprotected females, but here is a long *if.* The world is a very worthy old fellow, in his way, but rather too old for sentiment. Besides, he has a large family and too much business on his hands to spend much time, thought or money in Quixotic endeavors to relieve the fair, and the daintiest woman that happens to be thrown upon his mercy must take her chances along with the roughest vagabond that crosses her path.

One great difficulty in the way of professional women arises from the nature of the employments which are considered within the legitimate scope of female efforts. Those countenanced by public opinion are never such as lead to wealth or fame—never those in which success is attended with the *eclat* that often crowns the efforts of successful men. A law student may be sustained through the weary intricacies of Blackstone by visions of judicial honors, and even the dreary pages of theological discussion may be brightened by distant glimpses of satin and lawn, but what glory is to crown the success of a milliner or schoolmistress? Bread to eat, clothes to wear, with possibly a modest competency upon which to retire in old age, with a temper soured by petty cares—this is the most a professional woman has to expect. I am aware that many fine things may be said about the sustaining power of duty, the glory of woman's influence, and all that, but the question at present is not of the feelings that ought but of those which do most naturally influence the human heart, and we all know that the prospect of honor, fame or riches will sustain our exertions more effectually than an humble desire to "do our duty in that state of life to which it has pleased God to call us." So far from encouraging ambition, however, most of the professions in which women are countenanced by public opinion are little trifling affairs, whose success will not count much one way or another. The most a woman can expect to do by her own exertions in any of the orthodox feminine vocations, such as sewing, teaching, &c., is to maintain her independence, and perhaps earn a modest competency for herself. As to social advantages, a working woman is more apt to lose than to gain by her profession. Now, I do not wish to be understood as disparaging working women or their vocations. Such a course would ill become one whose own countrywomen have given such noble proof of the grace with which genuine ladies can descend from the most exalted stations in life to work at the humblest callings; but, at the same time, no one can deny the fact that the working women of any community do not constitute the leading members of society. We may theorize as we please about the true basis of social position, and lay down most equitable rules on the subject, but we cannot make the world abide by them any more than we can alter the fact that milliners, dress-makers, school-mistresses, &c., do not, as a class, compose the aristocracy of any community. However honorably a professional woman may sustain her social position it never receives *eclat* from the profession. I grant that many a milliner may be superior to the best of her customers, that the most injured of governesses may be far more of a lady in feeling than her employers; that does not alter the fact as to their actual position in the world, which certainly is not one of advantage. At the same time, it would hardly be fair to accuse society of snubbishness because its highest honors are not generally accorded to people who have little or no time to devote to its requirements. Society is the only sphere outside of home where women are permitted to play a conspicuous part, and society requires leisure. One who is closely occupied in any kind of business has not time to visit or be visited, to entertain or be entertained, and as the highest successes of ordinary professional women are never attended with any very dazzling *eclat* to attract the public attention, it is natural that they should drop out of public society without anybody's knowing exactly why. There are certain purely masculine professions, such as the law, diplomacy, divinity, the army, &c., in which any very decided success will bring a man before the world in a blaze of glory; but the ordinary vocations of woman, standing as they often do in square opposition to mental culture, and calling for no exercise of talent, give no occasion for brilliant results. School-teaching, the most intellectual of them, and I suppose the best, as it seems to be much in favor with reduced gentlewomen, is merely a sort of mental tread-mill, and its tendency is to contract and narrow the mind, by making it travel continually the same dull road over and over again. It calls for the exercise of no higher powers than a good stock of patience and various degrees of acquired knowledge.

But the nature of women's employments is not so much a matter of regret to the generality of those who have to engage in them as the narrow range of vocations open to the sex. While millions of men are making a comfortable living out of professions that are closed to women there is scarcely one of ours which is not equally open to them. Yet, while this unequal distribution of things places the working-women at a disadvantage, the difference is more than made up to the sex at large by the fact that men have to work for us, and if they possess advantages over us they use them for our good. This much must be said for the men, not one of them in a thousand is working for himself alone. Whatever goods he acquires, a man is always ready to share with some woman—if not with a wife, then, with a mother, a sister or daughter; so that I think it fair to say that, upon an average, at least one woman profits by the exertions of every man in the world. If it is hard for us to acquire wealth or fame for ourselves, we have the compensation of knowing that all men who gain either share them with some woman, and I think there are few of us but must acknowledge that we owe more to the efforts of a husband or a father than we could have gained in a lifetime by our own exertions, if the whole range of masculine employments were open to us. The present arrangement of things, it seems to me, goes to prove not that society is ready to impose upon women, but that it expects men to provide for them. Now, though this is a very pleasant arrangement for the generality of women, it is a little hard upon those few unfortunates who happen to be left out in the cold, and have to take care of themselves. Their situation is one that society does not seem to have contemplated, and hence the hand to hand struggle of a woman with the world, will always be a very unequal, and consequently a very hard one.

There is one noble profession within the legitimate scope of female faculties, which public opinion has very unreasonably, it seems to me, closed against the better class of women: I allude to the stage. It is esteemed little short of madness, for a respectable woman to think of appearing on the boards, and many an honest man will suffer his daughter to starve on the pitiful salary of a country school mistress, or toil at the needle till her thread of life is stitched away, when as an actress, she might not only had a comparatively easy life, but won riches and renown. Even the unambitious *role* of a second or third rate actress, seems to me far preferable to the wretched existence of a needle-woman or a country school mistress; and yet I have known women that might have rivaled Rachael or Ristori, who chose to earn a miserable pittance by selling embroidery or giving music lessons, rather than submit to what they consider the degradation of displaying their genius to the world. It is strange to think what histrionic talents are sometimes buried in the earth; and stranger still, how idle prejudice can deem it a disgrace to become the living embodiment of a poet's dream, to put life and action into the divine creations of Shakespeare and Goethe, or to give vocal utterance to the heavenly strains of Donizette and Bellini—honors of which the proudest might be proud. As to the morality of the stage, it must be confessed, that has sunk extremely low in these days of *Black Crook and White Fawns*—a circumstance hardly to be wondered at, since the effect of public prejudice is to banish respectable women, and abandon the stage to such as are indifferent alike to public opinion and public decency. But that a profession whose business is to give life and reality to the conceptions of genius, is not essentially degrading in its influence, such characters as Mrs. Siddons, Mrs. Mowatt, Miss Bellamy, Garrick, Ristori and Jenny Lind, amply prove. As to the awful bugbear of appearing in public, it must be remembered that a good actress appears on the stage only in the character which she represents, and her personal life may be more retired than that of many a ball-room flirt. It is not Miss A., B. or C. who is fixing the attention of a crowded theatre, but Lady Macbeth, Juliet or *Marguerite.* Herself, is the very last person that a good actress ever presents to her audience.

It must be remembered, too, that the mere fact of appearing in public, is a very small matter; our manner of appearing there is the thing to be considered. While no one will contend that public life is the sphere of action for which women are peculiarly fitted, yet this is no argument that they should not emerge from obscurity when there are good reasons for so doing. No person whatever, man or woman, has any right to claim the attention of the world, unless he can show it something worth attending to. Publicity is a thing which must justify itself, or it becomes impertinent notoriety. Retirement is not intrinsically more proper for women than for men, but the business and pursuits of men oftener justify publicity. A mere vulgar love of notoriety is as ugly in one sex as in the other. The criminal folly of Herostratus would not have been more culpable in a woman—or, to draw an illustration from our time, the female half of a certain ridiculous couple who contrived, a few years since, to gain a transient newspaper notoriety by going up in a balloon to be married among the clouds—was not a whit more absurd than her whiskered partner. The main difference between the sexes with regard to their manner of living, is that women's employments so seldom call for the abandonment of private life, that the chances are, one is wrong in bringing herself prominently before the world, while the occupation of men place them so openly and naturally in contact with it, that the odds are small, but their position, whatever that may be, will justify itself. Yet, as I have said before, when circumstances do warrant a woman appearing conspicuously before the public, she is no more out of her proper element than one of the other sex. Mrs. Siddons was no more out of place when standing before the curtain to receive the thunders of applause which were the just meed of her glorious performances, than were Garrick and Sheridan, in a like situation. It is always the circumstances, not the mere fact of a woman's appearance before the world, that must justify or condemn her. Queen Victoria may, with perfect propriety, read a speech at the opening of Parliament, but a very different comment would be passed upon the conduct of any one of my fair countrywomen who should attempt the same at the opening of Congress. The wife of a certain gallant Confederate General, compromised nothing of feminine dignity when she rushed through the streets of Winchester, regardless of Yankee shot and shell, striving to rally her husband's flying columns,[2] but I could not

---

[2] Miss Andrews's remark about "the wife of a gallant Confederate general" refers to Fanny Rebecca Haralson, who in September 1854 wed John Brown Gordon at the age of seventeen (Ralph Lowell Eckert, *John Brown Gordon: Soldier, Southerner, American* [Baton Rouge: Louisiana State University Press, 1989], 10). During the war, Fanny kept close to her husband as he rose in rank in the Army of Northern Virginia, from captain of an infantry company to brigadier (November 1862) and major general (May 1864). As part of Jubal Early's Corps, Gordon's Division fought in the Shenandoah Valley, including the battle of Winchester, September 19, 1864, in which the Southerners were badly whipped. Fanny, staying in town, was appalled to see Early's men, including some from her husband's division, fleeing through the streets. General Gordon tells what happened:

"I saw Mrs. Gordon on the streets of Winchester, under fire, her soul aflame with patriotic ardor, appealing to retreating Confederates to halt and form a new line to resist the Union advance. She was so transported by her patriotic passion that she took no notice of the whizzing shot and shell, and seemed wholly unconscious of her great peril. And yet she will precipitately fly from a bat, and a big black bug would fill her with panic" (John B. Gordon, *Reminiscences of the Civil War* [New York: Charles Scribner's Son, 1904], 42). How Frances

say as much for any of my gentle readers who should play the same part in a street riot. Again, to multiply examples, no one feels that Queen Elizabeth transcended the bonds of womanly duty, when she rode through the British lines at Tilbury, and encouraged her troops in that admirable speech, which has never been surpassed by any patriotic oration, before or since; but it does not follow that any of my female readers would make an equally dignified appearance, if she should present herself the next time General Grant reviews his troops, and commence a patriotic address to the United Sates army.

It may be objected by some, that the example of Queen Elizabeth is very *mal a propos* to the present case, as she was a woman of strong and masculine temper; but after all, I question whether she was not more conspicuous for feminine follies than masculine vices. Her love of dress was proverbial—her coquettries unrivaled in the annals of flirtation, her vanity the plaything all around her. It is true, she was somewhat addicted to cursing and swearing, and would box the ears of offending courtiers now and then, but these practices, far from being fostered by the exalted position she occupied, seem rather to have been faults of the age in which she lived, and were restrained rather than encouraged by her public station. Had she been the daughter of a private gentleman, she would not have been able to swear at princes and cardinals, nor to box the ears of gentlemen, but she would no doubt have tried the same exploits, with double vigor, upon less illustrious victims.

Andrews/Elzey Hay knew of this incident decades before the general's autobiography appeared and could write about it in *Scott's* in January 1869 is suggested by her *War-Time Journal.* "The Gordons and Paces are here on their way home from Virginia," was Fanny's entry for May 27, 1865. Haywood, the family home at Little Washington, was always taking in visitors, family, and friends. "The general dropped in to see us," she wrote. John and Fanny Gordon stayed for two days; Miss Andrews saw them off at the depot on Monday, May 29. It is therefore likely during this time that Frances Andrews heard first-hand the story of General Gordon's wife at Winchester. Her article mentioning it for *Scott's Monthly Magazine* is arguably its first appearance in print.

What has been said about the legitimate appearance of women in public, will not, I hope, be construed into a defense of what may be termed the school of female radicalism, advocated by Mr. J. S. Mill and his followers. Because some women may, under certain extraordinary circumstances, leave the retirement which is their natural and appropriate sphere, is no reason why others should force themselves into political assemblies, join their acclamations with those of a thousand rowdies, and send their bonnets into the air along with the hats of clowns and rogues, as is the fashion with certain representatives of the modern "Woman's Rights" school. These advocates of what they term their rights, are the real authors of all women's wrongs. By their unreasonable and unwomanly conduct, they have prejudiced the world against even the legitimate appearance of woman in public, and pointed the shaft of ridicule against efforts which often merit better treatment. In contending for political rights, they would give up social privileges which are more than worth them all. It is unnecessary here to make a question of woman's capacity for the exercise of political freedom. To judge from the acts of a certain Congress, which has for a longtime presided over the destinies of a great nation, one would hardly think it possible for woman to exhibit greater incapacity for government than men sometimes do:—but that is neither here nor there—the question may be settled on more convincing grounds. Women have their own part to play in the economy of creation, for which they are especially adapted by Providence, as are the other sex for theirs, and any attempt to make them fill the place of men, would be as unreasonable as to expect a railway locomotive to do duty for an ocean steamer. The Saturday Review very justly remarks that you cannot make men of women, nor women of men, and any attempt to establish the one for the other, will end in degradation of both. The higher a woman rises in those qualities which make woman truly admirable, the further is she removed from any touch of the distinctive characteristics of the other sex, and vice versa. A masculine woman, an effeminate man, are equally terms of reproach and scorn.

But aside from these considerations, women should lose far more than they could gain by acquisition of those rights which Mr. Mill and his adherents are so eager to confer upon the sex. In our present position, we enjoy privileges and immunities that would never be accorded to demagogues and politicians. Men would never lavish those delicate attentions, those tender cares, that respect and deference which they now regard as due the very name of woman, to creatures whom they had seen strutting around the polls on election days, jostled by roughs and blackguards. It is now our privilege to take precedence over men, in all that concerns our real comfort. The best accommodations in all public places are reserved for our use; we occupy the best rooms at hotels, the best seats in theatres, the best berths on steamers. It is our privilege to sit when men have to stand, to ride when they have to walk, to stay comfortably at home when they are exposed to the hardships and dangers of war—and shall we exchange such privileges as these for the miserable right to lounge about street corners, and talk slang in bar rooms? It is our privilege to enjoy comforts which it is men's business to provide, our privilege to claim the protection of strong arms and brave hearts, where it is the duty of men to struggle and overcome. Who would forego all these for the poor right of claiming one thirty-millionth part of a share in the government of a nation—a right which the lowest blackguard among all those thirty million people possesses in an equal degree with you! a right that will not even pay a dress-maker's bill, or buy a new bonnet, and which rather lays you open to insult, than protects you from it—a right which is as often used to wrong others as to protect the possessor—a right which the best of men often scorn to assert, and which the basest hold so low that they will buy or sell it for a drink of mean whisky! No, no, give us woman's privileges, and we will do without the rights; rights which would degrade our sex, without elevating the government of our country. Whether circumstances may sometimes justify women in appearing conspicuously before the world, an ambition to figure in republican politics is not one of them. In other countries, women may be sovereigns with honor and dignity, but they cannot, without degradation, be numbered among the "sovereign people" of a republic.

There seems to be something essentially vulgarizing in the influence of republican institutions upon society, as any one must acknowledge who has observed their effect upon the manners of the ladies of our republican courts. There is something too *prononcee*, too independent, about them, to suit very refined tastes. They are not all positively coarse and unfeminine, but there is about the best of them, an excess of ease, so to speak, which is not exactly consistent with our notions of perfect feminine grace. They have the air of being used to be stared at, and not minding it—nay, some of them seem rather to like it. Now, I would have a woman, while she is perfectly easy and graceful under the ordeal of being stared at, look, at the same time, as if she would rather not be so, if she could help it. Madame de Stael has hit the right thing exactly, in describing the appearance of Corinne, when she was crowned at the capital. "Son attitude sur le char e'tait noble et modeste; on apercevait bien qu'elle e'tait contente d' etre admiree, mais un sentiment de timidite se melait a sa joie, et semblait demandee grace pour son triomphe."[3] Now, it is the want of this timidity, this "seeming to ask pardon for their triumphs," which detracts so much from the charms of the class referred to. Some of them even go beyond the mere absence of positive refinement, and acquire a sort of swaggering, demagogue manner that savors strongly of election days and country politics. If the demoralizing influence of republican politics is so perceptible upon women who are brought in contact with them only through the medium of their husbands and fathers, what might we not fear, if they should ever take an active part and appear in person on the arena of political excitement!

But to return from this digression. There is one of the higher professions which seems to be common ground between the sexes but even here, in the field of literary labor, men have decidedly the advantage.

---

[3] "Her attitude on the chariot was noble and modest; you could clearly see that she was happy to be admired, but a feeling of shyness mingled with her joy, and seemed to ask for mercy for her triumph."

To those of mediocre powers, the lower walks of literature, such as corresponding and reporting for newspapers, are open, but as women have no facilities for acquiring the information necessary for such undertakings, their literary performances must always be of an ambitious character, in which failure is certain, except to persons of real genius, though it must be confessed, that literary aspirations are by no means confined to these last. Women of the present day have a perfect mania for book writing. As an English reviewer declares, no woman seems to think her education complete, till she has sent a manuscript novel or poem to the editor of some leading periodical. The great mistake of these aspirants is, that instead of testing their powers first on a modest essay, or a simple story for children, they plunge headlong into a three volume novel, and, of course, break down at the very start. Little as ordinary readers may realize the fact, novel writing is the very highest branch of prose literature, and ranks next to dramatic and epic composition, in its demands upon the creative faculties. There is not one person in a thousand likely to succeed in such an undertaking, and, hence, the reason why so many female aspirants for literary honors make ridiculous failures, and bring contempt upon the efforts of the sex. The mere suspicion of female authorship will prejudice many people against a book, before they know anything else about it—a prejudice for which the folly of pretenders who aim at what is above their powers, must be held responsible, and which only an established reputation like that of Charlotte Bronte or the author of Adam Bede is sufficient to overcome. It is this prejudice which leads so many female authors to veil their first efforts under masculine names, as the only chance to get fair play—a practice which has the sanction of such remarkable precedents as Currer Bell, George Elliott, and George Sand.

Public opinion as to the merits of ordinary female writers, is pretty generally divided between two classes—those who take it for granted that anything penned by women is sheer nonsense, and those undiscriminating literary prigs, whose blind veneration for everything in print, leads them to entertain a mighty respect for the intellect of any country miss who has sent a copy of verses to the nearest village newspaper. Even a really clever female writer must, at certain periods of her career, run the gauntlet of both classes of critics, and before she can vindicate her claim to the respect of the one, run the risk of being made ridiculous by the exaggerated and undiscriminating applause of the other. There are some people, such as country critics and professors in female colleges, who think the mere fact of having written a book, is enough to cover its author with immortal glory—no matter whether the book be Milton's Paradise Lost, or one of Miss Braddon's novels— it is all one to them. The silent contempt of people, who won't read your productions, is really less annoying than the stupid veneration of those who, if they read, can not understand them, for the former is at least a negative and unaggressive sort of injury, while the latter becomes a positive wrong by making one seem a pretender, in spite of oneself. Suppose for instance, my fair reader, that you have induced, for some better reason than a mere desire to see your name flourishing in the papers, to write and publish a book. It may be that you are conscious of having written a very poor book—a mean story, perchance of which you are heartily ashamed, and which you were only induced to publish, because you were sorely in want of funds, and the editor of some fifth-rate magazine, with a large circulation among journeymen laborers and servant girls, offered a good prize for your performance. It may be that you are particularly anxious to keep the secret of your authorship, and to mention it in your presence is like talking of the gallows to a man whose father has been hung. The idea of having written that silly story (you have grown a good deal abler since it was published) hangs over you like a night-mare, and you are never allowed to forget it. Go wher-ever you will, you are heralded as the lady that has written a book. You are invited to visit some friends in a distant part of the country, where neither you nor your writings have ever been heard of before, and where you fondly hope to keep the latter in the background, so that you may, for once, escape the necessity of figuring as a blue-stocking. But, unluckily, some injudicious friend at home, with worse taste than intentions, happens to have an acquaintance in the place where you are going, and thinking to do you a great service, sits down and writes of your projected visit to his town, informing him, at the same time, that you are a lady of remarkable literary attainments, and once had a story published in the "Weekly Repository of Moral Reading." This person spreads what he has learned from your *maladroit ami*, and when you arrive at your destination you find yourself already known as the lady that has "written a book of not less than three hundred pages." You go to a ball the night after your arrival, and soon become uncomfortably conscious that everybody is watching you, and that some of the company are quietly expecting a little amusement at your expense. The men all stand off, afraid to approach you, thinking they would have to talk about books and metaphysics to a learned lady—and we all know that men don't go to balls to talk metaphysics, any more than ladies go there to talk to each other. You stand toying with your fan, and feel so foolish that it would be hard to make your situation more uncomfortable; yet this is done by some one in the company who pretends to a great deal of *savoir faire*, and who brings up a person with formidable red whiskers—probably the editor of the village newspaper, or president of some female college, and introduces you to him by your *nom de plume*, as the author of "Florabel, the Lost Maiden of Elfindale." Everybody looks very complacent at this stroke of policy, and feeling satisfied that the right thing has at last been done, in bringing two such congenial spirits together, you are left to the mercy of your companion, who, having posted himself for the occasion, quotes newspaper poetry and extracts from your own productions till you wish yourself a man that you might pull his nose. Finally, when he bids you good-night, as the assembly is breaking up, and you begin to hope that your troubles are over for that evening, he caps the climax of your woes by asking you, in a loud voice, so as to be overheard by everybody in the house, to write some poetry for his paper! You feel the more inclined to resent this injury, because you know it never enters his head to think of paying for your productions; he takes it for granted that the glory of appearing in the Bumpkinsville Gazette ought to be sufficient remuneration for your labors. Next day he comes to bore you for two hours, and calls again in the afternoon to take you out driving. Everybody turns to look as you pass through the village, and when you meet the sarcastic Miss MacBee, riding with the fastidious Mr. MacDee, you cannot help perceiving that they appear highly amused as they pass you, and that they are going to say something satirical as soon as you are out of sight. Even here your troubles do not end. In the next issue of the Bumpkinsville Gazette there will appear an editorial notice of the "gifted young authoress now sojourning in our city," or, worse still, in the poet's corner some doggerel lines to Miss ———, signed by the red whiskered editor's initials, and you may consider yourself happy if he does not take it into his head to make love to you.

Nor are country editors and female college professors the only persecutors you have to encounter. Some day, when you feel particularly inclined to be indolent, there comes a delegation from Miss Aspasia William's select school, to inform you that the young ladies are going to have a May party next week, and you are expected to write speeches in verse, of a hundred lines each, for the May Queen, Flora and four personified seasons. Then comes Miss Cecelia Dunn, with a request that you will write acrostics on the names of twelve favorite authors in her album. You are constantly annoyed by pert school misses for comic or sentimental compositions on subjects of their own choosing, to be read as their own productions at public examinations, while some fond mamma makes the modest request that you will teach her daughter to write poetry. In short, the annoyances entailed by a small literary reputation are incalculable, though these are counterbalanced if one succeeds in the profession by greater and equally numerous advantages.

The great beauty of anonymous writing is to protect one against bores and the other annoyances of a small reputation, till one can claim the advantages of a great one. Under all circumstances, it is wisest to feel one's ground first, before advancing boldly upon it, and for a timid or reserved person there is nothing like a pseudonym, which throws a veil over one's identity, and stands like a tower of defense to shield one's private life from the invasions of public curiosity. If by the public were meant merely that vague assembly of individuals which makes up the world at large, one would care very little about it, save in so far as one's interest was concerned in pleasing its taste, but each one of us has a little world of his own, bounded by the circle of his personal acquaintance, and it is the criticism of this public that literary novices dread. Within this circle there is always some one individual who, to young female writers in particular, is the embodiment of public opinion. One could not write a line without wondering what this person would think of it, if the blessed anonymous did not come to one's aid. Safe behind this shield the most timid writer may express himself with boldness and independence. This I take to be the only legitimate use of anonymous writing. An honorable man or woman will never use a fictitious name as a mask for the utterance of things to which he ought to be either afraid or ashamed to fix his own.

Though there are trials and difficulties attending even the most honorable professions in which women can engage, this is no argument against their entering the lists with resolution and perseverance, when occasion demands it. Home and society are the legitimate and natural spheres of woman, but where fate has denied one the cherished privilege of being taken care of the next best thing she can do is to take care of herself. We have all known women who, without a stiver of their own in the world, continued somehow, by dint of sponging and a certain sort of graceful imposition upon their friends, to fare as well as the richest and grandest in the land. No one can tell how they manage it, but, like the lilies of the field, they toil not, neither do they spin, yet Solomon, in all his glory, was not arrayed like one of these. And the very women who lead this sort of existence are the ones that feel most complacently the superiority of their position in society over that of their less fortunate sisters who have to work for a living, while, in reality, they are far less respectable than the honest servant girl, who eats her brown bread and owes no man a "thank 'ee" for it. The most despised profession in which a woman can engage, if it be but that of a kitchen scullion, is more respectable by far than a position of cringing dependence, or even a magnificent sponging upon those to whose protection she has no special claim. Independence is not particularly to be desired for a woman, if she has those to whom she can legitimately look for support and protection; but even then it is often better to help by a little honest labor for one's own than to hang a dead weight upon the hands of an aged father or an invalid husband, and lead a starvling, beggarly life at home, for the poor grandeur of not having it said that one is obliged to work for a living.

The Art of Lying[1]

A certain French writer reflects with admiration upon the ease with which a well bred woman can tell a lie. Without endorsing his approval of glib mendacity, it must be admitted that the art of lying has been carried to a high state of perfection among men and women of the world, who often practice it so skilfully as scarcely to be conscious of their own prevarications. A successful lie must, of course, be an unde-tected one, and should not be called by ugly names; hence, in fashion-able circles, where the ninth commandment is avowedly not always interpreted with Quakerish fidelity, the breach of it is veiled under the softer names of tact and *diplomacie.* To give his due to a certain per-sonage who is popularly supposed to stand in close relationship with the whole family of lies and liars, it must be granted that well-bred falsehoods are generally prompted by, or at worst, practiced in imita-tion of amiable impulses, and so far from conflicting with the com-mand about bearing false witness *against* our neighbor, their tendency seems rather to bear false witness in his favor. We have all been taught to hold, theoretically, that lying is essentially a malicious practice, whereas, it is probable that good nature and kind intentions are the parents of more falsehoods than envy, hatred and malice, all combined. One must have reached a very low state of moral turpitude before he can deliberately utter a malicious lie; but thousands who would shrink with horror from such meanness let slip little food natured fibs every day, without a scruple—the end, in their eyes, justifying the means. Yet, while there are undoubtedly more people who will prevaricate through good intentions than the opposite, it is to be feared that less amiable motives are often at the bottom of what we like to consider our tenderness for the feelings of others, and perhaps, after all, mere moral cowardice or a selfish regard for our own popularity are as com-mon incentives to social insincerity as a kindly wish to give pleasure or

---

[1] *Scott's Monthly Magazine* 7/4 (April 1869): 265–71.

avoid pain. We flatter ourselves that we are too polite or too considerate to tell the truth, when we really have not the courage to do so; and
many of us will suffer a friend to make a fool of himself rather than run
the risk of offending him by a little plain talk. Good nature may prevent us from telling a pretty girl that her love story in "The Ladies'
Own Magazine" is sad nonsense, or from informing a worthy parent
that the son who writes such pious letters from college when his funds
are low is a hopeless young scapegrace; but what is it that deters you,
my amiable reader, from giving a candid reply to the friend who asks
your opinion of a stupid essay, or a silly poem, when by doing so you
might possibly deliver him from the more pitiless candor of the publisher or the public? Is it tenderness for him, or for yourself, that
prompts you to shun the thankless task of unfavorable criticism? You
doubtless wish, for his own sake, that your friend could know the truth,
but aware, at the same time, that men are never particularly grateful to
friends who disclose unwelcome facts, you prefer that he should learn
it from somebody else, and you leave him to do so. Too wary to run
the risk of making yourself obnoxious, and unwilling, perhaps, to tell
a direct untruth, you shuffle about and evade the point by some remark
which you consider very non-committal, but which leaves your friend
under as great delusion as if you had come out at once with a good,
honest lie, and told him that his performances were superb.

The ingenuity with which falsehoods are sometimes painted over
to look like truth is one of the greatest curiosities in the art of lying.
There are many people who would be immediately shocked at the bare
idea of telling a direct lie, but from whose consciences all sense of guilt
sems to vanish if they can only manage to deceive themselves at the
same time that they are deceiving others. It is curious to observe the
pains and ingenuity which these worthies expend in doing what an old
saying, in plain but expressive language, calls "whipping the devil
round the stump." I once knew a pious mamma, who wished her
daughter to avoid receiving a certain visitor, but whose conscience
would not permit her to use the formula "not at home," till she had
first sent the young lady to walk in the garden. The same person was

once appealed to by another mamma for her opinion with regard to a marvelous daub of a painting, the work of mamma's daughter. The lady appealed to had too much taste to feel and too much conscience to express directly the admiration which mamma's complacent tone seemed to invite; but, unwilling to wound the other's feelings by showing a want of appreciation for her daughter's supposed genius, she exclaimed with an air of surprise, "Why you don't tell me, my dear Mrs. T., that this is really Lucy's work!" her manner at the same time feigning all the admiration which her lips had hesitated to utter, and thus telling as flat a lie, to all intents and purposes, as if she had spoken out at once, without circumlocution, and declared that Miss Lucy bid fair to surpass Rosa Bonheur. The latter course would seem to possess at least the merit of not deceiving yourself, which is more than can be said in favor of your little slippery evasions. If one is going to deceive it seems to me much more convenient, and not a whit more criminal, to lie it out manfully at once; your painted falsehoods amount to the same thing in the end. A painted lie is doubly false, for while it deceives as effectually as the blackest of its species, it declares itself at the same time, not to be a lie. It deceives the very people who would have the greatest horror of it, if they could see it in its true colors. Somebody has said that an evasion is the worst kind of falsehood, being a lie plus a shuffle, and he might have added that it is the most cold-blooded and deliberate, for the greatest labor and ingenuity are often requisite in order to lie against the *spirit* without contradicting the *letter* of truth. Honest people are sometimes surprised into lying by the suddenness or unexpectedness of the temptation. Some question is asked to which a candid reply might not be pleasant or proper, and having no time to patch up an evasion, they whip out an unvarnished falsehood before they know it, and then suffer agonies of remorse which would never have been felt had the lie only been plastered over with a little semblance of truth. In such cases the plain lie has at least the advantage of being detected and repented of, while a painted one might be sleeping on one's conscience forever. Hence, it is plain why only hardened consciences can digest acknowledged falsehoods, while the tenderest sensibility does not always shrink from pointed lies and evasions.

After all, I question whether there are many people, either in society or out of it, who are perfectly truthful always, and under all circumstances; nor, perhaps, is it desirable that they should be so. Your very candid people are generally very disagreeable, and always disliked, which proves that candor is not such a popular virtue as some of us like to think—when we happen to feel particularly well pleased with ourselves. It will do well enough so long as it confines itself to a candid appreciation of our merits; but the best of us do not find it so very agreeable to be reminded of our defects, which is the thing your very candid people chiefly take upon themselves to do. It is hard enough to look at one's faults, even when the knowledge of them may prove beneficial; but to be informed, gratuitously, of defects which you cannot remedy—to be told, for instance, that your nose is too long, or your hair too red, that your teeth are irregular, that your lips are too thick, that your movements are ungainly, or, worse still, to be informed that you are not so clever as you think yourself, that you made a silly speech at Mrs. A.'s dinner table yesterday, and Mrs. B. pronounced you a very dull companion for a *tete-a-tete*, that everybody was saying how ill you looked at the ball last night, and Mrs. D. thought your dancing ridiculous. All this may be perfectly true, but is neither profitable nor pleasant; and you naturally conclude that the candor which calls your attention to such facts is more the result of ill-nature than of a friendly desire to correct your faults. Truth points the weapons of malice as often as falsehood. With some people, candor is only another name for ill-nature. They love to say spiteful things, and their sincerity is rather the offspring of malice than of a disinterested love of truth. I cannot see that this world would be either the happier or the better if we were all as eager to reveal unpleasant facts as good nature and good breeding are to conceal them. It benefits no one to be informed of faults which he cannot remedy, and which may rather be ranked as infirmities or misfortunes. A dull student will learn none the faster for being assured that he is a dunce, and a plain woman will appear none the better to-morrow for being told that she is looking exceedingly ugly to-day.

It is almost as unpopular, though perhaps not so ungracious an office, to open the eyes of our friends to faults and mistakes which, if known, might be remedied. I, for one, would not be the person to tell a lady that she *rouged* too highly, or to inform a theological student that he would make a better blacksmith than clergyman, however much it might advantage him—not to mention his future parishioners—to become convinced of the fact. It is not always wise to be over-candid, even when one is so from the very best of intentions, for few people will apprehend such intentions through the disagreeable medium in which they are conveyed—the medium of our weakness and follies. There is no part of our moral nature so tender as self-love, and nowhere else does a wound smart so keenly or rankle so deep. We all like to say fine things about the noble virtue of sincerity, and most of us persuade ourselves into the comfortable belief that we are above being cajoled by the insidious arts of society; we entertain a lofty contempt for flatterers and sycophants (if they are not too sharp to appear such); we despise adulation, and hate insincerity, we the immaculate; we honor truth and candor; we love the honest man, who is not afraid to tell us of our faults, but who, with manly fidelity, points out to us, &c. This is all very well, so long as our insidious flatterer and our noble specimen of manly frankness exist only in the abstract; but just let some honest, good fellow appear in reality, and volunteer the friendly information that we made a precious fool of ourselves at Mrs. D.'s last night, or that we had better not write any more such stuff as our last article in the "Universal Review," if we have any regard for our reputation, and see if we really admire his candor more than the good taste of the gentleman who envied us our flow of spirits at Mrs. D.s last night, and entreats us to favor the public with another of those charming articles in the "Universal Review." We may talk as we please about our love of frankness and sincerity, but until we are all so perfect that truth can never offend, facts will belie our fine professions, and the peace of society will still require an occasional departure from veracity. What is it that makes John Bull so unpopular with all the rest of mankind but his blunt, unvarnished tongue, while his mealy-mouthed neighbors over the water, whose charming hypocrisy would persuade you that the most cherished wish of the nation is to give you pleasure, always send travelers home enraptured with French affability? Yes, it is pleasant to hear agreeable things, even though you labor under an uncomfortable conviction that your good sense ought to doubt their truth; it is pleasant to have a French *modiste* look admiringly into your plain face and declare that you are *ravissante* in the bonnet which she ties under your chin—*qui vous va si bien*; and though you may be turned of forty-five and conscious of appearing fully fifty, you cannot repress a slight sensation of pleasure when she asks "if madame has yet twenty-five years?" She puts you in a good humor with yourself and with her, for although she may not succeed in convincing you that what she says is true, you think it not quite impossible that she may believe it herself. In the social code rudeness is the highest of crimes. The manners of a highly convivial people like the French are influenced more by social than by moral considerations, and hence, a thorough-bred Frenchman will murder truth, and lie past all hope of redemption, rather than be guilty of what he considers a rudeness.

Without pretending to justify social hypocrisy on moral grounds, I think the most rigid moralist must grant that it arises mainly from the perversion of an amiable desire to give pleasure or avoid pain, which, though not a very lofty trait in itself, cannot, in its legitimate exercise, be deemed a very bad one. In the days of my youth I used to receive instructions from an amiable old French master, who taught at a large boarding-school in the village where my father lived. I went three times a week to recite my lessons to him, but if I happened to be a moment behind time, Monsieur would make it convenient to suppose that his pupil would not be there at all, and betake himself to a drinking saloon hard by where he would pass an hour with his toddy and tobacco much more agreeably than in poring over Ollendorff or Fasquelle. I frequently met him on his way to this favorite resort, and though I knew that he was greatly disappointed at seeing me, and he knew that I knew it, yet he always turned back towards the scene of his labors with good grace, saying, with a smile, "Ah, mon leetle friend, I just took a promenade for to meet you and carry your books for you, because I know you be fatigued from so long a walk." My childish morality may have been at fault, but I confess that I liked this much better than if he had been candid enough to scold me for coming too late, and so begun the lesson by putting both of us into a bad humor. And children are not the only people wheedled by such adroit turns of manner. Little as we may feel inclined to acknowledge the fact, it is nevertheless true that there are very few of us who do not like people the better for a little insincerity. The morality of society might be improved, but I question whether its agreeableness would, if every member of it were always, and under all circumstances, perfectly candid and straight-forward. Suppose, for instance, that nobody ever took pains to conceal chagrin at having to receive an unseasonable or a tiresome visitor—are you perfectly sure, my moral friend, that you yourself would never be made to feel unwelcome? We all have to know and visit a few tiresome or uncongenial persons, and we are all liable to stumble upon our friends at inconvenient seasons—nay, further, little as we may relish the fact, it is more than probable that we are ourselves tiresome to some one or other of our acquaintance, and might be made to feel exceedingly uncomfortable now and then, if people were always too sincere to welcome an unwelcome guest. If instead of a smiling "How do you do, Mr. A.; I am very glad to see you," there should be only a pouting "Good morning, sir," followed by a sulky silence, to every visitor who happened to be a little tedious or inopportune, how very uncomfortable many worthy people would constantly be made to feel! I have often thought it would be curious if the countenance of a well-bred woman could be photographed just before and just after passing the drawing-room door to meet an irksome or unseasonable visitor. I have seen fair ones, when roused by the door-bell from an afternoon's *siesta*, bounce from their soft couches with an exclamation of impatience, quarrel, pout and scold at imaginary bores through the various stages of a hurried toilet, grumble all the way down stairs, turn to make

a parting grimace at the parlor door, and then enter to greet the unconscious object of all these hostile demonstrations with a beaming
countenance and the most engaging suavity of manner. A philosopher
would smile at such an exhibition of human bitterness; a moralist
would make it the text of a pious disquisition on the sinfulness of human nature, while a man or woman of the world sees in it nothing but
the most simple and natural occurrence of everyday life. But for all
their assumption of superiority I cannot see that the philosopher or the
moralist would improve matters in the least by carrying their sour looks
into the drawing-room, though they might not be wrong in advising
others never to wear sour looks nor to use cross words at all—advice
which may be had by the bushel from any "Society for the Promotion
of Morality and Virtue." Even then I hardly think we would do away
with the necessity for a little make-believe, because a bore would still
be a bore, and our beaming countenance and cordial manner would
still be a lie, though we never unmasked, even in secret.

From what has just been said, we may see no grosser fallacy was
ever uttered than the old maxim which declares that politeness costs
nothing. Does it cost no effort to sit talking with a stupid visitor till
past midnight? Does it cost nothing to lay aside a pleasant book and
go shopping with a country cousin on a summer afternoon? Politeness
does often cost infinite pains, numberless sacrifices of our own tastes
and inclinations; and, more than that, it no unfrequently demands a
sacrifice of truth, or, at lease, of sincerity. If an honest divine, who happens to be a guest in your house, should ask what you thought of his
three-hour sermon on free will and predestination, could you possibly
give a reply which would be, at the same time, perfectly candid and
perfectly polite? If you are made of common flesh and blood, perfect
sincerity would probably require you to confess either that you had
slept though the worthy man's discourse, or were horribly bored at it.
But would this be polite?

Very palpable insincerity, however, cannot be either pleasing or
polite. Social falsehood must wear the garb of candor, else it fails to
answer the purposes of society, and becomes more vulgar than a

homely truth, exposed stark-naked to the eyes of those who least desire to behold her. An awkward, bungling lie has much the same effect on well-bred minds as the misplaced finery of a country belle who appears at church in a sky-blue dress and white satin slippers. The one would be polite if it could, the other would be fine, if she only knew how. A well-bred falsehood always adheres religiously to the eleventh commandment—"Thou shalt not be found out." This is especially the case when the object of the falsehood is to pay a compliment. Gross flattery is the most ill-bred thing in the world, and must be disgusting to all but obtuse or vulgar minds. There is not one of us but likes a delicate compliment, so softly insinuated as to lose the air of flattery; but to be told that you are the handsomest woman or most talented man in a ball room, and then overhear the same remark whispered by the same person to somebody else—to be told that your hostess might dispense with gas for one night, as the brilliancy of your eyes was sufficient to light her rooms; or, as I once heard a creature in paper shirt collar and yellow gloves declare, that if you were in Heaven the angels would dethrone God and worship you—what rational being can endure? The insult to one's taste and understanding implied in such fulsome stuff is more offensive to a sensible person than the flatterer would have his compliment agreeable. Flattery is an implement that must be handled with the greatest care, for while none of us are proof against the influence of an adroit compliment, there are few who will not be disgusted by an awkward one. Gross flattery, far from approaching the standard of well-bred lying, set up by our French writer, strikes one rather as the bungling work of a pretender, totally unversed in the fashionable art to which he aspires. While a delicately insinuated compliment is sure evidence of tact and good breeding, an awkward, unsuccessful effort at flattery bears on its face the marks of low breeding and a coarse mind. The only persons accustomed to society that ever condescend to gross flattery are those whose own inordinate vanity will swallow any sort, and who, in knocking you down with an overloaded compliment, are only doing as they would be done by. You may very safely take it for granted that a man who compares you to Venus will not object to being

258

told that he is himself an Apollo. Delicate flattery, even when a little transparent, may be pardoned as the result of an amiable desire to say agreeable things, and may still be very soothing to that little foible of self-love from which none of us are free; but coarse, fulsome adulation always falls wide of its mark, and disgusts by its vulgarity even more than by its palpable insincerity. Instead of awakening us to an increased appreciation of our own good qualities, it merely arouses us to a sense of the coarseness and vulgarity of him who utters it. Flattery, to be entirely successful, must hide itself under the appearance of sincerity. Hence, an implied compliment is always more grateful than one plainly spoken, and a flattering manner more insidious than fair words. It is curious to see what opposite effects the same cause can produce when acting in different degrees. How we all detest flattery, which we know to be such, and how we love to be wheedled without knowing it! Skillful flattery not only adheres quietly to the command "Thou shalt not be found out," but says to its object, "Thou shalt not find thyself out"—the chief merit of the art thus consisting in the artifice with which it is practiced.

To flatter gracefully and acceptably requires not only a nice tact but considerable knowledge of human nature, or, at least, a quick and correct perception of character. You must know a man's sensitive part before you begin to tickle him. In no respect does the much villified Earl of Chesterfield display his subtle knowledge of human nature more forcibly than in some of the advice given to his hopeful son on this subject. "Observe," says he, "and you will find, almost universally, that the least things either please or displease most, because they necessarily imply either a very strong desire of obliging, or an unpardonable indifference about it." And again, "Observe the little habits, the likings, the antipathies and the tastes of those whom you would gain, and then take care to provide them with the one and secure them against the other; give them genteelly to understand that you had observed they liked such a dish or such a room, for which reason you had prepared it; or on the contrary, having observed they had an aversion to such a dish, a dislike to such a person, &c., you had taken care to avoid presenting them." Of women, he remarks that they must generally be flattered about their persons, because beauty is the quality which they value most; but he sagaciously adds, "An undoubted, uncontested, conscious beauty is, of all women, the least sensible to flattery upon that head; she knows it is her due, and is therefore obliged to no one for giving it to her. She must be flattered upon her understanding, which, though she may probably not doubt of herself, yet she suspects that men may distrust."

I once saw the wisdom of this assertion aptly illustrated by the blunder of an amiable person who undertook to compliment two sisters—one of whom was remarkable for an uncommonly handsome face, and somewhat awkward figure, while Nature had compensated the other for a very plain face by casting the rest of her body in a faultless mould. Instead of flattering each one on the point about which she was most dubious, as the penetrating Chesterfield would have done, this maladroit person commended the pretty girl's face and the ugly one's figure, thus contriving to make each one feel uncomfortable by slighting the very point on which she would most like to be reassured. The same want of tact is apparent in the half-patronizing, half-apologetic air with which some good people flatter the intellect of plain girls. It is so much a matter-of-course to speak of women as clever, or "smart"—as our American phraseology has it—when we cannot in conscience call them handsome, that a compliment to one's intellect often amounts to nothing more than a polite apology for not passing one to her person, and as such a plain woman soon learns to receive it. If one really wishes to say agreeable things, and is afflicted with no scruples of honesty, he should flatter people upon the qualities they would like to have, rather than upon those that they really possess. It is amusing to see how well meaning people sometimes stumble in their attempts at flattery, and fall upon its opposite—like the worthy old gentleman who commended a young lady for her good sense in refusing to take the part of a peri in *tableaux vivants*, on the ground that she was not handsome enough. A lady friend of the writer's once flew equally wide of her mark in praising the good sense of a university student who had declined to publish his prize speech. When he became old enough to look upon his college boy productions as the *veal* that they really were, he no doubt appreciated the lady's compliment, but at the time it was made I dare say he would have been better pleased had she flattered his eloquence at the expense of his good sense. Perhaps the most thoroughly candid people in the world are those who are so without intending it. Kind-hearted men and women, untrained in the path of fashionable discrimination, are very apt to lose their way in the deceitful mazes, and blunder, without knowing it, into the straight but rugged track of sincerity. While their frankness does not professedly occupy itself in pulling moats out of other people's eyes, like that of your candid prig, they often make one painfully sensible of a beam which might else have been ignored. It is well, however, that honesty does sometimes find its way into places where it is least expected or desired. A little truth is essential to the health of society, and indeed, as a courtly Parisian once said to me, "It is never necessary to tell a lie, except when the truth will not answer your purpose just as well." Even Chesterfield allows that it is hard to say which is the greatest fool, he who tells the whole truth, or he who tells no truth at all. While the comfort of society may require that all its members should not, under all circumstances, be solely intent upon telling "the truth, the whole truth, and nothing but the truth," it does not therefore follow that they should always be equally intent upon telling lies, and nothing but lies.

Origin of Good Manners[1]

GOOD manners are not indigenous to human nature—a fact which the reader will readily admit when he looks back upon his own boyhood, and reflects upon the laborious process of artificial training by which the principles of decorum were drilled into him. Children are born with a natural antipathy to good-breeding, as to book learning, and boys, in well-regulated families, probably get more floggings for bad manners than for bad lessons. A boy in his raw state is the rudest thing in nature, and a girl in the same state, not much better. Did you ever dine at the same table with a large family of small children, and watch their mother during the repast? "Johnny, don't eat so fast." "Take your elbows off the table, Mary." "Don't take such big mouthfuls, Joe." "Stop smacking your lips, Julia, and take your knife out of your mouth." "You, Frank, what do you mean by dipping your own knife in the butter?—with molasses on it, too! Leave the table this minute." "And you, Jack, stop eating with your fingers." These, or such as these, are the utterances that fall from the lips of a careful mother with almost every morsel that goes into her mouth; and the little savages to whom they are addressed require the same drilling over and over again, line upon line, precept upon precept, from day to day, from year to year, till nature is overcome by habit. Where there is no one to instill the artificial principles of good breeding, the grosser propensities of nature flourish unrestrained, and the incipient savagery of childhood develops into the fearful enormities of the grown-up "hoosier," who spits tobacco-juice upon your carpet, dips his dirty fingers into the salt, and slaps his own knife into your butter-dish, first making it clean by licking off the gravy and molasses that may have stuck to the blade.

There seems to be something in the mere act of eating peculiarly favorable to the development of any latent vulgarity that people may have lurking in them. As it is the only one of our purely sensual

---

[1] *Scott's Monthly Magazine* 8/1 (July 1869): 517–20.

enjoyments which has been converted by good society into a graceful and elegant entertainment, it is necessary to regulate the etiquette of the table with scrupulous nicety, in order to draw the line as distinctly as possible between the dainty feeding of the epicure and the hungry voracity of the brute—two different phases of the self-same act. The artificial refinements attendant upon the etiquette of eating make it more difficult to teach children decent table manners than almost any other branch of good breeding; and a neglect of them is more disgusting to people of refinement than any other species of mere material rudeness, because it is so easy to make eating vulgar. An under-bred man appears worse at a well-ordered dinner-table than any other situation he can possibly be placed in, while the graceful etiquette of a fashionable dinner-party shows off the manners of a well-bred one to the very highest advantage. Now, if eating is naturally a vulgar and sensual operation—as one might justly conclude, from the manner of its performance among those whose habits of life approach nearest to a state of nature—whence arose that elaborate etiquette by means of which it has been converted into an elegant social pastime, and reduced to a state of almost artistic refinement? If it comes so natural for people to put their knives into their mouths, how did we ever learn to consider such a practice vulgar? If men in an uncultured state prefer wiping their mouths on their fists, or on their coat-sleeves, how did doileys and pocket-handkerchiefs originate? Where did good manners come from? Who first invented them? The most direct answer that suggests itself to this question is, that good breeding originates with and depends upon civilization. The latter necessarily gives rise to the former; and a people's manners, either as nations or as individuals, will always be governed, to a certain extent, by the state of civilization at which they have arrived. Before knives were invented, it could hardly have been considered vulgar to eat with one's fingers, and where silver forks are unknown, it would be very unreasonable to find fault with a man for putting his knife into his mouth. Adam and Eve are not usually regarded as essentially vulgar people, yet they never heard of a spoon or a fork; and if the forbidden fruit were really an apple—as those ancient theologians, our nurses, so confidently assert—they must have divided it in the way that schoolboys describe as "bite about by turns." While the human race was still clad in fig leaves and coats of skins, men were not ashamed to blow their noses with their fingers, or to wipe their lips on their fists; but as civilization advanced, pocket-handkerchiefs were invented; and finally, when some brilliant genius discovered that it was not exactly the thing to blow one's nose and wipe one's lips on the same cloth, napkins and doileys came into use. An artificial state of civilization necessitates an artificial state of manners, and children have to be taught the latter just as they are taught the various arts and sciences incident to the former.

But there is something more than mere external civilization concerned in the formation of good manners, as is apparent from the fact that different forms of civilization give rise to very contradictory points of etiquette. For instance, with us, it is the height of ill-breeding even to rest one's elbows on the table, or to lean back in one's chair,—while the ancient Romans always took their meals in a reclining posture. Yet there are some points of etiquette common to all nations and ages, and independent of any form of mere material civilization. For example, it has always been counted a rudeness, among civilized people of every age and nation, gratuitously to contradict another, or interrupt the thread of his discourse. Such ideas seem to go beyond mere artificial culture, and take their rise from natural instincts of decency or propriety. Civilization may invent knives and forks, and teach a man not to eat with his fingers; but his own instincts of decency—or somebody else's, if he has none of his own—must suggest the propriety of avoiding rude language and unpleasant personalities.

It seems then, though good manners are not indigenous to human nature, there are some latent germs implanted in the race, which are capable of being developed into what we term good breeding. These germs or instincts, and the courtesies that result from them, are based on the two simple feelings of consideration for self and consideration for others. All good breeding has its foundation in these two principles, and every little point of etiquette—even those which are apparently the most artificial and arbitrary—can be traced back to one or the other of them. For example, consideration for self suggests the propriety of putting a fork into one's mouth rather than risk slitting one's lips by drawing a sharp blade between them; and consideration for others would make any man of moderately delicate stomach think of a butter-knife, after eating bread and molasses with his own. Consideration for others teaches the impropriety of smacking one's lips like a pig, in eating, or sipping one's coffee with a loud, swilling noise; while consideration for self, after one's first bad cold, would naturally suggest the distinctive use of napkins and pocket-handkerchiefs. Even such trivial and seemingly arbitrary points of etiquette as taking off your glove to shake hands with a lady, or refraining from a second plate of soup at a dinner-party, are based on feelings of consideration for others. It is not to be supposed that many diners-out, with the prospect of a dozen courses before them, will feel inclined to load their stomachs at the outset with a double quantity of soup and he who keeps the rest of the company waiting, and delays the other courses while he surfeits himself with the first, interferes with the comfort of other people in the same manner, though not in so great a degree, as if he had arrived too late, and kept the dinner waiting.

I would not be understood as advocating a rigid and unconditional adherence to certain fixed rules of etiquette, always and under all circumstances. One of the best evidences of high breeding is the ability to set aside rules of etiquette with a good grace whenever occasion may require. There is a certain independence of manner—a sort of well-bred impudence, so to speak—that is peculiarly fascinating in gentlemen, when not carried too far. It is as different from anything like vulgar impudence or pertness as are the manners of Belgravia from those of Billingsgate; yet so narrow is the line which divides them, that there is often but a single step between independence and pertness. A thoroughly well-bred man is equally averse to a slavish submission to rules and a boorish disregard of them. He has confidence enough in himself to feel that he is the master, not the slave of etiquette; and can judge for himself when to obey her requirements—when to set them aside. It is this confidence in himself, tempered by a proper regard for the rights of other people, that gives the graceful ease and self-possession which are so much admired in a man or woman of thorough breeding. What we call ease of manner is wholly due to a nice balance of the two feelings of regard for self and regard for others. In order to be perfectly easy and self-possessed in any company, one must entertain a proper self-respect, tempered by a just regard for those with whom one associates. Awkwardness and *mauvais honte* result from an underestimation of self or an over-estimation of other people; while the opposite error gives rise to that vulgar ease of manner, that intense self-assertion, which are so common in Methodist preachers' and politicians' wives. The kind of self-respect that belongs to good-breeding arises not merely from a consciousness of personal merit, nor from the assumption of the vulgar republican theory that, "one man is just as good as another, and a ___ sight better, too," but from the possession of those external and acknowledged merits or advantages which assert their own rights in society. An honest tinker may possess and be conscious of as much personal merit (barring the intellect) as General Lee; yet he could never feel at ease in the society General Lee moves in— because he knows himself to be deficient in the peculiar merits, culture and refinement, which that society demands. No man can feel at ease in any society for which he has not been fitted by education and early associations. He feels that he is among his betters, and respect for others outweighs his respect for self—so that he will either suffer from *mauvaise honte*, or try to bully good breeding, like Mr. Brunderby.

It is a great mistake to assert, as some people do, that any man of correct morals and fine instincts is a *gentleman*. He may be ever so noble a *man*; but the *gentleman* is something artificial—something that requires culture and external polish, rather than innate merit. The basest rascal living may be a perfect gentleman, for all the purposes and requirements of society, if he has the training and manners that make a man agreeable in company; while the noblest specimen of humanity that ever breathed under a fustian coat is not a gentleman, in the proper acceptation of the word, if he spits tobacco-juice on the carpet or wipes his mouth on the table-cloth.

One of the greatest absurdities of modern democracy is the practice of dubbing all sorts of people as ladies and gentlemen. Your cook must be "the lady what stays in the kitchen," and your coachman "the gentleman as 'tends to the hosses." I have even heard very respectable dissenting ministers, ignoring the beautiful simplicity of our prayer-book language, make use of these much-abused terms in performing the marriage ceremony; in other words, they marry the artificial acquirements of this person to the artificial acquirements of that one— while the native man and woman are left unwedded. It can surely be no insult to the *man* to tell him that he is not a *gentleman,* for you merely assert that he does not possess certain artificial acquirements necessary to shine in a particular kind of society; and it is no special compliment to the *man* to declare that he is a gentleman, because the man is his natural self—the gentleman only the artificial part of him. The man is born,—the gentleman is made; and if General Lee himself had been bred in a baker's shop, he would not be, in the strict acceptation of the word, a gentleman. Some men cannot be made into gentlemen by any amount of training, while others possess a great natural aptitude for it; but in every case, the article is manufactured, not a natural product. It takes at least three generations' remove from a state of poverty and ignorance to make a thoroughbred gentleman. The man who works his own way to fortune or distinction has no time to spend upon those smaller refinements which make up the breeding of a society-man; and his son cannot have them in perfection, for lack of refined and elegant associations at home; so that his son's son is the nearest descendant whom the rising man can expect to make into an accomplished gentleman—except in certain cases of extraordinary aptitude. After all, it is home associations that make or mar a man's breeding, and their impress will remain upon him to the end of his days, whatever may be the associations of after life; and whatever company he may see abroad, his manners will still take a tinge from what he has been accustomed to at home.

Of the two natural instincts from which our ideas of good manners are developed, consideration for self is much more strongly marked than the other, and will generally thrive with very little cultivation. Consideration for others is weak enough in most natures, and will die out altogether, unless it is kept alive by careful training. That indescribable something which we call *tact*, and which so few possess in perfection, results from a free development and constant exercise of the principle of regard for others. True tact never does an unkind or an unpleasant thing. It is the embodiment of the golden rule, "Do unto others as you would that others should do unto you," and springs not only from the power of imagining ourselves in the situation of others, but from an amiable desire to render that situation as agreeable to them as we would like to have it for ourselves. Good breeding, in the abstract, is simply good feeling reduced to an art, and practiced till it seems a second nature. This art almost any one may acquire in some degree by proper training, but an essentially ill-natured person can never display that delicate refinement of tact which springs from an honest desire to make others comfortable. I once saw the kindness of native tact most beautifully illustrated by a young lady, who, seeing a blind man offer his hand to a person who had not observed his movement, quietly place her own soft fingers in his outstretched palm, and thus spared him an awkward reminder of his infirmity. In polite society, when the *art* of good breeding (though not always the *virtue* of good feeling) is cultivated to the highest pitch, one main object of it is to make everything work as smoothly and pleasantly a possible—to ruffle nobody's feathers, and to rub everyone's fur down the right way. It is true polite society sometimes sanctions what we may term, at the risk of seeming paradoxical, a well-bred rudeness. To utter a sarcasm or administer a rebuff gracefully, is one of the nicest achievements of social culture. The main difference between a well-bred rudeness and an ill-bred one rests on the fact that the latter is always unprovoked and aggressive, while the former is purely defensive, and is never resorted to except to resent an insult or put down an impertinence. Any gratuitous display of ill-feeling or ill-temper, any unprovoked sarcasm or ill-natured remark is a very great breach of good manners, and one who indulges in them commits social suicide. Society belongs to the gay and light-hearted, and all that is harsh or uncouth in the affairs of common life must be banished from its enchanted pale. Society was instituted for pleasure; and from its shining precincts, the sorrowful, the vexed, the disappointed, must either withdraw themselves, or banish their sorrows, their vexations, their disappointments. The same good breeding which demands the concealment of our own grievances requires us also to overlook, or appear to overlook, the foibles and infirmities of others, and to hide at least our perception of them from their own eyes. Everybody's little mistakes and failures, short-comings and over-reachings, must be covered with the mantle of social charity, and only the best side of themselves and their affairs held up for their own inspection. This amiable purpose would suggest itself, naturally enough, to amiable people; while the others, admiring their lovely conduct, or envying their popularity, would naturally take pattern after them in a course so well adapted to the ends of society; and hence, good society always keeps up the appearance, at least, of good nature. Thus, then, it seems that, after all, good manners originated first in good nature, and good-natured people were the first inventors of them.

Mercenary Matches[1]

The subject of this essay was suggested by a conversation that took place, not long ago, in the drawing-room of my friend, Colonel ____. I entered just as a very seedy-looking young man, who had once possessed great wealth, and been a dashing major in the Confederate army, was playfully lamenting that he could not fall in love with a rich young girl. At this remark, master Arthur, the colonel's eldest son, a fast young man of eighteen, looked up with the air of one who knew a thing or two, and meant to give us "old fogies" the benefit of his enlightened views.

"Well, I think," said he, with great emphasis on the *I*, "that if a *feller* is going to marry at all, it isjust as easy to fall in love with a rich woman as a poor one. I intend to marry some rich old widow, who will die soon and leave me her property. A man is a fool to marry for anything but money."

Nobody appearing very much shocked, master Arthur looked disappointed, and subsided for awhile.

"I have known young men who married old widows that were *not* rich," said Arthur's mother, who sat sewing by a window; "women old enough to be their mothers."

"You never heard of such a marriage except in the case of a college boy boarding with a widow who had no daughters, did you?" asked the major, who, by the way, was something of a wit.

We were all obliged to confess that we never had.

"Very well, then," he continued; "the thing is easily explained. Collegiate towns always abound in poor widows, who take boarders, talk scandal, and make matches for their daughters. It is a law of nature that every college-boy, at a certain stage of his existence, shall fall in love with his landlady's daughter; and if she has no daughter, what can he do but fall in love with the landlady herself? But how," he

[1] *Scott's Monthly Magazine* 8/3 (September 1869): 673–77.

continued, "can you account for such matrimonial freaks as that of the lady who ran away with her father's coachman, or the pretty heiress who fell in love with the Dutch gardener?"

"By a natural depravity of taste," said the colonel's pretty daughter, Kate, who had hitherto not taken part in the conversation. "There is no excuse for well-bred women to marry beneath themselves because the men who come in contact with them are generally in a situation to have obtained like advantages, and make suitable associates. A woman who goes so far out of her way as to fall in love with a shoemaker or a carpenter, proves that she is not worthy to move in good society."

Kate had been reading Bulwer's novels, and had very aristocratic notions.

"But suppose the shoemaker and the carpenter were really men of education and refinement, who had been forced by circumstances to engage in these humble callings?" said the major; and I thought there was something pathetic in the look that he cast at his own rusty shoes and threadbare sleeves as he spoke.

"In that case," said Kate's mother, "a prudent woman would count the cost, and decide for herself whether she would sacrifice her ease or her affections. Prudent people always have many considerations to influence them in deciding upon matrimony."

"Oh, I hate prudence," cried Kate; "it is a mean, selfish, Yankee sort of virtue, fit only for merchants and tradesmen. I am determined never to make a *prudent* marriage. I always did detest these nice, quiet, exemplary young men—these good, safe matches that papas and mammas approve of so highly."

"Brave, Miss Kate!" exclaimed the major, himself more chivalrous than prudent. "My sentiments exactly. Prudence is the daughter of Selfishness and Avarice, and her parents too often cloak themselves under her mantle. I must confess to a very small respect for all your dull, plodding, puritanical virtues—such as prudence, patience, frugality, and the like; they lean too much to error's side, and often run into their kindred vices. A frugal young man is very apt to make a stingy old one."

"Prudence," said the colonel, rousing from his after-dinner nap in the great arm-chair, "like many other good words, has been so much abused that we have almost forgotten its legitimate signification, and we suspect it of cant, just as we take a philanthropist to be a cheat and a scoundrel, or a woman with a mission to be a scolding wife and negligent mother—though prudence, philanthropy, and even missions, may all be very good things in their way."

"No, no,—I protest against *missions*, in every sense of the word," said the major. "Mr. Jellyby was right; a woman with a mission is—."

The conversation was interrupted at this point by the arrival of visitors. I went to my room, and amused myself with reflections on what I had heard; and here are my thoughts about
MERCENARY MATCHES.

There is probably no young lady, past the novel-reading, castle-building age of sixteen, who has not sometimes pictured herself the happy wife of a poor man. Visions of white-walled cottages, with latticed windows and vine-covered porch, will at times steal upon the imagination, and demolish for an instant those more ambitious structures which the fertile fancy of youth is so prone to rear. Eugenie de Guerin says in her journal: "I have never dreamed of grandchildren or of fortune, but oftentimes of a little cottage, far away from towns, very neat with its wooden furniture, its shining crockery, its trellis at the door, hens in the yard, and me there, with—I do not know who, for I would not like a peasant such as ours, who are rough, and beat their wives." We have all had our cottages, as well as our castles in the air, and have seen them, perchance, as ruthlessly overturned by the uncompromising hand of reality as Eugenie's dream of the Languedoc peasants, who "beat their wives." It is to be observed, that our dreams are always of a poetical, comfortable sort of poverty, very common in books, but not often found in real life. It is very pleasant to dream of jessamines, plenty of fresh butter, fat hens, etc.; but poverty in a miserable hovel, in sickness, dirt, and rags,—poverty with a morsel of bread, among rude men, who "beat their wives,"—this is poverty as we have it in real life; this is what our cottages in the air are so apt to become as soon as they touch the earth. Romantic young ladies are not always aware of this, and hence a world of anxiety for prudent papas and mammas.

I am afraid I incline somewhat to my friend the major's opinion of the virtue of prudence in the abstract; but you must not imagine, readers, that I am going to advocate a total disregard of it in affairs of matrimony, and treat all pecuniary considerations as too mean and prosaic to be worthy of a thought. I doubt whether there are many matches, after all, entirely unmercenary. It is true old Dame Nature will sometimes in a fit of perversity make briefless young lawyers and rattle-brained dragoons incomparably more attractive, personally, than the most exemplary young men of business; it is true the dimpled cheek and sparkling eye of a penniless beauty, or the glossy moustache and dashing ways of some incorrigible *mauvais sujet*, may often cause un-calculating young hearts to palpitate; yet wealth has its influence, too, even over innocent, unselfish minds,—and the eye must be very bright and the demeanor very enchanting which can outshine the glitter of gold. Money acts very extensively, I think, by the unconscious influence which it exercises on the imagination, like rank, fame, or any other earthly good, investing its possessors with a sort of fictitious lustre, so that rich belles and beaux really do seem more interesting than those unaided by the glitter of the precious metal. We have all seen instances of very ordinary men and women who derived a certain importance from circumstances of advantage in which they happened to be placed, so as to seem for the time as though they really possessed some inherent superiority over other people; and we feel a sort of respect for them,— we hardly know why. Wealth, like any other advantage, exerts this sort of unconscious influence, so that people are often attracted by money, without being aware of the fact, who would be thoroughly disgusted with themselves if they suspected it. We are not all such philosophers as to regard every temporal good with indifference, and the best of people are not exempt for the little hidden weaknesses of human nature. I do not wish to take a cynical view of society; but facts must speak for themselves, and we all know that, other things being equal, rich girls are much more courted in society than poor ones, and rich coxcombs are often tolerated where penniless worth would not be. The world becomes more and more luxurious every day, and the importance of money grows with the love of luxury.

The generality of people are, however, *necessarily*, more or less governed by pecuniary considerations; and, as I have said before, there are probably few marriages wholly uninfluenced by them; but we must not therefore conclude that the majority of matches are mercenary in the odious sense of the word. A man may love a woman sincerely, and yet be deterred from making proposals of marriage by the fact that his own fortune and prospects are not such as to warrant him in undertaking the support of a family, unless the woman has property of her own—in which case he may seek her hand, even when he would not otherwise have done so, without justly incurring the charge of venality. Such conduct—though our Kate might stigmatize it as *prudent*—is very different from addressing a woman merely because she has money, without being at all influenced by higher motives.

Women have even more reason for taking property into consideration than men. If a man is old enough to suit a lady of marriageable age—which suppose we place anywhere from twenty up—he is certainly old enough to have made at least a start in life. I take for granted that a man ought to be older than his wife; indeed, public opinion is so well settled on this point that it is scarcely worth mentioning. If, then, a man of marriageable age—say from twenty-five to forty—has not done something for himself, if it be but to carve out future prospects, it is reasonable to suppose that he never will make anything, nor ever will raise prospects for anybody else. Even if a woman has property of her own, she may justly hesitate to trust it in the hands of such a man, who would probably fritter it all away, or at best would not increase it as fast as the necessities would increase for spending it. If, however, a man has made anything, and lost it through circumstances beyond his control—such as the convulsion which has recently overwhelmed our country—then the case is different, and a woman need not fear to trust him with her possessions, as he has already given evidence of his capacity for managing property; and the loss of his own, not being through his fault, casts no reflection on his sagacity as a man of business.

Thus, after all, we come back to character as the main thing to be considered. Even in a worldly point of view, a man's capacity for managing property is a matter of greater moment than the mere amount of his possessions. In purely mercenary matches, this point is often overlooked—the glitter of gold blinding the eyes to every other consideration,—so that calculating avarice overreaches itself, and loses the wages of hymeneal perjury by the unforeseen dissipation of the fortune that was to be its reward. Purely mercenary matches are, I hope, not more common than their opposites, and they certainly meet with little sympathy from the world, even when they do not fly in the face of our sentiments of right and decency, as is sometimes the case. We have all seen rich young men made the objects of innumerable tea parties and quiet dinners at houses where there were marriageable daughters, and we remember the sneering comments of society, in which we ourselves have probably joined. We all know the feeling of disgust which both parties inspire when blooming youth sells itself to toothless age, or when the still greater disparities of mind and heart are covered over with gold. We all know, too, the pleasure that is felt when two fortune-hunters take each other in, and we have all doubtless applauded the social verdict, "Served 'em right." Mercenary marriages are thoroughly and deservedly odious; but I think we must grant that a little prudence is very necessary in matrimony. Prudent matches are often the very reverse of mercenary ones. A rich young lady cannot do a more prudent thing than bestow her hand on a poor and worthy man of talent, and we all like to see rich men marry good girls who have no fortunes of their own. Such matches cannot be mercenary—on one side, at least—though both parties may justly be influenced by pecuniary considerations, in so far as the fortune possessed by one enables both to carry out their inclinations, which they could not have afforded to do if both were poor.

Opposed to these discreet and rational marriages—for matrimony is not all a *romance*, except in the fancy of young girls—are those reckless, headlong alliances, of the order to which runaway marriages usually belong, into which men and women, as well as girls and boys, sometimes rush, regardless of consequences. There are only two classes of people who can afford to leave pecuniary considerations entirely out of the question—those who are rich enough to be above, or poor enough to be below them. A man who feels able to support a family in the style in which he is himself content to live, can afford to make a purely mercenary match; and one who is so poor that his anxieties and perplexities cannot be increased, even by the care of a family, may afford to do the same. People who do not mind work, and who have never known anything but poverty, need not be afraid of entailing greater hardships upon themselves by matrimony. In Prussia, there is a wise law forbidding men to marry unless they can prove their ability to support a family. This is but an act of justice to society, for no man certainly has a right to bring children into the world for other people to support; and as the burden of feeding for paupers falls mainly upon the government, it has a right to take means for the increase of them. Extreme poverty can afford to disregard consequences for its own sake, but society must suffer for them. I once knew of a released convict from the State penitentiary, whose eleven children were supported almost entirely by charity. He certainly had no right to entail any fresh burdens upon society; but when his wife died, he married another before she had been in her grave three weeks, and in a few years had four more children for the public purse to provide for.

If the people who make foolish marriages were the only or even the chief sufferers for their folly, no one else would have a right to complain; but the worst of it is, that their friends and relations are always involved in the consequences. When a young man of no fortune, and with no prospect for making one, marries a wife as helpless as himself, and brings a lot of children into the world for her friends or his own to take care of, it is a clear encroachment upon the rights of others.

Poor people, with the tastes and habits of rich ones, are of all creatures the least independent of pecuniary considerations in their matrimonial affairs. A single man or woman, if not burdened with much delicacy of feeling, can sometimes contrive to lead a very comfortable life, by dint of sponging and borrowing, and getting presents, politely called so. But with a house full of children on their hands, they would find it not so easy to live upon nothing. It is not always safe for even an industrious man to trust to making a fortune after marriage, because the expense of raising and educating children is so great, and children are one of the consequences of matrimony that all people, especially poor men and preachers, can count upon with a good deal of certainty. True, the necessity of maintaining a family will often inspire the father of it with an energy and determination which no other motive can give, besides furnishing powerful incentives to economy and self-denial— virtues which few are inclined to practice, unless urged by some strong inducement. If we look, for instance, among those about us who have been ruined by the late war, we shall find, as a general thing, that married men have set about the work of repairing their broken fortunes with more vigor and determination than those who are free from the responsibilities of matrimony. It is not, however, the question of a man's willingness, but of his ability to support a family, that is under consideration here. Even wives without children are sometimes very expensive appendages, as every man is fully aware who has ever settled a dressmaker's bill or paid the price of a new bonnet.

Part 2

Selections from Eliza Frances Andrews's 1870 Journal

Editor's Introduction

After the war, someone described Frances Andrews as of middling height, slender, and graceful in her movements. She was also a striking redhead, probably with freckles. Of this she wrote, again as Elzey Hay, in "A Plea for Red Hair," an article written a few years after the war and republished in 1870:

> The world positively refuses to admire red heads and freckled faces, or to regard them as marks of either physical or intellectual superiority. In vain are nymphs, fairies, angels, and the good little children in Sunday-school books, always pictured with sunny tresses; the world is so perverse that it scorns in real life what it pronounces enchanting in books and pictures. Now this inconsistency is the main cause of quarrel that we red-heads have against the rest of the world.[1]

Miss Andrews was not afraid to criticize prevailing fashion, especially if it suggested false pretense, such as men who wore cheap paper collars on their shirts, rather than the genuine article sported by gentlemen. "Paper-Collar Gentility" also appeared a few years after the war and criticized the cheap shirt collars sported by so-called "gentlemen."

> They are suggestive of a small shopkeeper, second-rate boarding-house state of society...of plated forks and printed cards of invitation; of bad cigars and cheap perfumery...and worse than all, they are suggestive of a mind to save washing-bills; of a desire to keep up the "outward and visible signs" of decency without the "inward and spiritual grace."[2]

It was this spirit of cynicism that we see so abundantly in Miss Andrews's observations on Yankeedom in summer 1870.

---

[1] Elzey Hay, "A Plea for Red Hair by a Red Haired Woman," in Rushing, ed., *Journal of a Georgia Woman*, 100.

[2] Elzey Hay, "Paper-Collar Gentility," ibid., 104–105.

August–September 1870

That summer Frances Andrews and her sister Metta, accompanied by a "male protector" named Hobbs, left Little Washington, traveled to Charleston, and from there set sail for New York. They were going to visit Elizabeth Littell Ward, cousin of their mother. "Cousin Lilla," as Fanny called her, was married to Richmond Ward, a wealthy businessman who lived in a fashionable section of Newark, New Jersey.

Fanny began the journey north about the time of her thirtieth birthday; Mett was five years younger. The war had been over for five years, and Reconstruction in Georgia and throughout the South was in full sway. Miss Andrews was still getting used to the reality that the old Southern social order had been knocked on its head—a fact that we see in her published journal of 1870–1872 on its very "first" page. Kittrell Rushing, who discovered Frances's narrative in a handwritten ledger in 1998, notes that the first 114 pages had been cut out from their binding. Hence, we don't know why the two Andrews sisters had determined to visit Cousin Lilla and her family. Because Eliza Frances Andrews did not oversee publication of this postwar diary, as she did with *The War-Time Journal* in 1908, we have no formal name for it, but will settle for Professor Rushing's *Journal of a Georgia Woman, 1870–1872*. The latter entries—twelve under various dates from July to December 1871 and just one for February 25, 1872—offer much detail on Miss Andrews's activities in Washington. But they do not deal with Yankees, with whom the lady from Georgia had much contact during her seven-week sojourn in New York and New Jersey, August 1–September 21, 1870. It is this colorful array of impressions and opinions to which we shall now turn.

Fanny had not even left Charleston when, "on stepping into a street car, we have our first experience of practical social equality": there was "a negro passenger" on board. Three years before, in April 1867, the president of the Charleston City Railway Company had ended its Whites-only policy for city streetcars.[1]

One of the most striking aspects—perhaps *the most* striking—of Miss Andrews's journal of August–September 1870 is that she composed it frankly and honestly as a travelogue on Yankeedom. Like Mark Twain's *Innocents Abroad* (which was written about the same time, incidentally, and published in 1869), Fanny Andrews's postwar journal is an unabashed and observant recording of the strange, exotic people and things with which she came into contact, with chauvinistic commentary.

Fanny and her sister would have known that Elizabeth Ward lived a wealthy, privileged life. Her husband, Richmond, was a successful businessman in Newark. But it was the kind of business in the North he was engaged in—manufacturing consumer goods made by hired laborers—that drew acidic comment from our journalist, who had grown up in a household where social position and wealth in the South rested on land, cotton and slaves.

In short, Fanny and Mett were being thrown in among a bunch of Yankees, and the older sister did not like it much at all. "There were many Yankees among the passengers," she noticed aboard the steamship taking them north, but "it was amusing to see the tacit understanding by which they and we rebels avoided each other." The avoidance was made easier by the very sounds of speech that could be heard on board the steamer, *Manhattan*, bearing them to New York; Miss Andrews bristled at the sound of Yankee voices. Mortimer Ward,

---

[1] Walter J. Fraser Jr., *Charleston! Charleston!* (Columbia: University of South Carolina Pres, 1989), 285. Some modern historians, such as Kittrell Rushing and Jean Berlin, have characterized Frances Andrews and her writing as "racist" (Rushing, ed., *Journal of a Georgia Woman*, xxvii, xli). Here we will refrain from such anachronism. The word had not even been coined in 1870 (it was 1928, and in common use from 1935, just in time for Hitler's Germany). To apply it to earlier times is to fix upon them an artificial and purposeless context—sort of like labeling the ancient Romans as "war criminals" for their destruction of Carthage and killing of its inhabitants in 146 B.C. The concept of war crimes would not be developed for another two thousand years.

Cousin Lilla's son, was kind enough to meet Fanny, Mett, and Hobbs at dockside. "He had a pleasant face, with beautiful teeth," she remarked, "but my heart sunk within me when I heard his awful Yankee lingo."

Here it was, half a decade after Confederate defeat, and Fanny Andrews was still a *Rebel*. Here it was, five years into postwar sectional reconciliation, and the author of this journal still felt more comfortable staying away from "those people," as General Lee used to say.

Thus it may well have been that this Georgia girl, as she styled herself in her *War-Time Journal*, in 1870s New Jersey was more than casually disposed to notice differences between how *her* people and *those* people did things. A few days after their arrival at the Wards' elegant, four-story mansion in downtown Newark (Broad Street), the Andrews women were visited by a Mrs. Phelps, a resident from Warrenton, Georgia (near Washington), who had traveled with them from Charleston. Arriving in the afternoon, possibly earlier, the fellow voyager was invited by Fanny and Mett to stay for dinner—as Southerners were used to doing. Not Northerners, though. "When anybody takes trouble to come from a distance to see us, we expect them to stay all day or night, as the case may be," she writes. "But Yankee ideas of hospitality are very different, and our rich cousin seemed a little embarrassed at having unexpected company to dinner." She went on: "I like our old slipshod Southern way, that don't mind if things do go a little wrong, much better than this Yankee primness."

Everything is so different from home that I could almost fancy myself across the water. But I like the old home ways best—this is all very grand and rich, but they don't understand genuine comfort here at all. Everybody cleans their teeth over the wash basin, and then turn on the water cock. I can't stand that and long for the slop tubs at home. Then, we never wipe on the same towel twice at home. Here no fresh ones have been put in the room since we came. There we can scatter our clothes about the bedroom & fling a newspaper on the floor when we are done with it, here we have to keep even combs and brushes in the bureau drawers, and the newspapers must all be laid on a particular spot on a certain table, as soon as one has read them, and so I am in constant terror again, lest my disorderly habits may break out sometime, unawares, and shock all my Yankee kin.

Everywhere it seemed different. "There are no piazzas in this part of the world, and I never see people sitting on their front stoops," she noticed. Even the wildlife was different: "we have English sparrows here instead of mocking birds and Jorees." And so were the plants: "the turf here is of a vivid green, that we have nothing like at the South, and they have some lovely evergreens, such as Norway spruce, Scotch fir, and yew, that will not live in our climate." Moreover, even when they had a beautiful tract of landscape, Northerners could not help but tinker with it. "We had a delightful ride this afternoon," Fanny wrote on Friday, August 26, "to see a glorious view from a place called Eagle Rock, some five or six miles from Newark. How these Yankees do fix up everything!" After a visit to New York's Central Park, Miss Andrews described it as "a wonderful exhibition of skill and industry"—but not of nature. "I like the works of nature better," she remarked, "with all its art, Central Park is not half so beautiful as the grounds around Haywood. It is admirable in its way, but there is an artificial air about it that would weary me if confined to it always, as a substitute for Nature."

On September 2, the group took a trip on a steamboat up the Hudson River, but here too our journalist could not help but draw contrast.

I like the flowery swamps, the wild tangled scenery of our Southern rivers better. The dear old South, in its wild uncultivated state, has more of Nature: the hand of man does not obtrude itself there in every corner as it does here. The miserable, money loving wretches that these Yankees are: they even have the impudence to paint their advertisements of paper collars and patent medicines upon the Palisades and the rocks that jut from the Highlands of the Hudson.

Niagara Falls was even worse. "Well, at all events, the Yankees have Niagara, and that is a possession a world might be proud of—though they have done their best to spoil that," she wrote the next day.

> Above the falls on the American side, the river is disfigured with paper mills, and all sorts of ugly manufacturing houses.... It was all glorious and grand, but everywhere the hand of man was too obtrusive. I would like to see Niagara a wild solitude, as Chateaubriand saw it. It is one of Nature's sublimest spots, and the pitiful efforts of man to improve and beautify it, are simply contemptible. There ought not to be a house within ten miles of Niagara, and as for suspension bridges over chasms and steam elevators upon the sides of precipices of a thousand feet, they are very convenient to tourists, but not consonant with my ideas of congruity. I believe I would rather risk my neck clambering down the sides of precipices as we did at Tallulah in Georgia, than see the grand gorge at Niagara disfigured with an unsightly wooden structure for my convenience.

Further cheapening the sight of natural sublimity was that it came with a price tag: "How pitiful it seems to pull out your purse and pay a dollar or two for every new view of that incalculable wonder!...to pay for looking at Niagara—what a desecration!"

Traveling across New York state, Fanny and Metta experienced anew the faster pace of life in the North (rather, "at," as Fanny liked to put it). At a stop in Rochester, they had breakfast cut somewhat short; she would have enjoyed it more if given a bit longer, "but these rapid Yankee schedules allow no time for anything of that sort. A fifteen minutes breakfast or dinner is a barbarity that would be unheard of out of Yankeedom." The Yankees themselves knew that a quarter-hour was a short time indeed to be served and enjoy one's meal at a railroad trackside hotel or tavern. In western New York Fanny's attempt at dining led to this sharp passage (dated September 5):

> At Gnoguchamna, where we dined, a rascally Yankee trick was played upon us. In barbarous Yankee fashion, we had only fifteen

minutes for dinner. It was an elegant eating house, and we were ravenously hungry after a 5 o'clock breakfast and a mean one at that. After bolting a few mouthfuls, we were startled by the cry "All aboard," and there was a general rush for the cars. There stood all the train officials and the hotel proprietor, enjoying the joke, but not one of them volunteered to inform us that we had still 8 minutes—and we did not find it out till we had paid our fare, and were on board again. There were some angry travelers then, I mean. If I had the time, I would write an account of it to the World, and expose their rascality.[2]

Train travel not only confirmed Yankees' rascality, but also their rapacity.

It is all a humbug about the cheapness of travel at the North. It is true, a R.R. or steam boat ticket can be bought for less than half of what it costs to travel the same distance in my country, but there are so many extras that by the time one has traveled a hundred miles, he is swindled out of more than would carry him a thousand at the South. When you buy your ticket at the South, you pay for everything, but here they won't look at a piece of baggage without charging extra for it, nor let you look at anything else. They are a nasty, miserable, sniveling, driveling cheating, swindling, humbugging, vulgar minded set of snobs and skinflints, these Yankees, and if there is another rasping expletive in the language, I wish somebody would tell it to me, for I have exhausted my vocabulary.

Our journalist's mention of "my country" reminds us that in a strange or foreign land, pangs of homesickness can be ameliorated by the most unexpected encounters. For Fanny Andrews, it was the presence of Black folk. Although few and far between, they could be seen

---

[2] Though unsigned, Miss Andrews's article "Romance of Robbery" had appeared in the *New York World* in August 1865. Other pieces followed, and she apparently still had connections with the paper's editorial office five years later.

occasionally, as on the steamboat that took Miss Andrews and her party upriver to Albany.

> There was a party of negroes on board the steamer, but they were perfectly respectful, and I do not object to social equality at the North, because here, it is not a symbol of my country's degradation, and besides, there are not enough negroes to make the question one of any practical importance. A mulatto girl sat next to me at dinner, and I only felt amused. The fact is, I like negroes so much better than Yankees, that the sight of a black face in a crowd, gives me positive pleasure: it looks like home.

In Newark cousin Lilla lived in a gorgeous house. In her first days of writing, Fanny noted its abundant space and fine furnishings, "with mirrors, paintings, velvet carpets, statuettes, busts, damask hangings, glittering chandeliers, china and glass ornaments." "But," she also observed, "no piano, and but one case of books" (back home at Haywood, the family library filled an entire room). Indeed, to the young woman from Georgia "these Yankees, rich as they are have no time to enjoy life. Everybody seems in a hurry. The people on the streets go in a sort of trot that I shall never catch, and children are put through the park in as much haste as if recreation itself were a business."

Ah, Yankee business! Here, too, Fanny found her hosts most peculiarly un-Southern. Cousin Lilla's husband Richmond had made his fortune manufacturing patent and enameled leather ("cannot be worth less than a million," our journalist guesses). The Wards' neighbor, George Clark, owned a factory producing spool thread. It was the same all around, as Eliza saw in a carriage ride through Newark several days after her arrival. "We took a drive through the city yesterday afternoon, and saw some elegant residences in the suburbs, but they all belong to merchants or manufacturers," she sniffed—it was well known in the

South that the accepted callings for gentlemen were as planters or as soldiers.[3]

> Opposite one of the parks, cousin Lilla pointed out a row of ele-
> gant residences, every one of which was owned by some sort of
> *rich tradesman.* Metta and I could hardly restrain our laughter at
> the *naivete* with which she gave information concerning them.
> "See that brown stone front to your left—two of our most fash-
> ionable belles live there—their father is in the leather business."
> "Mr. Jones built that large double house over the way—he made
> his money in the shoe business—and there, just beyond it, live
> the Browns—they are the leaders of our society—manufacturers
> of spool cotton—worth two million at least. The lady living in that
> four stories front, behind those elm trees, has the handsomest
> diamonds in Newark—her husband owns a trunk *factory*—he
> came here twenty years ago, without a dollar in his pocket." We
> are expected to admire these men very much, for making their
> own fortunes, and I pretend to think it all very nice, but can't help
> thinking to myself all the time, how much more I admire our
> Southerners for the way they lost theirs, and I can't help con-
> trasting cousin Lilla's ciceroneship, with the way we show places
> in our part of the world—"that old house in the park, belongs to
> Judge King—the one who married Judge Pettigrew's daughter—
> no relation to your Roswell Kings, in Georgia, but a fine old fam-
> ily—Dungenesse, yes, that is the residence of the Nightingales—
> descendants of Gen. Greene—the Randolphs live over there, in
> that old brick house they are a branch of the Virginia family."—
> This is the way we point out places in Carolina and Georgia—
> without a word or a thought about the negroes formerly owned
> or the bales of cotton made there.

---

[3] Frances Andrews's assessments of the Northern men she met frequently hinged on whether they were gentlemen. Dr. Weaver stresses the importance of this distinction for antebellum Southerners: "The Southern ideal of educa-tion...was designed to produce the well-rounded gentleman" (Richard M. Weaver, *The Southern Tradition at Bay: A History of Postbellum Thought* [New Rochelle, NY: Arlington House, 1968], 75).

This passage is more than a critique of Yankeedom; it is an affirmation of the Southern ethos. The wealthy of Newark lived in houses whose financial underpinning everyone in town knew. In a tour of Southern mansions, the guide (*cicerone*) would not have to announce how they came to be ("without a word or a thought about the negroes...or the bales of cotton"), but the talk would be about the *family* who lived there, and to whom they were related. This emphasis upon who people *were* as the basis of society, rather than upon the money or things they *owned* that so featured in cousin Lilla's tour guide narrative, led to a frank admission by our journalist: "somehow, in spite of all their finery and my poverty, I can't help a feeling of superiority, which places me entirely above all temptation to envy on the one hand, or mortification on the other. I belong to a family of eminence and distinction, and am a much grander personage where I live, than gold or diamonds could make me here, but let that be."

Cousin Lilla has been showing me her diamonds and laces today, and they are magnificent. She has long pendant earrings, and a broach studded with gems, any one of which would make a handsome solitaire. Even her fan and parasol are covered with real point lace—Brussels point, and she has shawls of lace and cashmere, that almost make me stare with wonder. They sit well on her, because she is a genuine lady in spite of the lingo and the "leather business." She has the blood of Seaburys in her veins, and what is better still, instincts of nobility in her heart. She is a fine looking woman, and has cultivated manners. But I cannot get over my horror of that abominable lingo that all these Yankees have—It sounds so coarse, so unrefined, that I can hardly realize it is the language of ladies and gentlemen—for there are some real ladies and gentlemen, even among the Yankee.

Then there was "spool cotton Clark," the Scotsman in his midforties "who lives next door and is worth half a million." The more time she spent with the gentleman, owner of the Clark Spool Thread Company, though, the more she came to like, even admire him. After he dropped in one Friday evening in late August, Frances recorded in her journal:

> Our next door neighbor, Spool Cotton Clarke,[4] called too, and I never was more surprised in a man, in all my life. Instead of a vulgar old codger, with no thought beyond making money, I found him one of the most intelligent and cultivated men I ever met. He staid till nearly twelve o'clock, and I was perfectly delighted with him, though he is stout and bald headed, and a radical. But he has never been naturalized, and can't vote, so that don't hurt: he has just the faintest little touch of Scotch brogue in his voice, which is very pretty. I am not going to call him Spool Cotton Clarke any more, but, George A. or George W., or whatever his name may be. It shows he has good taste never being naturalized: I don't see why any man should ever want to give up his English birthright to become one of this horrid Yankee nation.

Miss Andrews's reference to George Clark as a radical—"a Scotchman, and an awful radical," she writes elsewhere—introduces us to a strain of Northern politics in the years after the war. During the conflict a Radical wing had arisen among Congressional Republicans. Generally, its adherents criticized Lincoln's slow pace toward emancipation and argued for a harder prosecution of war against the Rebels. In the several years afterward, they advocated a Reconstruction policy that punished the ex-Confederate states, championed rights for freedmen, and urged that adoption of civil rights measures for Negroes should be a condition for Southern states' readmission to the Union.[5]

Obviously, it was not George Clark's politics that endeared him to Frances Andrews. On September 12 she took a carriage to the Clark thread mill.

---

[4] Rushing informs us that *Clark* is the correct spelling of the Scotsman's name (*Journal of a Georgia Woman*, 113n.10).

[5] James M. McPherson, *Ordeal by Fire: The Civil War and Reconstruction* (New York: McGraw-Hill, 1992 [1982]), 268, 495.

He was there to receive us, showed us all over the place, explained the machinery, and when we left, gave us each a pretty little box of thread.... It was a very interesting visit—and heavens! How it opened my eyes! I will never turn up my nose again at a manufacturing of spool thread. Cotton planting is nothing to it. It is a really manly business to command such an establishment as that, and still more so, to understand all about it as Mr. Clark does—and still find time, with all that on his hands, to be one of the most cultivated and sensible gentlemen I ever met! What a fool I have been! I know now that cotton planting and soldiering are not the only occupations for gentlemen, and I have found out that rich manufacturers are not necessarily shoppies and upstarts. A spool of sewing thread seems a very insignificant thing but the process of making it is anything but insignificant. I'll never make a fool of myself again by feeling contempt for manufacturers.

Yet Mr. Clark was the exception, as one repeatedly sees in Miss Andrews's recording of her six weeks in the North.

The more we see of Yankee society, the less we like it. This is not mere sectional prejudice, for I leave politics entirely out of the question, in forming my opinions—indeed, most of the people I have met, have spoken very kindly of the South, so I have no reason to bear them a grudge on that score. But there is a stiffness, a want of cordiality, a want of something I can't describe, that makes their manners utterly unlike those of our Southerners who are to the 'manner born.' For instance, when I first met my cousin Mortimer—whom I don't know yet how to address—I thought it would be too stiff and formal, after all our friendly correspondence with his mother to call him Mr. Ward, so after introducing him by that title to some of my friends, I turned to him with a smile, and said "But you must give me a less formal name to call you by, for you know you can't be *Mr. Ward* to your cousin."

"That's so," he replied, through his nose, turned red in the face, commenced playing with his fingers, and said nothing more, so that I don't know to this day what I am to call him. How differently one of my Southern cousins would have done. We've had had pet names for each other in ten minutes, and he would have been joking with me about not giving him a more friendly greeting than a mere shake of the hand. But Yankees never joke. One of the trials of my life here, is, that they will take everything I say in dead earnest, while at the South, every other word we speak is a jest. When cousin Lilla showed me all the modern conveniences about her house, I laughed at myself for not having been accustomed to them before, and humorously exaggerated my own ignorance. But she took it all *au serieux*, and actually believed me so green, that she came in at night to show me how to turn the gas off! Mett and I buried our heads under the bed clothes and laughed till our sides ached, when she left the room.

There is undoubtedly much to be said in favor of the great conveniences of Yankee housekeeping. I have hardly seen a servant since I came here, while at home, half a dozen darkies are rushing in and out of one's room continually. Everything is served as if by invisible hands in an Aladdin's palace: turn a cock or pull a knob, and all your wants are gratified. But after all, I like our good old slipshod Southern ways the best. Water, sweet and fresh from the well, even if you do have to wait half an hour for a darkey to draw it, is much better than when brought for miles through lead pipes, and I sometimes feel as if I would be glad of a pretext to step out doors, if it were but to call a servant. There is a primness about a Yankee house, that keeps me in constant terror lest I should put something out of order. Everything is so tidy, that I can find no place to throw waste paper, and when I was vainly seeking for some place to brush my teeth over, Cousin Lilla pointed me to the wash basin, and told me just to turn the cock and rinse it out when I was done! Towels are folded up neatly and hung on the rack, everytime they are used, so that the same one is made to serve for ever so long, while we at home, never wipe our faces twice on the same towel. Napkins too, we have fresh at every meal, while here they are all put into silver napkin rings and numbered, so that the same ones will serve for a week. The Yankee way is much more economical and orderly than ours—but I can't help liking ours best. The tables are served in such a skimpy way that it looks like starvation, compared with our bountiful Southern boards. There is always enough—but nothing over—it is as if everybody's appetite had been accurately measured and allowance made for it. There is a little skimpy dab of butter on the dish, when we sit down, that I would be mortified to leave behind, on the table at home—and absolutely nothing left when we have finished. Yet I always get enough, and nobody seems ashamed to take the last slice of bread, or the last morsel of butter from a plate—while at the South, we would think it looked miserably stingy if our tables showed any perceptible diminution after feeding a score of people. The Yankees carry out everything on this little sniveling scale. In making change at home, we never think of so small a matter as a dime or a picayune, while here they are scrupulous down to the last copper, it is not uncommon for the children to buy a cent's work of candy, just as they would a dime's worth with us. I spend all my pennies as they call them, on the beggars and street musicians, since I find they are glad to get them. Most people drive away these vagabonds, but I can't send them off empty handed—especially the poor little children. I dare say I am very green, and these sharp Yankees laugh at me in their sleeves, but I am not used to such scenes and they touch my heart.

The first vagabonds that came in my way were two Italian boys who made very sweet music, and I threw them a quarter—just as we would have done at the South, feeling half ashamed too, at giving so little, but they seemed perfectly amazed at getting so large a sum. That was in the morning: late in the afternoon, as I was standing in the window they passed by again, and looked up at me with a bow and a smile. Next day, came a poor little boy with a fiddle, and began to play. Mr. Ward turned him out into the street: he could speak no English, but began to plead in plaintive notes on the poor old fiddle, that touched my heart more deeply than words, and so came more pennies out of my pocket. The next beggar was a horrid old Irish woman, whom I knew to be an impostor, but gave for the sake of a poor little child she was dragging around with her. Since then, they come so thick and fast that I have to put each one off with a penny. Pennies are not without value here where people think of such little things. I really do believe that this little skimpy way of caring for trifles, makes people sniveling and contemptible: I have not seen a manly looking man since I bid good bye to our Southern traveling companions on the boat. Mett and I have noticed what miserable little sniveling specimens of humanity pass along the streets: even Mortimer Ward, who is really good looking for a Yankee, is small and stunted, as if he had thought too much about pennies.

Evident here are six reasons for Fanny Andrews's dislike of Yankee society: its manners; lack of humor; prim style of housekeeping; measured, even skimpy meals; all-around cheapness; and hard-heartedness toward those in need.

While there was indeed a sectional prejudice in her observations—despite her denial above—the journalist's entry of August 13 serves up at the end of this snippet a genuinely admirable sociological truism.

The country around Orange and Montrose is a perfect garden of Eden—but the "trail of the serpent is over it all." The country is a Paradise—but the people!—the more I see of them, the more odious they are to me. Yankee society, the little I have seen of it, is horribly vulgar, and what I have seen, seems to be only a fair specimen of what I have not seen. Almost everyone of the elegant residences that have been pointed out to me are owned by people who have grown suddenly rich by the manufacture of shoe pegs, trunk straps, or some contemptible little thing of that sort—a Yankee manufacturing town like Newark is certainly not the place that one would choose for its society. Give me a thousand times over, our elegant Southerners, with their poor old dilapidated homes. I would rather today, marry a poverty stricken Southerner without a home, than be mistress of one of these splendid establishments with a miserable plebeian who knows nothing beyond the shoe peg and tape business, for its master. It is people, and not their surroundings, that makes society.

There was a word for these makers of shoe pegs and trunk straps: *shoppies*, as in "Mortimer is quiet and a gentleman, though not an elegant one, like Garnett. But the shoppies they live among are—awful, to use a Yankeeism." When even Yankees coin a word for the coarse tradesmen in their midst—"shoppies"—Fanny's criticisms find foundation.

> Well, it isn't their trades that I mind, but all these people do smell so of the shop—and the more diamonds and point lace they pile on, the more vulgar they seem. I am not ungrateful enough to mean any of this for my own relations who are so kind to me, for cousin Lilla is a genuine lady in manner and feeling and Julia is charming, though they do both talk in the harsh Yankee lingo.

To these familial exceptions—cousin Lilla and Julia Ward, cousin Mortimer's wife—were to be added sundry of the other nice people Fanny happened to meet in Newark. One of these was a Mr. Leslie: "he really is a polished gentleman, and not a bit shoppy." Such outliers, as we would call them, caused Frances to ponder the tension between her characterization of a whole group of people and the likable individuals who stood out from the rest. This realization she voiced in her entry of August 23.

> Upon the whole, I like my Yankee kin very much, and to tell the truth, the kindness and consideration with which Mett & I are treated by everybody, makes me feel quite ashamed of the way we snub Yankees "down South." I have heard nothing but expressions of kindness and sympathy for the South—except from that fool who didn't know any better: even those who think we were wrong, seem to feel a genuine pity for our misfortunes, and treat us with extra consideration, because we are Southerners, so that I feel quite compunctious to think of the extra contempt I feel for them because they are Yankees. Sometimes, when people who call on me, remark that they have a brother or a sister at the South, I feel half ashamed to think of the contempt with which all Yankees are treated there, and a kind of sneaky feeling comes

over me, as if I know something dishonest, in accepting the courtesies that are extended to me, when I have always treated their
countrymen with studied indifference and reserve. I am not going to do so anymore. Though I hate Yankees in the aggregate,
worse than ever, yet I am under obligations to individuals, and I
will not be ungrateful. In future, whenever I meet a decent Yankee at the South, I shall make it a point to be polite to him—
though of course, I don't mean to have anything to do with car-
petbaggers, and school marm's and radicals.[6] But I shan't encourage indiscriminate and wholesale proscription of them any more.

Writing in 1870, referring to Northerners as shoppies and sharp-
sters, Eliza Francis Andrews was playing on caricatures of the Yankee
that had developed in America decades earlier.[7] So well had these ste-
reotypes been honed and massaged in antebellum American popular
culture that our journalist could deftly reduce them to just a few words:
"money flash and vulgarity":

Everyday we have rides and drives and somebody to see. The
people here are perfectly horrid, and all that I see confirms my
former impressions of Yankee society. Money flash, and vulgarity. Thank heaven, I am a Southerner, and have Southerners for

---

[6] "Carpetbagger" was the derisive term used by Southerners to refer Northerners who settled in the South after the war (McPherson, *Ordeal by Fire*, 520).
"School marms" reflects the fact that even before Confederate surrender a number of Northern female teachers traveled South to provide educational services
for the newly freed Black children (Willie Lee Rose, *Rehearsal for Reconstruction:
The Port Royal Experiment* [Indianapolis: Bobbs-Merrill, 1964], 229–30).

[7] Fully a generation before the war, a pamphlet circulated that told the imaginary story of a Yankee descended into Hell. The condemned consignee was
charged with any number of outrages: selling wooden nutmegs, peddling as
"Spanish cigars" those really made of oak leaves, and pawning a well-worn pair
of footwear to a pious old lady as the shoes of St. Paul. Among the Devil's accu-
sations, too, was that of "stealing an old grindstone, smearing it over with butter,
and then selling it as a cheese" (Avery Craven, *The Coming of the Civil War* [Chi-
cago: University of Chicago Press, 1957 (1942)], 173).

my associates. The he-Yankees are as contemptible as their females are vulgar: little sniveling scrubby wretches—it would take
three of them to make a good tall Southerner. The only good
looking men I have seen since landing in N.Y. are the policemen,
who are big and strong at any rate, and I believe the little dress-
maker who fashioned my silk coat, and two poor little milliners
across the street, are the most thorough ladies I have met. Everybody is so loud and flashy. My cousin is a handsome, lady like
person; but she shuts us up in the dark to keep the sun from fad-
ing her carpet, and does other little skimpy Yankee tricks at
home, while she wears point lace and diamonds. There is the difference: we poor rebs make ourselves comfortable if we can't be
grand; we don't wear diamonds, but we don't mind if the carpet
gets spoiled: we'll get a new one, instead of diamonds. In this fine
house each person has a clean towel every Sunday morning—at
home, nobody uses the same towel twice. Everything is as me-
thodical here as clock work: there is one day in the week for
sweeping, another for washing windows, another for clean table
linen &c. At home we sweep the floors and wash the windows
whenever they get dirty, and change table linen every day.

Even in death the Yankees persisted in their "money flash." After
a carriage ride through New York's Greenwood Cemetery on Saturday,
the 27th, Fanny judged the experience decidedly unpleasant. "I cannot
describe the feeling that came over me when the guide would point out
a splendid mausoleum, and inform us, 'That's the family vault by John
G. Smith—he's in the hat and glove business—one of our richest men';
or, 'That monument Mr. Samuel Jones raised over his wife he made
his fortune in the pin and needle business.'" In her journal Miss Andrews wrote about the handsome monuments, interesting sculpture,
splendid mausoleums—and, of course, their cost, which was part of
the travelogue. The memorial for two of James Gordon Bennett's children "cost $50,000 the guide told us." "The garish splendors of Green-
wood affect me unpleasantly," she reflected. Case in point: "the most
costly of the vaults is a Byzantine structure in white marble, that cost
$30,000, and the prettiest, to my taste, a gothic edifice on a hill,

belonging to Stephen Somebody—one of the richest men in New York. So much for splendid tombs. I have forgotten his name already."

Going about in company of Lilla Ward, Fanny was mindful of the contrast between her and her host's outward appearance, especially their apparel. On a Sunday in late August she commented, "cousin Lilla herself is gotten up in such magnificent style and thinks so much of fine clothes, that I am afraid our shabbiness might be a mortification to her." Once Lilla offered to take Fanny and Mett to a certain posh place, but the sisters demurred: "our poor shabby wardrobes would never pass muster there...I would like to go, and see the sights, even with my meager outfit, but I would not like to make my good generous friends ashamed." But "shame" was a comparative thing. "Ah, there is one point on which I can truly boast of Southern superiority—nobody is ashamed of shabby clothes there: some of our greatest and most influential ladies in Georgia would pass for nobodies here, on account of their clothes—But enough."

Family history came to fore when Frances and Metta paid a visit to an estate, Tuscan Hall, seven miles from Newark, whose great house had happened to be built by the sisters' great-great-grandfather a century before. Walking about the kitchen she imagined that during the War for Independence in the 1770s, American soldiers may have taken food and rest there.

> What would the shades of those good old ancestors think if they had known that two of their descendants were standing there, who had given food and shelter and rest, and prayers and blessings too, to soldiers who fought against the flag those old heroes had loved? We have all been rebels together—only their rebellion was successful—ours was not.

The current occupants of Tuscan Hall were Germans—a wealthy brewer and his family. Two children translated for the older folk, who spoke no English. "Their elders flocked around, and received us with a heartiness that would not shame the memory of my hospitable ancestors.... They wanted to bring us some sweet milk, but we contented ourselves with a draught from the well where our ancestors had slaked their thirst," she recorded. "It was the coolest, purest water I ever tasted, and I loved to think that perhaps Washington's soldiers had watered their horses there. I wish Lee's soldiers had too."

"There is no doubt about it, the general tone of society here is perfectly horrid," Miss Andrews wrote on August 23, "though of course there are exceptions, like the Bruens, the Garthwaites, Mr. Leslie, and those charming Miller girls." (At one point, Frances remarked of Leonard, a younger Bruen brother, "his manners are just like a Southerner's," which was her highest form of praise for a gentleman.) Two weeks later, the Bruens came calling at the Wards' home, along with others. The soiree led to Fanny relating in military-like detail how at one point in the evening she "brought up my reserves, and gained at least a partial victory" over a dreadful Yankee shoppy.

SEPT 7TH WEDNESDAY. A nice quiet day and a charming evening. Julia and Morty took tea, Mr. and Mrs. George Bruen, Mr. Clark, and the Howells called afterward. Mr. Bruen is perfectly charming, and old Mr. Howell is as fat and jolly as he can be, and I like him though he is an awful Radical. He behaved like a gentleman, and carefully avoided all allusion to disagreeable subjects, but one of his daughters, Lizzie, took a seat near me, and commenced conversations about the war. I made one or two efforts to change the subject, but she kept returning to it, and alluded to the South in a sneering manner that nearly made me boil over. However, I managed to contain myself and to answer her as much as possible in monosyllables, and I told her some rare lies too. She kept asking if I was not dreadfully afraid when the United States soldiers came where I was—and I told her no, I wasn't a bit afraid of them—which was about as flat a falsehood as ever passed my lips. I had a great mind to add that I was too much concerned about higher matters, to tremble at the prospect of having spoons stolen.[8]

---

[8] Under date of Tuesday, August 23, 1870, Miss Andrews wrote, "The fashionables are slowly returning to the city, and the Yankee swells are beginning to

Elizabeth Howell was "an awful snob," Fannie opined, "and like all these Yanks, measures everything by money." During the course of the evening Lizzie began boasting of her recent trip to Europe.

She spent three months in Europe last spring, and was constantly bragging in allusions to things abroad that she thought I could not understand: everything that was mentioned, she would hop to compare with something abroad, and was so anxious to bring in her foreign travels, that she did it once at the expense of comparing the elevator at Niagara with the steps in the Tower of London. She tried to talk over me to Mr. Clark, but he studiously addressed himself to me—only making a polite rejoinder to her remarks, and then appealing to me so as not to leave me out of the conversation. It was worthy of a Southerner: I felt so grateful to him, and fortunately, my reading has made me so familiar with all the real points of interest in Europe that I was really more capable of keeping pace with Mr. Clark than was Miss Howell, and had the pleasure of turning her down two or three times.

But Fanny's real triumph over Lizzie Howell came a bit later— not so much a *coup de main* as a *coup de pied*, as we see in this passage, whose particulars our journalist clearly savored.

---

call on us. We had three last night, one of them, Mr. Peck, was really a nice gentleman, but there was one little prig named Scott, who entertained us with the exploits of his brother—a staff officer of one of *Beast Butler's* generals." Union major general Benjamin Butler served as military commander in New Orleans, and to keep order among an openly hostile populace he issued decrees that led the citizenry to call him "Beast"; Butler was not possessed of handsomeness, anyway (Chester G. Hearn, *When the Devil Came Down to Dixie: Ben Butler in New Orleans* [Baton Rouge: Louisiana State University Press, 1997], 106). Another unflattering nickname was "Spoons," which Southerners derisively began calling Butler upon word of Federals' theft of families' dinnerware (Charles Dufour, *The Night the War Was Lost* [Garden City, NY: Doubleday Company, 1960], 354)— hence Miss Andrews's sly allusion to "having spoons stolen."

I saw her give a long contemptuous stare at my poor Japanese poplin, and when I looked at her elegant Paris made dress, banded with exquisite lace and then thought of my own shabby toilet, I began to think she had the upper hand of me then, and the battle was lost on that ground. But luckily, she soon uncovered her weak point, and then I brought up my reserves, and gained at least a partial victory. I don't know whether it was accidental or intentional, but she contrived some way, to expose her feet. They were no bigger than all the other women have in this region, but perfect clodhoppers compared to an average Southern foot. I saw my chance at once, her shoes were beautiful bronzeo, trimmed elaborately with bows and buckles: mine, only simple black kids with a little embroidery about the tips, but very pretty, and I know that my feet would look like pigmies in them compared with hers as I contrived while talking very earnestly to Mr. Clark, to put my feet out from under my dress—very carelessly, as if I were perfectly unconscious of the act, and let them rest straight along of hers—still talking earnestly all the time, as if perfectly unconscious of what my lower extremities were about. Presently she looked down, and I could hardly keep from laughing out, to see how quickly she drew her clodhoppers in. Oh, what wretches we women are—and yet, it is fine fun. I never engage in these ridiculous contests voluntarily, but when challenged to it by a Yankee shoppy, I'll fight to the death. I wouldn't mind her snickering at my poor dress, but when she presses to turn up her pitiful Yankee nose at my country and to speak sneeringly of my beloved South, I'll put her down if I die for it.

The *drole de guerre* between Miss Andrews and Miss Howell was not over, for Lizzie gave Fanny one final opening for "a few hot shots."

Miss Howell returned to her politics after awhile and very gratuitously boasted that she was a Republican, pitched into the Democrats, and finally sneered at some man she had met on the steamer as nothing but a Southern Judge. I am no more of a Democrat than I am of a Republican, but as the Democrats are allies of the South, and I the daughter of a Southern Judge, her remarks were more personal perhaps than she intended. I said nothing to provoke a quarrel, but, secretly resolved to pass a few hot shots into her the first good chance that offered. It was not long before my turn came: I found occasion in telling some little anecdote or reminiscence, to make some off hand allusion to "respectable merchant sort of people—prosperous tradesmen and manufacturers you know, very worthy people of course, whom I am always careful to treat politely, but not, you know—" &c &c. taking care to address her as if taking for granted that she was one of the *elite*, who was entitled to look down on vulgar prosperity, though I know, as well as she did, that her father made his fortune in the leather business—that is, as a tanner on a large scale. I wouldn't have made such a snobby speech to anybody but a snobby fool, and took care that nobody else should hear—but it served my purpose: I think she will hold her tongue about Southern Judges in future.

Wednesday, September 21, 1870, was Fanny and Mett's last day at the Wards', the day they prepared to go to New York and steam back toward home. Even amid sincere goodbyes and heartfelt expressions, Yankees had a way of showing their smallness of spirit, as one sees in this passage from Frances's journal under date of September 26, after the two sisters were back at Haywood.

Cousin Lilla cried, when she bid us good bye, which was very sweet—especially, as the very last thing I did before leaving her house, was to break a vase. It was too bad to think I had spent six weeks among all that finery without doing any mischief, and then to go and lose my character at the eleventh hour. It was worse than turning the ink stand on Mr. Jenning's linen sheet: I would rather burn down the house of a Southerner than break a pin belonging to a Yankee: they have no tact, and do make one feel so dreadfully. Cousin Lilla never once said, "oh it don't matter," or "I don't care half as much as you do," as any poor starving rebel would have done, if I had broken his last plate with his last dinner on it, but said "what a pity"—and "you didn't mean to do it, of course," and "I hoped it was nothing more than the lamp shade, when I heard the crash," and finally wound up my pleasant feelings by saying "I wouldn't mind it so much if I had not painted the vase myself—it was my own work."

I said nothing, but inwardly resolved to replace the vase if it took the last dollar out of father's pocket—I didn't have any in my own. Fortunately, at our journey's end, Mr. Phelps returned me 12 dollars that were left from my traveling fund. The vase I broke could not have been worth more than $2.00 at the outside, for I saw its counterpart at the Dollar Store but I will replace it with a $12.00 pair, and I will give them as a present not as a reparation—that will be doing things as a Southerner....

She did not mean to be rude, for she is really one of the kindest hearted women in the world—but she is a Yankee, and had not tact enough to abstain from apologizing for her [smudged] at the expense of her guests feelings. The truth is, Yankees have not a spark of genuine hospitality about them. A Southerner will share the poorest dinner he ever sits down to, with a friend, and bid him welcome, but a Yankee only entertains for his own credit—to display his fine things and make a show: he is selfish, even in his hospitality. At the South, we entertain for the pleasure of it, and think more of making our guests comfortable than of making a creditable display for ourselves. I never heard mother apologize for a dinner in my life, though company had often taken us unawares, and during the war, our fare was often of the poorest, and there were many good reasons why it was no better—but the reasons were never given—our guests fared as we did, and were supposed to be content. But Yankees are a vulgar minded set of whangsniffling...and as for their being Yankees and talking whang-nosed, they were born there and couldn't help it.

"I thank the Lord I am not a Yankee, whatever other faults I may have," Eliza Frances Andrews affirmed, as she concluded this portion of her journal.

Postlude

Fanny Andrews (1870–1931)

Frances Andrews was just twenty-four when, in February 1865, she wrote in her journal about "the career I have marked out for myself." A few months later, in June, she deferred Capt. Spenser Semmes's request for her autograph until she had become "a celebrated female."

By these clues, we can figure out that early on, Miss Andrews had staked out for herself a career as a writer: articles for newspapers, essays in literary magazines and, of course, novels. As early as September 1870, during her seven weeks' visit to relatives in New Jersey—possibly earlier, according to Dr. Rushing[1]—Frances was at work on her first novel, *A Family Secret*. She worked on it for quite a while; Lippincott's published it in 1876.[2]

After the war, living in Washington, Fanny sought to support herself by teaching. She didn't like it; in autumn 1871 she recorded in her journal her disdain for "a black-board and twenty stupid children." Additional income came from her articles for *Scott's* and other publications. It is clear, however, that writing the novel was her passion, as she confided in her diary on October 1, 1871:

> I have written my book a dozen times over in my head. I can't help living in my romance at all odd moments, as when I am walking, or sewing, or sitting idle at night, but the trouble is, that I never think it twice alike. Sometimes I make out an exciting scene, or a sprightly conversation, and when I come to write it down, it is all different from what I thought: I get the very words fixed in my head, and then, don't even use the ideas. So characters and events change under my hand in the same way. People

---

[1] Rushing, "Introduction," *Journal of a Georgia Woman*, xxx.

[2] Rushing, "Editor's Introduction," in Andrews, *A Family Secret: A Novel* (Knoxville: University of Tennessee Press, 2005), xi.

that I meant to be very important, sink into insignificance, and others that I hardly intended to mention by name, grow into the most prominent characters in the story. In short, I don't manage the tale atall, but it manages me, and the very people I make in my own head, take the reins out of my hand and turn out something very different from what I intended them to be. I don't know what will become of it: if I had time to sit down and put my story in proper trim and mold it according to a fixed model in my head, it might turn out something worth writing, but cobbled up in this irregular piecemeal fashion, I do not know that it will ever serve any other purpose than to amuse me and father. I do wish it would turn out a famous story, just to see how delighted father would be—but that is a wild thought—it takes genius to make famous stories—and it is not likely that a little country school mistress should have genius—or rather that one should have genius and be nothing better than a country school teacher. Mercy! How I do hate that schoolroom and what slavery it is to be poor![3]

Frances's mother, Annulet, passed away in January 1872; her father, Garnett, died a year and a half later at the age of seventy-four. Shortly thereafter, with her brother's help, in 1873 she got a teaching job in the girls' high school in Yazoo City, Mississippi, where he was practicing law (more successfully than farming; he was forced to sell the family's cotton plantation). Upon her return to Georgia in 1874, Eliza lived with her married sister Metta in Washington until 1881, while she served as principal of the Female Seminary. In the early 1880s, illness drove her to Florida. During this time, she developed a keen interest in botany. She outlined her love of the "fad" in an article published in *Popular Science Monthly* in 1886. She herself had been an invalid in Florida so she wrote from experience in "Botany as a Recreation of Invalids." Her instructive essay is here reprinted in full:

In a recent number of "The Popular Science Monthly," the writer of an interesting article, on "Thomasville as a Winter Resort,"

---

[3] Rushing, ed., *Journal of a Georgia Woman*, 41 (entry of October 1, 1871).

mentions the want of public amusements there as a subject of regret from a hygienic point of view. The criticism is a just one, and unfortunately applies to most of our Southern health resorts—St. Augustine, with its yacht club and sea-bathing, and Jacksonville, with a few other cities large enough to attract theatrical companies, forming possible exceptions.

Invalids, as a rule, have a great deal of leisure on their hands—more of it than they like—and to fill this time pleasantly is a question involving a good deal more than mere amusement. The importance of mental distractions to invalids is a fact too universally recognized to call for comment here, my object in this paper being merely to suggest a mode of distraction that, in my own experience, has not only been attended with the happiest results physically, but has proved a source of intense and never-failing pleasure. I allude to the study of botany—not the tiresome, profitless study of text-books, but of the woods, and fields, and meadows.

The beauty of this pursuit is that it takes the student out-of-doors, and throat and lung troubles, as has been truly said, are house-diseases. I am speaking, of course, to those who have begun to fight the enemy before he has captured the inner defenses, and who are supposed to be strong enough to do a reasonable amount of walking, and some solid thinking. For botany, though the simplest of sciences, can not be mastered without some effort. You are met right at the threshold by that fearful, technical vocabulary which must be conquered before advancing a single step—a labor so formidable and repellent, when undertaken according to the old school-book method, that I do not wonder so many have shrunk away from it in disgust or in despair.

But even this task, apparently as formidable as learning a new tongue, can be made a pastime if rightly undertaken. Don't try to learn definitions or commit long strings of names to memory from a book, but get some simple work and take it out into the woods with you. Don't worry with writing schedules or trying to draw outlines of the different kinds of leaves, but gather as many as you can; then, by reference to the book, describe them to yourself in botanical terms, and keep on in this way till you can give a scientific description of any plant you see, without the book. In a few weeks you will find that you have mastered, almost without knowing it, the dreadful bugbear of botanical language, and got a good deal of solid pleasure out of the process to boot.

You are now ready to take up the classification of plants, and to study their habits and relationships—and this is where the real pleasure begins. Don't worry about species at first, but be satisfied for a time with referring the different plants you meet to their appropriate orders and genera; specific distinctions are often perplexing, and can be attended to later. Gray's "Manual" and Chapman's "Southern Flora" are the only hand-books you will need—the latter for Southern Georgia and Florida, the former for more northern latitudes. I have seen Northern amateurs puzzling over Gray in Florida, and wondering that they could find so few of the plants around them described there, never seeming to realize that a manual of the flora for the Northern States would not answer just as well for an almost tropical region.

Florida is a specially interesting region for the botanist on account of the peculiar forms of plant-life to be found there. I wish I had time to introduce the reader to some of my friends of the forest and jungle, though I dare say he will find it more profitable to seek them out for himself. Botanizing in Florida, however, has this drawback: the pine-lands are so poor that, for the most interesting specimens, you must go to the swamps and hummocks, at the risk of getting more malaria than plants, as I can testify to my cost. But in Southern Georgia there is no such danger. The soil of the pine-lands there is richer, and the whole earth becomes, in spring-time, an Eden of beauty and fragrance. There is no need to go into malarious places; you can hardly set your foot down anywhere without treading on flowers. At a place near the railroad, between Albany and Thomasville, I once stood and gathered seventeen different species without moving out of my tracks. The Houstonias, Atamasco lilies, and yellow jasmines, make their appearance in February, and from then on till June the most diligent collector will have had as much as he can do to keep up with the rich succession of plant-life constantly unfolding itself to view.

And, all the while that one is pursuing a delightful study, he is getting abundant exercise in the open air, without the dreary consciousness of exertion for exertion's sake. One can walk for hours on a botanical ramble without fatigue, when twenty minutes of an aimless "constitutional" would send one home fagged out in body and mind. The parlor gymnastics recommended by Mr. Youmans may have their value in some cases, but for myself the most dismal moments I have ever spent were while laboring conscientiously with dumb-bells and Indian clubs in the name of exercise. Physical exercise, for its own sake, is intense and profitless, and often, I believe, pernicious labor. Give yourself a motive for exertion, and it then becomes exhilarating. The study of plants supplies just such a motive as invalids need. It is too useless (from a practical point of view) to be suggestive of labor, and yet so exceedingly fascinating as to make you ready to undergo any amount of labor in the prosecution of your favorite "fad." I remember once exposing myself to a terrible danger in endeavoring to get possession of a rare and (to me) new plant. I scarcely thought of the risk then, though now the bare recollection of it makes me shudder. This enthusiasm, which the science of botany awakens in all who devote themselves to it, is not its least valuable hygienic factor, for a little genuine enthusiasm will put more life into a sick body than all the drugs in the dispensary.

After all, the proof of the pudding is in the eating, and in conclusion I can only urge fellow-sufferers, who have a moderate amount of strength and patience, to try my simple prescription. As an old negro nurse once said to me anent some "doctor's stuff," "If it don't do you no good, it don't you no harm," and will at least prove a wholesome diversion from the imbecile fancy-work, and still more imbecile gossip, that make so large a part of the daily routine of life at most resorts of health and pleasure.[4]

---

[4] Miss E. F. Andrews, "Botany as a Recreation for Invalids," *Popular Science Monthly* 28 (April 1886): 779–81.

Having regained her health, Frances was prepared to return to teaching. In 1885 Wesleyan Female College in Macon offered her a position; she served on the faculty there, teaching literature as well as French until 1897. In her last decades Frances wrote articles on botany for scientific magazines, as well as textbooks. Her *Botany All the Year Round* (1903) was used in schools across the country. After translation into French, her *A Practical Course in Botany* (1911) was also used as a text in that country.[5]

Fanny Andrews's literary output was impressive. *A Family Secret*, her first novel, became a best seller in 1876, with her publisher listing it as by both Elzey Hay and Eliza Frances Andrews. Then, again carrying both of the authors' names, came *A Mere Adventure* (1879). *Prince Hal; Or the Romance of a Rich Young Man* was published three years after that. These novels earned positive comment in the newspapers of the day. In *Prince Hal*, Henry Grady, editor of the *Atlanta Constitution*, claimed he saw "the most powerful work" written by a Southerner in years. And this was in the heyday of Joel Chandler Harris, Thomas Nelson Page, and others whose fiction was gracing the pages of Northern journals throughout the Gilded Age.[6]

Miss Andrews lived out her days in Rome, Georgia, sustained by royalty income from her textbooks. She departed this life on January 21, 1931, and is buried in her family's plot in Washington's Resthaven Cemetery.

Decades earlier, she had deprecated herself as "nothing better than a country school teacher." Of course, we know she was much more than that: the author of a wartime journal that ranks among the best in Southern literature.

---

[5] S. Kittrell Rushing, "Eliza Frances Andrews (1840–1931)," *New Georgia Encyclopedia*, October 6, 2019, www.georgiaencyclopedia.org/articles/arts-culture/eliza-frances-andrews-1840-1931/; Barbara B. Reitt, "Eliza Frances Andrews," in Kenneth Coleman and Charles Stephen Gurr, eds., *Dictionary of Georgia Biography*, 2 vols. (Athens: University of Georgia Press, 1983), 30; Rushing, ed., *Journal of a Georgia Woman*, xxxvii–xxxix.

[6] King, "Introduction," xv; J. V. Ridgely, *Nineteenth-Century Southern Literature* (Lexington: University Press of Kentucky, 1980), I: 93,99.

Index